ALIVE AND FIXABLE

A Road to Love and Recovery

A MEMOIR

FRANCIE LOW

The events and conversations in this book have been set down to the best of the author's ability, although some names and details have been changed to protect the privacy of individuals.

First paperback edition: December 2018

Book Design/Illustration by Andy Bridge

Book Interior Design by Laura Boyle

Author Photo by missygoldwynphotography.com

ISBN 978-0-9980272-1-0 (paperback)

ISBN 978-0-9980272-2-7 (ebook)

www.francielow.com

Contents

For my Super Family: Tony, TJ and Alex.
And to angels everywhere.

PROLOGUE

The Crash

I THOUGHT I KNEW HOW BADLY my husband Tony was injured in the crash, but I didn't *really* know. Part of me didn't want to hear the gory details, so I avoided them for years. I was given varying accounts of the crash from doctors, a fireman, and cycling friends. I can remember some things from his ride that day: I knew the path he took and how he loved cycling; I can picture some of the passing scenery and imagine how he felt pedaling along. And then I stop.

It was July 30, 2010, just before one p.m., when I poked my head into Tony's home office. He was finishing up a work call on speaker-phone while simultaneously pulling on his bright green-and-white Team Taleo bike jersey. Telecommuting had its perks. Nobody could tell what was going on while wrapping up end-of-the-quarter sales deals and compiling reports, one of four of the most important days of the year for him. I dreaded the long day almost as much as Tony did—his intensity was palpable. His quick, clomping footsteps into the kitchen to refill his coffee mug in a flurry and the forceful way he opened his office door to dash to the bathroom two steps across the hall meant he was in the "zone" and anything else could wait.

"Taking a break?" I asked once he was off the call, knowing the answer before I uttered the words.

"Yeah," he replied while tapping out a text message. "I'm late. My teammates should ride without me."

"Last minute customer order?" I knew the answer to this question too.

"As usual. The quarterly report can wait an hour. I've been on the phone nonstop since seven a.m., and I need to get out. I'm going to take a quick ride to Danville and back, just twenty miles," he said, giving a last tug on his jersey and moving a few steps from his desk to his bike stand. He looked for the pump to inflate the tires, part of his ride prep routine. Tony operated like the Tasmanian Devil, whirling through work and household tasks, always running late because he had to finish just one more thing.

It was unusual for Tony to ride at lunch. Most days, he rode in the wee-dark hours of the morning, before holing up in his office for the day or going to a Little League game on the weekend. But having skipped the morning ride so he could handle a few sales calls, he wanted to get some fresh air and spin out his legs, which had become tight from sitting all morning.

"Bye!" Tony called. He was out the front door and turning the lock with his key before I could reply. He beat me out of the house by almost thirty minutes. A dull ache stirred my core. I dismissed the eerie feeling and continued scratching out my grocery list for whatever might please a babysitter and two adolescent boys for dinner.

"I'm running to the store. I'll be back in a bit," I called out to TJ, my twelve-year old son stretched out on the couch in the family room watching his favorite TV show, *Psyche.*

"OK," he droned without looking up. His preteen apathy was growing by the minute.

I drove our giant white Sequoia SUV slowly through our neighborhood of mostly beige-painted ranchers with manicured, velvety-green lawns, taking the main route to the store. Traffic was heavy, and the sun was high. It was a typical Northern California July day, just starting to get hot by early afternoon. I thought about Tony and how the sun must have felt good on his skin, browned from routine rides. Tony complained about how sunscreen didn't do much for his already dark, Asian complexion. I smiled, knowing how quickly Tony could feel his stress start to lift with each turn of the crank. The ride would do him good.

Tony and I rode together a couple of times until he got too fast for the rides to be fun for either of us, so I was familiar with the route he was taking to Danville. I could picture him, with the other riders who had become his tribe, descending Snake Hill, known for its tight, steep curves and leading out to the flat, open bike lane at the bottom after a sharp right-hand turn. From the time he started cycling, it hadn't taken him long to become fast and begin racing. He could really fly on the flats, his favorite terrain for his red-and-white Cervelo, one of three bikes in his collection. Since amateur racing was his exercise, hobby, and release, he had a bike for every kind of competition. The Cervelo P2C was his time-trial bike and the envy of his cycling mates. The sleek carbon frame and handlebars cut through the wind like a fighter jet.

At 22 mph, he could sail past the town of Walnut Creek, down Danville Boulevard to the community of Alamo in minutes. He always slowed at the busy shopping centers, keeping his eyes peeled for road hazards like people, tree branches, potholes, or man covers. Riding was exhilarating but not without risks. Tony's quick brain never stopped scanning for danger. I knew this from trailing Tony on my bike, he was careful not only for himself but also for anyone else who rode with him. Tony used his right index finger to draw imaginary circles around threats for the rider behind him, the etiquette of cyclists.

From here, I could only piece together the rest of his ride with a smattering of facts shared with me weeks and years later, from his friends, a doctor, fireman, policeman, *and* Tony.

The neon-green accents of his racing team jersey caught the eye of Tony's teammates returning on their way back from their preplanned route. They exchanged quick hellos and salute-like waves acknowledging one another, but never taking their eyes off the road for more than a split second.

Tony rode on, but as he approached a busy shopping center, he tempered his speed, taking extra precaution for cars that often unexpectedly pull out in front of cyclists for one reason or another. Hugging the right curb of the bike lane, he detected a car edging up uncomfortably close on his left. A large Escalade SUV pulled up beside him blocking his view like a rolling black wall. Tony slowed, waiting for the vehicle to make a move, jump ahead or drop behind—he wasn't sure what the vehicle was trying to do. Was it trying to turn into the parking lot? Was it a distracted driver on a cell phone? Was it slowing to tell him something or worse yet, to curse at him for riding in the street? Instead, the vehicle matched Tony's speed, driving parallel to him for a solid block, past the Ace Hardware, slowing at the three-way intersection past a Starbucks. Though there was no stop sign or stop light and Tony had the right of way, he couldn't go any slower or he would fall off his bike and wasn't sure what this vehicle wanted to do. Tony couldn't see around the SUV, but sensed the driver was allowing him to pass straight away through the intersection first so that the driver could take a right turn. Rather than stop and unclip, Tony cranked on his pedals and continued across the street.

Neither Tony nor the driver of the Escalade anticipated the uninvited guest coming from the left side, entering the intersection at the exact moment that Tony headed across. The only thing Tony saw was a bright flash of white before waking up in excruciating pain. The pain controlled him like a demon possessed. Writhing on the ground, he was coming in and out of consciousness, shrieking and screaming uncontrollably. Why was it so hard to breathe? Why couldn't he see? His head was pounded with bright explosions of red, orange, white and blackness, but the pain! So much pain. And why? What happened? Confusion settles in as crowds gathered around him and sirens grew louder. A stretcher. An ambulance. Flashes of hot. Flashes of red. Flashes of white. A hospital. And darkness.

CHAPTER 1

Getting the Call

The Day of the Accident,
Friday, July 30

MY CELL PHONE RANG. I pulled over. I never stopped for calls, and to this day I have no idea why I did this time. I was almost out of our neighborhood, barely in the car three minutes.

The caller ID read "Tony." *I just saw him thirty minutes ago! He's in trouble already? I bet he got a flat and didn't have a spare tube. That's unusual.* I began planning in my mind. *I can rescue him since I don't have any kids to pick up for at least an hour.* I answered the call.

"Hello Francie?" An unfamiliar female voice asked hesitantly, as if the woman wasn't sure who I was or she was scared to talk to me. My heart dropped. I knew instantly. Something was wrong.

"Oh no," I answered back, fear beginning to bubble in my gut.

"I'm going to pass the phone to someone." The woman said slowly and softly.

A man spoke, his tone restrained. "Francie. It's Damon."

Damon is a family friend and a fireman. *Why is Damon calling me on Tony's phone? Why is he calling me at all?* He had coached my younger son, Alex, in Little League—taught him how to pitch. Our boys hung out sometimes, so it felt strange talking to him as a professional now. He told me Tony had crashed, near Starbucks in Alamo, thirty minutes away. I thought I heard him say a bike had hit Tony, but my mind was reeling. Nothing was making sense.

"Um, Tony is OK. He says his scapula hurts. Um, let's see. His eye is cut." Damon was trying his best to tell me what was wrong, but I could tell he was choosing his words carefully. "I wrapped Tony up good," he said. He would take him to the ER. *Ugh. I hate the ER. All that waiting and wondering.* The last time I was there with Tony, TJ was a baby. Tony's lungs had swelled up from some virus; ibuprofen was the solution.

"What do I do?" I asked evenly. It didn't feel real. Nobody in our family had ever been taken to the hospital in an ambulance. *Do I go to the hospital or go home and wait for a call? Do I cancel our dinner later tonight?*

"Meet us at the hospital. You'll probably beat us there." Damon was gentle and calm. He also told me he had Tony's bike and his shoes.

"OK," I answered. My mind was foggy. Nothing seemed to stick.

I pulled away from the curb, slowly driving the same route Tony had just ridden. My brain started swirling. *Where do I begin? Hit by a bike? It can't be bad. He'll be fine. It's his collarbone I bet. Breaking a collarbone is common for cyclists.* We'd seen it happen many times to cyclists who crashed on a casual ride or in a race. *The ER will take a long time. It's one thirty. We might make dinner. What about the kids? I will be gone all afternoon.* I kept thinking of all the things I had to arrange, hoping we would be home later that night.

The battery was low on my phone. *Shoot.* I plugged the phone into the car charger and called my eldest son, TJ, first. He was alone at home, waiting for a tennis clinic.

"Hey, TJ."

"Yeah," he said with annoyance. I'd probably interrupted another episode of *Psyche.*

"Dad was hit by a bike. He will be OK, but he has to go to the ER. I'm sure it will take hours so I won't get home until about six p.m.

Ride your bike to tennis at three. OK?" I informed him with slight irritation because I didn't know very much about Tony's condition yet and the day was in shambles.

"OK." TJ's mood was flat. It was always flat. He was almost thirteen.

I called my friend Carol. "Tony crashed." I knew she'd understand because her husband was also a cyclist.

"Oh, those bikers," she said, half kidding. We knew someone who'd been killed recently while riding his bike, so we had a certain amount of trepidation about our husbands riding. Carol agreed to get Alex for me. My ten-year-old played tennis with her son at our neighborhood club, two minutes from our homes. He could stay at her house until I could pick him up later. *Oh good. One less thing for me to worry about.*

I kept driving. I called another friend. I left a message: "Tony crashed on his bike. I think dinner is off. I suspect Tony won't feel up to it. Sorry to ask, but if you have a minute, could you bring me a phone charger? I'll be in the ER. Oh, can you let Mandy know? My phone is about to die." I couldn't spare my battery for another call, but I dreaded telling Mandy dinner was canceled as well. We had planned dinner months ago for a new restaurant in Berkeley. All three couples loved dining out, looking for the next foodie haven.

I found my way to Ygnacio Valley Road, just off the freeway, fifteen minutes from my house. I drove this busy six-lane road often, mostly to Target. I saw the red bulls-eye from the first stop light. A deep-red medical truck was just ahead and to the left of me. I knew it was my husband. The lights were flashing and if the sirens were sounding, I couldn't hear them. Everything around me was so eerily quiet and slow, as if I were in a dream. The truck drove through the intersection smoothly when the light turned green. I followed. I could almost talk to the passengers; I was so close. I strained to see Damon, but I needed to watch the road. The paramedics pulled ahead, farther and farther from me. *They will arrive first,* I thought. There were so many cars and so many traffic lights slowing me down. My hands tightened around the steering wheel. My eyes were scanning the lanes for a quicker path. *Darn it! This road is always jammed.*

I saw the hospital and an emergency sign. I pulled in to park, only to find the ER lot full. I didn't know where to go, so I drove around the hospital perimeter until I spotted an attendant.

"I don't know where to park," I called out to him. He stood outside a tall white box with windows, similar to a telephone booth. He looked out of place in his sharp white dress shirt and black pants, too much for the hot July sun. His dark skin sparkled with perspiration.

"Where are you going?" he inquired.

"The ER."

"How long?" he asked. I winced. *I don't know. Who can predict what happens in the ER?*

"Four hours?" I offered. He didn't really listen; he was getting it now.

"Don't you worry, miss. You can take as long as you need. Parking is free too," he said in a soothing voice as I handed him my keys. "ER is on the other side of the campus. I'll call a courtesy van to take you there."

"Thanks." *Good. I won't get lost trying to find my way.*

Within minutes, I arrived at the ER entrance, welcomed by a small trail of people in front of a desk. *Do I wait in line? This is a serious emergency. It doesn't seem like I should have to wait to see my husband?* A guy in front of me was coughing. I cringed, hoping I wouldn't get sick. I turned my head to avoid breathing in germ-infested air. As I waited, I looked around at the glass walls. I could see out to the hills, a blanket of long grass bronzed from months of sun and heat. Shadows of scrub oak, craggy and massive, dotted the landscape, all marks of a typical Northern California summer. The street below the hillside was bustling with cars. Chairs lined the perimeter of the waiting room, and a chattering TV had been placed high in the corner where anyone could watch it.

It was my turn now.

Do I sit at the admittance desk at all? Maybe I just gave my name. A large, young lady with, wavy, dark-blonde hair appeared a few feet away. She was dressed for an office, black pants and a beige blouse.

"Francie?" She called my name in a soft, friendly voice. I had no idea who she was, but somehow, I knew she would help me.

We stood by two big swinging doors to the ER. It was like she was expecting me. *Did Damon tell her about me?* She smiled slightly, taking my hands and asked, "Can I get you some water?"

"Sure." As I held the small paper cup, she told me I'd need to wait a little longer until my name was called again. She kept tilting her head, looking closely at my face, searching for something. Nobody gave me any information about my husband. I did what I was told. I didn't want to be rude since I felt more like a guest in somebody's house.

I sat in the chair facing the window out to the dry, grassy hillside. The TV was blabbering on and on. I didn't care to watch. I stared straight ahead, looking at nothing really. My phone rang. It was my friend Carol's husband, Mike.

"Do you want me to come?" he tentatively asked.

"Sure. I guess. Company is good," I replied, not convinced I knew the right answer. *I don't know what to do. Who do I call? Do I need anyone?* All I could think of was the TV show *Melrose Place*. Somebody was hurt once, and everyone from the apartment complex came to the hospital. *Who were my apartment-complex people*? I didn't want to call my family. My mom was gone and my dad was eighty-four and hard of hearing. I didn't want to scream into the phone so he could hear. *I need to wait until I know more. Family is stressful, and they are mostly in Colorado anyway. Tony's family will have to wait too. I don't want anyone to fret.*

I wasn't worried; at least I tried not to worry. *I'm sure it's a simple break.* I didn't cry or panic because I didn't really know what was wrong. *He's alive. He isn't like the other cyclist I knew—the one that died.* My mind wandered, avoiding the tragic what-ifs. I was glad I had showered and dressed in comfy, cute clothes: gray cotton chinos and a fitted black, long-sleeved tee with pale-pink stitching around the seams. Usually I wore a sweaty tennis skirt.

It wasn't long before the young lady was back. She was with an ER doc in bright-blue scrubs, matching surgeon cap, and wire-rimmed glasses. He was my age, fortyish. He took both my hands. It felt awkward. He walked slowly with me, our hands still entwined. The girl followed. We found an empty room. It was cold and dim. The doctor sat close to me while the woman settled in across from both of us. She kept looking at me with supposedly-sad eyes, like a bad actress. The doctor started to talk. His voice was gentle and slow. My eyes darted between the two of them, back and forth. *Can't they just spit out what's happening? Why aren't we in the ER with Tony?*

The ER doctor wasn't sure what happened, stating Tony was probably walking his bike because Tony's legs were fine. An SUV had hit him, he guessed, going on to list off the injuries. Tony had lacerated his eye lid. He'd dislocated his shoulder. He'd broken three ribs. I didn't cry. Instead, I soaked in the information. What he was telling me seemed bad, but they were all commonplace injuries that would heal. *An SUV? A mom hit him. She was in a rush, drinking a latte, I bet. That could be me. How awful for her.* I looked at the woman. She turned on her "sad" eyes again. She still wasn't saying anything, and I wondered why she was in the room.

The doctor raised his left arm. He showed me his black sports watch with a silver ID plate wrapped along the plastic wristband. "Your husband needs to wear an ID bracelet or watch. So we know who to call."

I looked at him, a bit confused by his comment. "He does; it's on his ankle." The doctor was flustered. He hadn't seen the ID. *Why tell me this now?* I wondered.

"We are still working on him. You can come in soon. He will repeat himself because he hurt his head," he continued, returning to telling me about my husband's condition. My body felt chilled and stiff despite their attempts to comfort me.

The woman was still quiet, tilting her head to one side again. She was trying so hard to look concerned. Her brow furrowed. Her mouth was downturned and closed. I felt like they were not telling me something. They seemed nervous. Hesitant. The doctor gave me Tony's wallet, phone, and a yellow plastic bag. I didn't want to look inside that bag. I dreaded seeing Tony's bloodstained clothes, even though I wanted to know about the injuries. It was hard enough for me to look at his phone, knowing he always kept it in his jersey pocket. A spiderweb of cracks spread across the screen, and it made me wonder. *How the heck did this happen? How is it even possible it still works?*

I sat in the waiting room with a clipboard of hospital forms. A policeman in a tan, sharply pressed uniform squatted down beside me and introduced himself. I don't remember his name. He apologized for the bad timing of his visit, but he needed to ask me some questions.

Could I talk about my husband's injuries with the officer? I repeated what the ER doctor had told me. "What was he wearing," he asked. I told him a green-and-white jersey. He seemed to think the colors were dark and unsafe. I opened the bag to show him the brightness of Tony's racing jersey. Seeing splotches of dried blood, I didn't pull it out. I held the bag out for the officer to inspect, turning my head like I would during a gruesome scene of a movie. Next, the officer examined the crushed, bloody helmet. After each inspection and response, he scribbled notes into his small black notebook.

I was alone again. I called my friend Carol to give her the update.

"It wasn't a bike. They think an SUV hit Tony. I'll be here awhile," I said unemotionally. "I don't think I can work my volunteer job at the swim meet tomorrow."

"Hit by an SUV? Boy. You'll do anything to get out of your job," she joked, knowing I drove an SUV. I tried to laugh. I had been whining about my swim-meet commitment all week.

"Can Alex go to the pasta feed with you?" Our swim team hosted a pasta dinner the night before a big swim meet. Carol would handle it all for me. Another worry checked off my growing list: Alex would get dinner and be with his friends.

My phone rang again as I tried to complete the intake forms. A girlfriend told me our friend Jules was coming to the ER since she was already at the hospital, visiting a sick friend. "OK," I said, and we hung up. I stared out the glass doors. I saw my friends Sharon and Steve walking from the parking lot. I spotted a white string. *Phone cord! My dinner pals have come!* I was so happy to see them. I immediately plugged my phone in by the TV, the only outlet I could find. I filled them in on what I knew about Tony's injuries, not getting very far on the forms. They both took in the injury update like I did, calmly. I don't think they could believe their ears either.

My phone rang again. The TV was too loud to hear, so I unplugged my cell and stepped outside. It was HR from my husband's company. A lady gave me so much information I couldn't absorb the words. *Tony has just been injured. How did she know to call?* She talked about forms. *Leave of absence? Does Tony need it?* I wrote down phone numbers and names. I tried to press what she was saying into my memory.

Friends called nonstop. More friends dropped by the ER. I called a few moms I could depend on. Left messages. TJ needed a place to stay; this was taking too long. Insurance forms went unfinished—too many interruptions. *How is the word getting out so fast?*

"Francie Low?" I heard my name called. I jumped from my chair to walk back with the doctor. Sharon grabbed the clipboard. She would finish filling in the forms for me, as much as she could.

I was scared to see Tony. Surprisingly, he was very clean, and there wasn't any blood. He was lying on a gurney, wrapped up tight in crisp white sheets, as if he were a human burrito. His right eye was sealed shut like a boxer's, black and blue and puffy. A white rectangle bandage rested on his cheekbone, a wide dash. I was afraid to touch him.

"Thanks for coming," he said right away. He looked up at me with his left eye. *What? Of course I would come.* "I'm sorry I'm messing things up. You go to Portland without me." *I can't believe he's thinking this way.* We were supposed to go on vacation in a week. Then over and over he said in a raspy whisper, "I don't know what happened. I just don't know what happened."

"An SUV hit you," I answered. I looked hard at him to see if my words registered. I was scared to tell him too much.

"Well, that's fricking obvious." He was alert and feisty. Apparently, he knew more than I thought; he knew he was in an accident and could not remember how he was hit. He was so careful when he rode. Desperately, he tried to recall every detail. Find the flaw—his engineer mentality.

A doctor came in, blonde with a thick mustache, wire-rimmed glasses, and jeans. He talked to me as if we were neighbors, standing over a diseased tree instead of my mummy-wrapped, banged-up husband.

"His brain is fine. Spinal cord is OK. He cracked three neck vertebrae, but they are all perfectly aligned," he said, pointing to the X-ray. My mouth dropped. My eyes popped. This was so much worse than I thought.

"Do you not know?" the doctor asked, looking at me now. He must have seen the look on my face.

No, I didn't. He went on to say Tony had broken the hooks on the spine, a clay-digger's fracture he called it and explained the term. Useless fragments of bone that can snap off while shoveling dirt. He might need surgery. I was stunned.

Another doctor entered. He wore a white coat. I stared at the navy embroidered stitching of his name. *Spanish*, I thought. He was friendly. His accent sounded like Ricky Ricardo, his tongue thick around English words. I glanced up at his face, framed by dark, slightly graying, slicked-back hair. We looked over at Tony in his dazed state. He told me Tony's lung was punctured, so he needed to insert a tube to let the pus building up in his lung drain. Tony would move to ICU—a precaution. *ICU? He is not going home tonight.* Everything was stated matter-of-factly. He obviously said these words often.

"I guess we will be working together a lot," I tried to joke with him. I wasn't sure how long Tony might stay in the hospital, but I knew his care was up to this doctor and me. Each mention of an additional injury slid off my brain, like I had a protective shield to deflect any feeling.

"When can he ride again?" I asked, trying to think of normal things. He told me Tony should be back on a bike in three months, maybe more. *Three months isn't too bad. We can get through this.*

CHAPTER 2

ER to ICU

The Day of the Accident,
Six Hours Later

"WHAT'S NEXT?" someone asked. All eyes were on me. I stood in the waiting room, my friends hovering around me, anxiously anticipating news of Tony's condition after my visit with him in the ER.

"Tony will go to the ICU, just for observation. When he's ready to move, someone will come for me," I reported, looking off into the distance more than at any individual. I didn't want anyone to get too close or the compassion in their eyes might trigger a flood of tears. I needed to stay strong. Sort out the details.

Tony was assigned a bed in the NICU department. *What did that mean?* I tried to imprint NICU into my brain, repeating the letters over and over. *Did I remember the order of the letters?* My brain was numb. I didn't pick out, I-C-U, **I**ntensive **C**are **U**nit. The *N* confused me. I had to let it go.

My friends sat on either side of me in a quiet row. Nobody knew what to say. All the colors in the room seemed dull, gray, and black, including my friends' clothing. My phone interrupted the silence.

"Hi. It's Denise. Can I do anything to help?" she chirped.

I paused. Denise was a spiritually minded friend. She could help me get God in on this one. I hated asking for prayers, a sign of vulnerability to me. I'd rather divulge my weight, but I wanted to cover every base, whatever it took to get Tony better.

"Can you call my church? Is that OK?" I asked.

"I'm opening up the yellow pages right now," she assured me.

It was something I should do, but I didn't want to admit it or ask myself. Within minutes, a minister called me. I told him what I knew. He said a prayer over the phone with me. Even though I'd asked Denise to call the church, and no one could hear, I squirmed and stared at the ground.

My friends were watching me as we waited. No tears slid down my cheeks. No cloud of gloom enveloped me. "You are taking this really well," one said.

I didn't really know how to respond. If I were hysterical, they would tell me to get a grip. I was not hysterical, and somehow this felt wrong too. I knew Tony would be OK. I was happy my kids were being taken care of by friends. I was happy to have other friends with me. I was happy so many wanted to help.

I confessed something on my mind. "Ya know, when Tony rides, I say a prayer. Today I didn't." I wasn't blaming myself. It was just that the thought stuck in my mind and made me wonder.

It was getting late, so Sharon and Steve invited me to have dinner at their place. I couldn't eat in public. I couldn't face anyone. *What would I say to people?* A couple of friends would meet me in NICU. *Did I remember the correct letters?*

I found the right place, the one labeled, "NICU." The doors were locked to screen for family members only. I pushed the buzzer. I told the voice that answered that I was there to see my husband, Tony Low, and magically, the double doors opened. I walked into a room with beds arranged in a half-moon shape, each one with small machines wired to the wall and the patient. The nurses' desk faced the patients. Midway was my husband's bed. I exchanged hellos with the nurse. She seemed spunky and cool. I didn't know if I could even talk to Tony. *Is he in a drug-induced sleep?*

Raspy, Tony piped up, "Take a picture. Take a picture. The boys. They'll be curious." I snapped a few shots. I had no intention of ever showing the boys photos of their bandaged and bruised dad. I didn't want to look at them either.

Tony had sleep apnea, so he asked for his sleep machine. *How did he think of these things in his state?*

And as if on cue, a lung doctor sauntered into the room. He had a graying beard and a set of wire-rimmed glasses. It was like a uniform, those glasses. The lung doctor said he could fashion a mask for him to help him sleep like the machine he had at home. He went on to tell me Tony had broken nine ribs, on one side, not the three I was told about in ER. Humans have eleven on each side. Tony's punctured lung prompted the doctor's visit.

"Your husband is very, very fit. If he weren't, he'd be on a respirator right now." That gave me pause.

"OK." I didn't know what else to say. I should have been relieved he didn't need a respirator, that he was so strong, but I couldn't feel. *Is anything really sinking into my brain?* The lung doc wandered out as quietly as he arrived.

The nurse gave me permission to go home, assuring me Tony would be fine. With so much medication, he wouldn't remember whether I stayed or not. Funny, I thought because he sure acted like he knew the score, bossing everyone around. "Take a picture. Get my sleep machine."

"I like your nurse. I think you will be in good hands," I assured Tony. I didn't want him to worry if I didn't stay. I kissed him on the cheek. I couldn't say much because the nurse was standing right there, and it felt weird to say anything mushy, like I was undressing in front of her or asking for another prayer. In any case, I needed to leave so I could tend to the boys. I needed to eat; my energy was fading.

From the hospital I drove straight to Sharon and Steve's home. Before I went inside, I checked on TJ. *Did TJ need a toothbrush or pillow from home?* I called the friend's dad caring for my son.

"What? Unless he has favorite jammies, we are fine," the dad laughed. Dads were so different than moms. I asked to talk to TJ.

"Dad is worse than we thought, but he'll be fine. He's in ICU." I dropped the *N*. I didn't know what to do with it.

"Is he on life support?" TJ demanded to know. No, I told him. *How does he think to ask that? What are you watching on TV?* He took the news well.

My phone rang and rang as I ate with Sharon and Steve, spaghetti with meatballs, and a much-needed glass of red wine. I was tired and anxious. I didn't want to answer. Two calls were the same number, so I picked up. It was a mom calling me back about TJ; I had asked her if he could stay with her. She was cool, as in not pressuring me for information or weepy on my behalf.

I explained the situation for the tenth time in six hours.

By eight o'clock, I picked up Alex from Carol's house. I was upbeat and thankful for her help.

"You sure are taking this well," her husband commented on my calm demeanor. *Is there something wrong with me? This is the second time I've heard this in one day.*

"He's alive. I'm sort of going with that one," I stated flatly.

Before we slept, I filled Alex in a little more, but I didn't make a big deal out of it. Jules, one of my many friends who'd flocked to my side at the hospital had channeled her therapist mother: "Tell the truth without a trace of worry. Listen and nod so they feel heard."

"Do I send Alex to the swim meet?" I didn't know where to send him otherwise. He was ten and the NICU only allowed children twelve and up to visit.

"Yes. Go about your life as normally as possible," she said reassuringly.

I tried out her suggestion on Alex. Earlier in the day, he burst into tears at the tennis courts when he was told his dad was OK even though he got into a bike accident. I braced myself. We settled into my king-sized bed, him taking Tony's spot. I needed someone close by, and Alex slept better with someone anyway.

Before I turned out the light, I matter-of-factly told Alex, "Dad will be OK. He just needs to stay at the hospital a while to get better." I didn't go into details. He seemed to take me at my word. If I wasn't worried, he didn't need to worry either.

With that, I turned out the light. As I lay there, I wondered if I *could* sleep. Emergencies kept people awake, a fact I remembered from a TV show or a movie. I ended the night with a prayer for Tony and the mom who hit my husband in her SUV.

CHAPTER 3

All About Us

YEARS BEFORE KIDS, Tony and I used to ride mountain bikes together through the winding trails of Marin County. We would pedal through the dusty switchback trails under a canopy of eucalyptus, pine, and oak, negotiating our way around ruts, rocks, and tree roots. Up, up, up we'd climb, me doing my best to avoid stopping or tipping over. Tony would ride ahead, trying to show me the easiest path. Sometimes he waited a long while for me if I fell or got stuck in a deep rut. If the hill was too steep to hop back on, I'd walk the bike up until I reached him on a flat stretch of trail where I could build up my momentum again.

Tony was always looking out for me on every adventure, sometimes surprising me in sweet ways. Since we liked the Disney movie *The Lion King,* he secretly placed a sticker of Simba, the lion cub, on one of my golf clubs, the driver. The idea was to calm me down before teeing off.

I cracked up the first time I saw it. "MISTER TWISTER!" I cried with a big smile, stomping my white golf shoe into the dry grass. We rarely used our regular names, Francie or Tony, because it seemed insulting, as if we didn't really know each other.

"He, he, he. Gotcha, babe," he beamed back with his giant gleaming grin. "Babe" started out as a cheesy name to call one another, like we were some lovesick couple. Then it stuck.

I played better golf because of that silly sticker. I smiled at every tee, looking at little Simba before sending my pink golf ball sailing down the fairway.

Tony pushed me to do things I never would have done on my own—harder, more daring things—like mountain biking up steep inclines or snorkeling far from shore. I practically swam on top of him on our first trip to Hawaii. I was scared to death of even the tiniest fish brushing my ankles while I nervously fluttered my fin-clad feet, admiring their world through darting, goggled eyes. He was my safety net for everything.

We were pretty much inseparable from the first time we met, on the dance floor during our last year at the University of Colorado at Boulder in 1987. Our group of friends loved dancing to New Wave music from mostly British bands like Depeche Mode, New Order, the Cure and the Police. Our favorite spot was the Boulder Express, a gay bar, but on Friday nights the straight crowd invaded the dance floor. Not many bars played our kind of music.

Tony had the dance moves and dressed well, important qualities I was attracted to in my early twenties. I swooned when he pushed back his oversized white blazer to put his hands on his hips and swing them in the most agile manner; I couldn't help but stare. He wore a tiny diamond stud in his left ear and gave me its mate six months after dating. His handsome Chinese features added to his cool factor: big brown eyes, caramel skin, and jet-black hair that he swept to the side and left slightly long in the back. Given my youthful reasons for being drawn to Tony, I joked later that I was lucky the rest worked out. He was very smart, an electrical engineer, and he had a big heart. He loved me a lot! I loved him a bunch too.

If there is truth to the expression "opposites attract," that would be us. An East meets West romance made in America. My pale freckly skin and strawberry-blonde hair gave away my Irish and German roots. I spiked up the bangs of my eighties big hair and wore navy eyeliner, drawn on thick, to make my blue-green eyes pop. I was slightly shorter than Tony in my pointed kitten heel dance shoes, but in my boyfriend jacket with built-in shoulder pads, our shoulders were almost the same size. We looked "mod," as my college friends and I used to say about our eighties linebacker fashion. I hoped Tony thought so too.

What I thought was a boring Irish-American upbringing, attracted me to other cultures and ways of life. Ironically, Tony was drawn to me for the exact traits I thought were ho-hum; I was different and interesting to him. We never ran out of things to say. In fact, the best man at our wedding commented on how much we talked and talked and talked. We could stand at the bar holding our long-neck Budweiser beers, completely absorbed in conversation. We learned everything about each other, like how I hated peas and he loved them. I loved pastries and he hated them. I liked purple and green and he liked green; I couldn't pick a favorite between the two colors. Tony thought that was weird. Our talks never seemed excessive; we just got along so easily.

We were very similar in our work ethic too, both of us were financing our college education with part-time jobs. Being with someone who worked hard for everything was very important to me; we were equals. We both wanted more for ourselves than what our parents could provide, which didn't take much, since neither of us had much. For starters, we wanted to own a car or a couch from the current decade. We wanted to travel and dine at cool restaurants. But in 1989, foodie experiences and quality jobs were almost nonexistent in Colorado. California called our names, a place with fresh baguettes in paper sleeves, fancy-named coffees like latte and cappuccino, and golden opportunities to finance it all. Tony took a position in high-tech sales in L.A., and I went to San Francisco, in hopes of finding a sales job in the wine industry. I ended up selling postage meters, as the glamorous world of wine couldn't cover the high rent. We stayed together, despite the five-hundred-mile separation, buying airplane tickets by the six-pack for weekend visits. After a year, Tony moved north to San Francisco, transferring within his company.

My mom wasn't very excited about me living somewhere far away and pricey.

"Do you really have to live some place so *expensive*? Why not Seattle where we have *family*?" she'd asked while she stood at the bathroom mirror, spraying Final Net over her head of white fluffed hair. I held my breath and walked away.

I wanted a different life, and I was willing to take a risk despite my parents' conservative thinking. Both my mom and dad, Judy and Frank, were depression-era survivors. They married in 1955, not wasting a minute to start their big family of seven children, a sign of a good Catholic. They imparted their penny-pinching tactics on my siblings and me on everything from hand-me-downs to margarine over butter, because it was cheaper. We learned to look for value, but if we wanted fancier jeans beyond J. C. Penney, we had to earn the money ourselves.

I wasn't afraid to go after my dreams no matter what my mother said. Moving to a costly city like San Francisco, without family, was one thing, but to be so enchanted with a Chinese guy really didn't go over well. My dad never said a peep. He kept his gray head behind the stocks and bonds section of the newspaper, sitting in his favorite recliner—*his* chair. He tended to stay out of parenting for the most part unless it cost money. But my mom, she was pretty good at looking straight into our souls. She knew Tony and I would get married before I did.

"He's very charming. I can see why you are smitten, but if you want to get ahead in life . . ." She was building her case against him.

"What are you talking about? He's smart and has a degree—two in fact," I shot back.

"Well, I just read in the paper that one hundred years ago Chinese were not even allowed into America," she said smugly.

"Mom! That was a *hundred* years ago." I rolled my eyes.

"Well, it carries over." She rested her case.

I shut my ears to her 1950s thinking. I just didn't see the problem. In the end, she was right about one thing: I did marry Tony. What she didn't expect was how much she would grow to love and respect Tony. He bought his dad a brand-new Buick LeSabre, exactly what his Dad wanted because his idea of living in America was to buy American, the best. My mom was very proud of her son-in-law after that gesture.

Both Tony's parents emigrated from China in the mid-1950s to make a better life for themselves and their future family. Their courtship didn't last long—three months. His dad, Jack, had already started a life in the United States, working as a janitor and saving his pennies to go back to Hong Kong for a wife. We asked him once how he met Tony's beautiful and elegant mother, May.

"A friend. He recommend," he told us sheepishly one night in the living room of Tony's childhood home in Colorado. Both of Tony's parents worked in the restaurant business, mostly at night, so Tony didn't pick up much Cantonese. In 1970s Wisconsin, where Tony was born, speaking anything other than English was taboo and just downright un-American. But Jack and May had family and friends in Milwaukee, so that's where they landed after marriage. The dampness and mold were too much for allergy-sensitive Tony, so they moved to Colorado for the drier climate, starting a new life waiting tables or tending bar in Chinese restaurants.

Tony's parents valued hard work and education, instilling their beliefs in their four children. The only other expectation his parents had for their kids: pick a mate with a college diploma. Tony didn't let his mom and dad down; he found me. His parents welcomed me into the family by placing a fork next to a plate for me the first time we ate dinner together. They didn't know I had been trained by the best, Tony, to eat with chopsticks from a rice bowl.

On one of our first dates, Tony introduced me to dim sum. The

Chinese dumplings were often served Hong Kong style from carts rolling past tables, stopping to unload a plate of shrimp and bamboo shoots wrapped in a sticky rice noodle or barbecue pork tucked inside a fluffy, cloud-like bun. He taught me the proper way to use chopsticks, holding them in the middle, not close to the tip like a pencil. And never should I let the sticks cross in the back, or I would surely offend the Emily Post of Asia. I loved experiencing a different culture. I probably didn't appreciate or understand what Tony was doing at the time, but he was letting me into the most precious part of his life. He didn't invite just anyone to dim sum. Tony's Chinese heritage is incredibly important to him and makes him proud.

I felt like I traveled the world with him right from the dinner table. On the flip side, my large family of seven kids was a trip for Tony. He was fascinated by our American traditions, waiting for my dad to slice up the roast beef for each person at the dinner table and saying grace before eating a bite. Sharing family dinners and holidays at my house was my pride and joy, Christmas my favorite. My dad and I taught Tony about playing Santa for our boys since Tony's family only celebrated with the tree-and-presents part of Christmas. We showed him how to take a bite out of the cookie set out for Santa, proof of his existence. Santa's presents were placed around the tree, unwrapped, a tradition my mom started because wrapping seven gifts for seven kids on Christmas Eve was too much work.

Growing up, dinnertime was entertaining even if we had to choke down economical suppers of flavorless meatloaf or tuna casserole. My teenage brothers and sisters told interesting and funny stories, making my parents laugh. They were five to nine years older than me, able to bus tables at restaurants or volunteer as candy stripers at the hospital. My younger brother and sister and I, the Three Little Guys, listened and laughed most of the time, even if we didn't get the punch line. I was always looking for an angle so I could say something funny too, but as a fourth-grader, I didn't have much material. As I got older, the dinner table banter became an even playing field and one I wanted to share with my favorite friends and my hip new Chinese boyfriend.

Tony loved that I would try new food and adventures with him. He admired my tomboy side, my willingness to try hard mountain-bike rides or play golf. In a big family, teasing was an art and survival an amusing and admirable trait in Tony's eyes. He appreciated my gumption and sense of humor, attributes I didn't think were a big deal, but to Tony, they were unique and fascinating.

"You're fun!" Tony would tell me. He was fun to me too. He could make me laugh even when he teased me. I was quite animated when I told stories, scrunching up my face in disgust or swinging my hip out to emphasize my point.

"Do it again!" he'd exclaim in his deep voice and bright smile. "I just love your antics."

"Noooo," I'd drone. My cheeks turned pink despite laughing along with him. He was like my brothers sometimes, getting a rise out of me for entertainment. I didn't get mad at him though.

We enjoyed seven years of apartment living in San Francisco, cooking, biking, golfing, working, and finally tying the knot in 1993. We always thought Colorado would pull us back when it was time to buy a house, but that moment never came. Somehow, we saved enough to stay in California, finding our first and probably our last house in the East Bay suburbs about thirty-five miles east of San Francisco. The housing market was nuts in 1997, "Monopoly money" pricing to me because the expense was so unreal and continually increasing. The streets in our suburban neighborhood were wide and flat, a welcome invitation for walkers, runners, kids on bikes, and teenage skate-boarders. We started a family right away, fixing up our small four-bedroom, 1964 rancher over the years and raising our two boys in a child-centered community with great schools and boundless extracurricular activities for sports and music. My sons loved all of it, finding their sport and musical passions. TJ, our oldest, played football and bass clarinet.

Alex, two years younger than TJ, settled on competitive swimming and singing tenor in two choirs.

Tony was fortunate to work from home, breaking into the new telecommuting frontier in 1997. He avoided the horrible rush-hour commute, saving him three to four hours a day in drive time. After our first was born, I never went back to work. We could afford for me to stay home, and I couldn't leave my baby. I always thought of myself as career driven, but my family became my focus instead. I looked at our situation as a business: I was in charge of "product development," and Tony was responsible for revenue. For the good of the family, this was our set-up, and we were happy to have the ability to live this way.

Always a planner, I volunteered in positions that would enhance my resume if I ever did go back to the office. My background was in marketing and sales, so writing school newsletters and fundraiser brochures fit my skill set. I never thought of myself as a leader, but my peers thought otherwise, talking me into serving as board president of the PTA and a local philanthropy group called the Lafayette Juniors. That was how I built my community: volunteering and parenting.

Like most people in the neighborhood, we had a nice life with our family and friends. None of us parents would miss a minute of watching our kids on the mound, diving off a swim block, or playing squeaky tunes in band, their tiny faces blocked by music stands. In between, Tony rode his bike, and I swam or played tennis for exercise. Our weeks were stuffed. That is, they were, until the day of Tony's accident.

CHAPTER 4

What Do We Need?

One Day After the Accident

THE MORNING AFTER THE ACCIDENT, I drove my son Alex to a friend's home, four houses away. At seven a.m. I couldn't think past packing food and towels for the swim meet Alex was going to be at all day. He was tired. I was tired. I didn't care if it looked like a scene out of *L.A. Story*, the spoof on Southern California culture where driving is the only mode of travel, even next door.

With Alex off and TJ at his friend's house for the weekend, my brain was free to plan how I would navigate my day, right down to my shoes. I tried to dress strategically: what would work at a hot swim meet and an air-conditioned hospital? Shorts would be too cold at a hospital, and my legs would stick to the plastic visitor chairs. I chose black yoga pants, a long sports tank, and a matching royal-blue pullover. I could take my first layer off if I got too hot at the swim meet. Sneakers would get me anywhere I wanted to go fast and comfortably.

I grabbed a green backpack from Alex's closet, the "diaper bag" for dad. It still had the changing pad along the back. I filled the pack with magazines, a notebook, water, and a lunch—roast chicken and goat cheese on a bagel. My sporty pullover didn't have pockets so I tucked my phone and Tony's cracked phone inside the waistband of my yoga pants.

I spent time straightening up the kitchen in case someone stopped by unexpectedly while I was out. I imagined TJ needing a change of clothes and his friend's parents standing inside to wait, plenty of time to look around. Why did I care? This was the one time I could leave the house a mess and visitors would understand, but I couldn't help it. I needed to keep busy, and I didn't want anyone to think we lived in constant clutter. As I washed the dishes, I stared out the window at the backyard and realized Tony had not mowed in weeks. The grass was at least four inches high, quivering in the soft morning breeze. *How am I going to manage the yard with everything else going on?*

I was ready by eight a.m., but I couldn't see Tony until ten. Visitors had to wait until after the night shift briefed the day shift. That left me plenty of time to go to the pool and see Alex swim his first race at nine. I was a little nervous about seeing people, wondering what people knew and what I should say. *Will people think I'm unfeeling if I go to the meet when my husband is in the hospital?* I tried to follow the advice from my friend: make my kids feel normal.

Crossing the parking lot to the pool was surreal. I felt disconnected, like I was watching my world through a window. Yet I was close enough to smell and touch the monstrous oak trees and neatly trimmed green grass of the surrounding park. My phone was set to vibrate, startling me when a phone call from Sharon buzzed my stomach. "The newspaper says Tony hit the hitch of a truck pulling a trailer and he was run over by the trailer." I couldn't believe I had just found out what happened to my husband at the same time as strangers reading the newspaper over coffee.

I took in what she was telling me, but I couldn't visualize how this could happen. It was not the SUV the ER doc told me about, the one I imagined with the rushed mom drinking a latte, that hit Tony. I couldn't picture a truck with a trailer in my head. My friend continued, "What are the chances he would hit the hitch? He couldn't do it again if he tried. This is a miracle." *Miracle? How could hitting a hitch be a miracle?* I guess she was thinking of worse ways the accident could have played out; I couldn't. All I could think was it was a miracle he was alive, and maybe this was the first time Tony didn't look carefully. But that didn't sound like Tony. Surely it was the driver's fault.

Walking through a heavy metal gate into the swim meet was surreal too; I felt like I was inside a bubble that separated me from everything. Squeals and chatter were muffled and sounded far away. I scanned the area around the pool, looking for our team campsite yet wishing I were invisible and hoping I blended into the background. The place looked like a Woodstock for families, with pop-up canopies, towels, and people spread across the lawn and bleachers facing the pool, "the stage." I felt eyes on me as I walked to the team campsite, my own eyes darted from little boy swimmer to little boy swimmer, trying to find my son in the sea of white team T-shirts and navy-blue swim jammers. Several people were reading the newspaper, waiting for the meet to begin, and that's how they were finding out about my husband, if not by word of mouth. My pool friends knew what had happened and hugged me right away.

Anyone who didn't know what happened the day before made me feel normal with questions like, "Hey, can I borrow some sunscreen?" or "Do you have a meet program? I want to see when my son swims." *Do I need to tell them?* I couldn't. Not talking about the accident kept it far away, as if nothing had happened. I wasn't sure what happened anyway, except that Tony was in the hospital and his future was uncertain. Nothing was really sinking in yet; the story was too heavy to tell.

Other parents started to offer meals and care for Alex. I was so grateful, I didn't know what to say. One friend flat-out asked what I needed from the store. I listed off a couple of things, coffee and orange juice. Alex was content hanging out in the shade with his friends, playing video games or listening to music like an Olympic swimmer getting into the zone before a race, but they were ten-year-olds.

After standing for "The Star-Spangled Banner," sung by a talented high school student, I watched Alex swim the first leg of the medley relay—backstroke, his best. Even as Alex launched his team to a first place start, I couldn't stop the feeling of tiny tendrils of guilt creeping into my skin or eyes penetrating my back. I was probably overthinking, as I often did, because I was hypersensitive to vibes, my sixth sense. Most of the time my sixth sense served me well, but in this moment, I needed to shut it off. Being there for Alex was more important. Tony would want me to cheer Alex on anyway. I watched his relay team sprint to a first place finish and left.

I drove to the hospital even though it was only a ten-minute walk. I needed to feel sheltered, as if in a cocoon, impenetrable to any noises, cars, or interactions with people. Somehow, I found my way from the garage to an information desk near an elevator. I had no idea where I was, since my only point of reference was the ER from the day before, like the *N* on a compass. A nice older lady in a pink volunteer uniform directed me to the NICU, an elevator ride up two floors. To my relief I remembered all the letters, and I didn't have far to go. Thank goodness for the ladies who assist numbed visitors like myself. Their calm grandmotherly care made it possible to function at a time when just choosing what to wear seemed overwhelming.

"Hi. I'm Tony Low's wife," I said to the wall intercom to the NICU. The magic voice-command words opened the doors. My eyes immediately caught the back of a man standing over my husband in a light-colored dress shirt and dark slacks. He wasn't talking, only staring at Tony. Oh no. My face scrunched up in worry. As I drew closer I recognized the person as the minister from our church.

Crap! I hope Tony doesn't see him! I'd kind of thought I'd taken care of the prayer business the day before. One of my biggest fears was Tony waking up to a face from church, believing he was taking his last breath. He could literally be scared to death! Luckily, Tony was sleeping peacefully.

The minister, of course, had the best of intentions. After our call, he only wanted to see for himself that we were doing OK, since he was leaving for a vacation. We sat in a corner of the cherrywood-paneled waiting room to talk, just a few feet away from the "security" doors to the NICU.

"Do you have enough help? Most of the church staff is out right now," the minister asked. He felt bad that he couldn't offer more assistance.

"I am doing OK. Lots of people are offering dinners and looking after my boys," I assured him. Sitting next to a minister who was there just for me felt weird, like I was sitting really, really close to an all-knowing and loving God I knew existed but preferred to keep at a distance.

"I'm not surprised, since you are so connected to the community," he said. I helped out a little bit at the church, but Boy Scouts and PTA took up my time and he knew that about me.

As long as I had an expert on Godly behavior at hand, I summoned up the courage to ask him about the struggle I was having, "I feel guilty that I don't feel sad. I believe Tony will get better, so I just don't think about the ugly side. I don't want to. But people keep telling me '*You certainly are handling this well*,' as if I'm broken or odd." I looked at the minister, feeling a little anxious about what he might say this meant about me.

"There is nothing wrong with being a positive person," he assured me. I liked his answers to my questions because they were short and supportive. He didn't try to drag me down into the dredges of tragedy in an attempt at empathy, to feel the pain I didn't want to feel. Instinctively, I knew I needed to be a rock for my family and for myself. If I didn't believe in a hopeful outcome, then how could anyone else?

Before he left, the minister suggested a website to help get the word out about what had happened to Tony, CaringBridge.org. I thanked him even though in my head, I immediately rejected the idea. I am not a techie, and I couldn't learn something new right now. Tony helped me with those sorts of things. I could barely take pictures with my iPhone, and I didn't really know how to find the photos after I took them. Tony was the family photographer anyway. We said our goodbyes, and I headed back through the magic doors. They seemed so ominous every time.

Tony's nurse for the day was from Alabama. Her bubbly southern twang was inviting and comforting. She wanted Tony to feel at home as much as possible, so she would let him have visitors, but only two at a time. Technically only family were allowed and children twelve and up. I decided neither of my kids would visit since one was twelve and the other ten. Both deserved to see their dad, at the same time I wasn't so sure either of them could handle seeing him all wired up and bruised. I could bring in special food too, she said—a huge relief, since Tony was very picky about what he ate; if it wasn't delicious, why bother. The only big rule: no cell phone usage, as it messed with the equipment.

As the nurse and I were talking, hospital staff came in to change the sheets on Tony's bed, while Tony was still *in* the bed. I winced with each push and pull of Tony's body to get the sheet out from under him and slide the new one back underneath. Tony wheezed. *I can't believe he's not saying anything.*

"Wait! His whole right side is broken! Can't you place a yellow sticky on him with the word 'injured' so people know not to touch him like that?" I blasted in distress at the nurse.

"We can't. HIPAA, the healthcare laws, protect patient privacy and won't allow patient information to be shared with nonmedical staff." *Insane! Stupid rule.*

"I certainly hope the pain killers are strong enough then," I said helplessly. "This is so wrong!" *How can I protect him if he can't speak up for himself?*

I sat with Tony a few more hours, mostly I watched him sleep, which he needed to help him heal and to forget about the pain. There weren't any windows or pictures to gaze at, only off-white walls, gauze-like curtains, and beeping metal equipment. I sunk into my head, remembering how Tony stayed with me after each of our sons was born, waiting on me and keeping me company. I felt more secure with him by my side, and I wanted to give him the same comfort. I was anxious but hopeful about finding a fast way to get him out of the hospital and help him to believe he could leave soon too.

During the afternoon shift change, I had to leave the room, so I headed back to the swim meet to watch Alex swim another race—the final event, the 100-yard free relay. Once again, his team sprinted into first place. Alex was content, happy to be with his buddies at the meet and then on to dinner at a friend's house. The mom told me later how polite Alex was, complimenting her on the meal: "That's a very nice presentation, Mrs. Kay." Food was heavily influenced at our house by cooking shows and Tony's passion for good eating.

I didn't feel as guilty being at the meet in the afternoon as I had been in the morning. Tony was resting and in good care, except for replacing the sheets. I couldn't do anything for him. I spent most of my time on Tony's phone with his family, his older sister and one of his younger brothers, finally able to fill them in on everything. They both asked if they should fly out to help. My mind wasn't ready to think about where family fit into our everyday lives, since we rarely saw any of them except for holidays. I told them I was OK; my friends were helping right now.

Thank goodness I have Tony's phone, I thought as I squinted through the spiderweb cracks on the screen, searching his contacts. I don't know how I would have called his family. Tony had all the numbers and did all the talking with his family, same as I did with mine. I wasn't sure I could talk to his first-generation Chinese mom because of the language barrier and tried to leave it with his siblings to handle. She called me anyway to hear the words for herself. With a lot of sighs and slow sentences in a low voice, she was like me, taking the shocking news in but not believing it. "Oh, OK. OK." I could feel her pain, like a darkness growing inside. He was her baby. Like me, she never imagined Tony would be hurt.

As I walked around the swim meet with the phone glued to my head, more people stopped to give me a hug and nod their sympathies. The simple gestures were soothing, just enough so I felt people cared and without needing to relive the accident through a conversation.

After the swim meet I went back to the hospital to sit with Tony. I stopped in the bathroom first, a single. I unpacked the iPhones from the waistband of my yoga pants and carefully placed them on top of the paper towel holder. I set my backpack down where I thought the floor was cleanest and went about my business. I grabbed my stuff, I thought, and left.

On my way back to the NICU, I ran into a cyclist friend of Tony's in the waiting room. I told him he could come with me to visit Tony.

"Just tell him you're my brother. They only allow family in here." I looked him in the eye to check that he understood.

With my Irish freckles and pale skin and my husband's Chinese-American heritage, I'm sure the nurses knew what was going on as I brought visitor after visitor who looked nothing like us in to see Tony. If they knew, they were kind enough to turn a blind eye. Cyclist buddies are loyal and supportive. The guys came in droves.

As I walked into the NICU with Tony's pale white friend, I stopped, panic shooting through my veins.

"I left the cell phones in the bathroom!" I ran back, not waiting for a reply. The phones were gone. I desperately looked around the waiting room, all around Tony's bed. Nothing. Tony's friend was still there. We questioned the nurses in the NICU, rather loudly so the whole room stood still looking at us like we just might do something crazy. Tony's friend ever so slowly reached into his pocket.

He spoke calmly. "I'm going to take out my cell phone now. Is that OK?" Everyone stopped, watching every move he made. "I'm going to call Francie's phone to see if we can get her phones back."

The room paused. Even I was in awe. He was breaking the no cell phone rule for me. A lady picked up the call on the other end; clearly, she had the phones. *Thank God!* I could breathe normally again, almost. We talked about where I could meet her—just down the hall. I almost broke into tears; I hate unsettledness. If I have too many worries or responsibilities, I crack. One of my strengths is planning, and if something goes off script, I can get riled or worse, start crying out of helplessness. Without both phones, I couldn't get the help I needed from my friends or stay in touch with Tony's work and his family. I didn't even want to think about what it would take to buy new phones right now.

I raced out the ominous doors that opened too slowly and ran down the hall. Two nurses were sitting behind a desk when I finally frantically arrived. My words spilled out quickly and loudly. "Where's the lady with my phones?"

"We don't know what you are talking about. What phones?" They stiffened at my intensity. I double-checked I was in the right department, scanning the room frenetically for any signage. The nurses and I looked nervously at each other, not really sure what to do next.

After several minutes that felt much longer, a nurse in purple scrubs with lunch coolers dangling off her shoulders wandered in, taking her sweet time to reach the desk. I practically pounced on her. It was all I could do to keep from grabbing the bags myself or shaking her to hurry up. She ever so slowly unzipped one of her lunch coolers and pulled out the phones. I let out my breath, like finding a lost child at last. Relief was an understatement.

Tony was still in and out of a fog, sleeping most of the time. I helped him through his dinner.

"How's the Jell-O?" I asked as he sucked the jiggly green blob off the spoon. He swallowed hard.

"Lime is not my favorite. The chicken broth is better," he whispered. After he sipped and slurped his dinner down, I stayed by his side and waited for his eyes to flutter to sleep. I kissed him goodnight and left.

On the drive home, my mind raced with a checklist of things to do: Where will the kids go after the weekend? How will we eat? How will I broadcast Tony's updates so I am not repeating myself to exhaustion? I had to make a plan so I could avoid random distractions or stressful people. Again, instinct told me my friends could help me through. They understood my life and where they could easily step in. My friend Suzanne had already offered to do laundry, and I almost cried at her generosity. Acts of kindness were overwhelming, like I didn't deserve it. My family would help if I asked, but the effort to teach them our routine and the risk of their pushing buttons only families know how to push was too much so I put them off for now. I wasn't ready for Tony's family to help either for the same reasons.

When I pulled up to the house after that second day, I could not believe the welcome sight. My lawn was freshly mowed and trimmed! Someone was looking out for us.

CHAPTER 5

Angels to the Rescue

Two Days After the Accident,
Morning

IT WAS ONLY FIVE A.M. ON A SUNDAY, but I couldn't sleep. My brain was still whirling from yesterday's chaos of lost cell phones, kid activities, and dinner plans in addition to my most important worry: Tony. I knew I needed help, but it felt weird to be the one to ask when usually I was the one to organize a meal sign-up or make a meal for someone in need. The enormity of my growing responsibilities ballooning inside my head was unnerving. I tossed and turned, twisting up in my sheets until I couldn't stand it anymore. I jumped out of bed to take matters into my own hands. This was my snap reaction when the urge to have a concrete plan was too great.

I threw on a faded pink sweatshirt over my summer jammies and a pair of baggy black sweat pants. The Bay Area morning fog still chilled the house. It would be hours before it broke into the sweltering heat of August. The coffee brewed as I fired up the laptop on the dining room table, my office.

In the quiet, I began to craft my e-mail plea to the people I thought would be good helpers. A couple of friends had already offered to organize dinners for us—one less thing to worry about. *How many weeks did we need?* I nervously typed in a request for two weeks to start, my best guess based on Tony's condition. I added, "if it's not too much to ask," to ease any pressure to help. In the next message, I felt even bolder as I asked two friends to coordinate kid schedules, a point person for each of my boys to cover rides to music lessons or provide a place to hang out. I picked two moms I once worked with on volunteer projects; moms I knew wouldn't flake. Commitment and reliability were really, really important—now more than ever. I could not afford to be derailed over a mishap in the middle of an already chaotic and intense situation. I chose my helpers carefully.

So many people were asking about Tony: text messages, e-mails, and phone calls. I was worn out trying to keep everyone up to speed on what was happening and how he was doing, and it had only been two days. *How can I broadcast updates on Tony's situation?* I remembered some friends had used a blog to update friends and family after a serious car accident. A blog could save me tons of time replying to the caring inquiries coming from friends and family near and far. This way anyone who wanted to could easily follow Tony's progress. I wanted to emulate my friends' example, be open about what was happening so people could speak freely around me instead of squirming in my presence, pretending not to know. I had to let go and let people into my life—not an easy thing for someone like me who preferred to be in control.

In 2010, blogs were not that well known in our circle. E-mail chains or digital newsletters were as techie as my mom world got as far as broadcast media. *How do I start a blog?* I wondered. Tony always tackled the tech issues, so I pondered: Who could possibly fill Tony's shoes? Two smart, computer-savvy dads came to mind for the job. The minute I clicked send on my e-mail request to them, the tension loosened in my neck and shoulders just a little. I noticed a couple of new e-mails sat in the queue. I could not resist the urge to open the first message. My friend Casey had heard about the accident, probably through the swim team grapevine. She sent me a link to a website called CaringBridge.org, the same site my minister had suggested earlier, the one I'd dismissed out of technological fear.

"I know you like to write, and this might be useful," Casey wrote. She was right about that. I worked on school newsletters and fundraiser brochures, one of my favorite aspects of my volunteer jobs. And if a second person was recommending the same site, I should follow the lead. I could easily handle clicking on the blue string of words staring me in the face.

I learned that CaringBridge.org was a way to share patient updates with friends and family who sign up using their e-mail address. Each new post was sent out to the list of followers; I didn't have to do anything but write—an instant blog. Not two seconds after sending an e-mail to the smart guys asking for help with a blog, an answer had landed in my digital mailbox from Casey.

After thanking my friend for the recommendation, she responded back immediately with yet another gift. "I'll go through the school directory to e-mail your friends the link," she wrote. I could not have known to ask for this kind of help nor could I know what an incredible gift the blog would become to me.

As I read through the steps to set up an account, I was actually setting it up. I answered questions about the hospital location and security access. With all of Tony's work experience designing safe networks, he was always worried about security, so I went for a medium security level. As long as a reader registered an e-mail address, they were accepted, and I knew who was reading. I hoped I made Tony proud with my decision.

The opening page asked, "What happened?" My fingers flew. I wrote about how he crashed into a hitch on a trailer. The list of injuries was so long I checked and rechecked to see if I'd missed anything: broken ribs, cracked vertebrae, dislocated shoulder, lacerated eyelid, and punctured lung. *Geez, I hope it doesn't get any worse,* I thought as I looked at the long list all in one place. Then I added how Tony was in the "ICU" for *observation only.* The *N* in NICU didn't mean anything to me; I thought it was like a hotel room number on floor "N" instead of a super-charged Intensive Care Unit for Neurological patients.

To counter messages from people that I called "trips to the dark side," where their message focused on the accident and what could have happened, I talked about Tony's alertness and bossiness. Looking for positive anecdotes to share came easily to me and helped me maintain a happier state of mind. The harder part was keeping my distance from anyone who could drag me down. So I added an important request: "To best help me, please be positive and don't worry." I couldn't be strong if the people surrounding me were falling apart. Fifteen minutes later, I was done. I started a blog all by myself, something I couldn't have defined even three hours earlier.

"You are an angel Casey," I whispered to myself. She really was, and she was part of a long line of angels who would help us—the start of a pattern I would recognize over and over. Already, friends were coming to the hospital to support me, and our lawn had been magically mowed. If I needed anything, I merely made a mental note and the solution dropped into my lap, or my e-mail box, in this case.

By six thirty a.m. I had set up a blog, asked friends for help, and made a breakfast burrito and sandwich for Alex to take for day two of the swim meet. I sent him on his way to Carol's, this time on foot. I straightened up the kitchen, *again*. The possibility of a random visitor motivated me to clean. This behavior would shock my friends more than my lack of emotion at the hospital. I organized schedules and people, not a house, until I absolutely couldn't stand the mess anymore. I hate cleaning. But my intuition was correct; someone did stop by unannounced.

Damon, the fireman, came by with Tony's bike gear. I had almost forgotten he grabbed the bike and shoes when he patched Tony up after the crash. I was grateful and impressed that he could be so considerate in such a stressful moment. The angel network was in action before I even knew it existed.

Tony had shown off his prized possession to Damon during a dinner party at our house a few months ago. The distinctive red-and-white frame with handlebars designed to let the cyclist ride in an aerodynamic position was ideal for short, fast races called time trials. Even though Damon was not a cyclist, he could appreciate the bike's beauty, what it was capable of, and the pride Tony had in his pricey acquisition—the envy of his cycling friends.

I never questioned big purchases by Tony since he never spent what we didn't have, and he earned it. Tony worked his butt off selling high-tech equipment, sometimes over sixty hours a week. The time trial or TT bike was part of his arsenal to become the best amateur cyclist possible, because Tony approached any endeavor at 150 percent.

After the accident, word got out right away that "the fireman" had held on to the fancy racing bike. Tony's loyal cycling friends surprised Damon with a visit to his house, grilling Damon on its whereabouts. There was no doubt why, first thing on a Sunday morning, Damon was at our front door with the bike.

Damon and I stood on the brick walkway with the morning sun warming my back. Damon was fit and slight, as if he cycled too. He was like an Italian version of Tony, about the same height with suntanned skin and thick hair. As glad as I was for Tony to get his bike back, I was even more grateful to finally talk with someone who had been at the scene of the accident. Lucky for Tony, Damon the angel came to his rescue. The first thing Damon saw when he arrived on the scene was the prized bike he'd seen at our house, so he instantly knew Tony was the downed rider before he saw him splayed out on the pavement.

Both of us were staring down at our shoes for a few moments, contemplating what to say to each other. I broke the silence first. "What exactly happened Damon? The newspaper said he hit a trailer hitch. Then the doctors said an SUV hit him while he was walking his bike. I just don't understand or know what to believe, and Tony doesn't remember a thing."

Damon unraveled the layers of crisscrossing facts. "Tony was riding south, in the bike lane on Danville Blvd, a very busy two-lane road for cars and cyclists in Alamo. A black Escalade SUV was traveling alongside Tony in the same direction. As they both approached a three-way intersection, the Escalade paused, waiting for Tony to clear the intersection before turning right from Danville Blvd on to a small side street."

"I'm with you so far," I said to Damon. I narrowed my eyes as if I was watching something I couldn't bear to see but looked anyway, hanging by a thread for his next words.

"On the opposite side of the road, a white pick-up truck with a hitch and a trailer, was waiting to take a left at the same intersection. There isn't a traffic light so the driver in the truck thought the Escalade was being nice, pausing for him."

"Oh no," I gasped. I knew what was coming, and I was still scared to hear the details.

"Neither Tony nor the driver of the pick-up truck could see each other because the Escalade blocked their views, like a dense, overgrown hedge. Tony collided with the hitch as the pick-up cleared the intersection."

"How could hitting a hitch cause so many injuries?" I stared at the ground, my eyes laser focused, as if I could find answers hidden in the brick walkway.

"Well, it wasn't just the hitch. Tony was thrown forward and the bike bounced backward. Thankfully the trailer was only filled with light debris, but it ran over Tony, smashing his face and body into the asphalt like a steamroller. I grimaced and shook my head. All I could do was continue peering at the ground and try not to picture the scene, just listen to Damon's words. Then he told me that there were black tire tracks streaked across Tony's jersey although the bike was barely scratched.

"Oh my God! It's a good thing I wasn't there. I would have screamed at that guy," I exclaimed. A distracted mom I could relate to, because I am always thinking of twenty things at once while I'm driving. But a young man—I figured he was a cocky and sloppy driver. I was mad.

"No, you wouldn't. You wouldn't. It was a young guy, and he was bawling," Damon responded firmly. I was stunned; I hadn't expected a sensitive, remorseful young man. I felt sorry for him now. It must have felt terrible knowing you'd run someone over.

At the time, Tony hitting the hitch did not seem like incredible luck to me. Two seconds later, he might have hit the trailer head on, bounced back with the bike or into the trailer with the debris instead of underneath; he wouldn't have been run over at all. However, had he been a few seconds earlier, the truck would have plowed into him, perhaps crushing him and the bike with no hope of survival. Had the Escalade simply followed the rules of the road and stopped behind Tony in the bike lane as if he were a car, nothing would have happened. To this day, Tony is adamant about sticking to traffic rules to avoid accidents.

Hitting the hitch *was* a miracle as my friend Sharon had said earlier in the week. It was another miracle Damon was at the scene and came to my house to deliver the bike, just when my head was swimming with questions about the accident. We continued talking while I led Damon inside to show him where to park Tony's cherished racing bike: Tony's multifunctional office. A bike rack dominated the room, like a pedestal for an esteemed trophy. Tires and tools were packed around computers on a desk, a big screen TV, and couch. The room tripled as a bike shop, telecommuting office, and gaming center for the boys. Tony often took conference calls with a headset on, leaving his hands free to grease a bike chain or change a tire. He called it his bike lab.

The rumbling sound of a car engine caused me to glance out the office window. A black-and-white police car was pulling up in front of the house. The same officer I'd seen in the hospital was heading up the brick walk; panic and irritation quickened my heart. *He was supposed to call me.* I met him at the front porch, greeting him warily; something was off about this officer. I was so relieved Damon was with me, right where he was needed, once again.

"How is your husband doing? Is he awake? Can I talk to him today?" the cop asked. He seemed genuinely concerned despite his tough cop persona. His tan uniform was sharply pressed, and his hands were on his hips like he was sizing up the place or looking inside for Tony.

"I don't know. I haven't been to the hospital yet. He's in ICU." I dropped the *N* in NICU again, like a useless article of clothing. "I can't even see him until ten." I answered with a sarcastic edge, still not trusting him despite his sympathetic questions. An uncomfortable pause hung in the air. I seized the opportunity to ask a burning question in my brain. "I was wondering, the guy in the truck is at fault, right?" I asked cautiously. I didn't want to seem anxious or guilty.

The officer looked at me tentatively. "Ah no. Your husband will get a ticket."

"A ticket for what?" I was dumbfounded. I tried to sound calm.

"Speeding," he said firmly. I couldn't believe it. Fury flashed through my body.

"What is the speed limit?" I pressed, steadying my voice to control my anger.

"Thirty-five miles per hour. He was going too fast for a bike and the conditions." If I remembered my driver's education correctly, a bike follows the same rules as an automobile. The police officer's explanation didn't sound right. His tan uniform represented the California Highway Patrol, not the local police. Maybe he was confused?

"How fast should he have been going?" I asked as unassumingly as possible. I didn't want to sound defensive or protective, even though that was exactly what was on my mind.

"Oh, five maybe ten miles per hour. You know, in case a cat jumps out or something." Every response from him was irritatingly slow and unemotional.

I looked at him incredulously. A road bike is not meant to go five miles an hour. There's a point where a cyclist can literally fall over if the speed is too slow, and if your shoes are clipped in to the pedals it can be nasty. After that, I knew for sure I could not trust this man. I didn't offer any extra information. I realized I had to be my husband's protector.

"Well, since I'm here can I get the serial number off the bike?" he asked coolly. Just then Damon walked up with Tony's bike shoes. Damon's timing was impeccable.

I introduced the two men but they didn't really say much, an odd vibe choked the air. We slowly walked into the house together to look at the bike. Damon and the officer commented on its mint condition, so different from my husband's fate.

"Must be the result of a low speed crash," Damon surmised. A flicker of anger sparked in my gut, my face remained blank.

Heavy silence.

The officer did not react to Damon's comment. He squatted to look at the bottom bracket and slowly took down the numbers into the familiar black book, the same one he held the entire time he questioned me in the ER. He stood up just as slowly, his uniform still perfectly pressed, and left the house. He pulled away from the house as if he were driving a hearse, commanding and dark.

CHAPTER 6

The Lawyer Angel

Two Days After the Accident,
Later that Afternoon

MY MIND WAS SPINNING while I quickly drove to the hospital. *Speeding ticket? You give the guy lying on the ground screaming in pain the ticket? The guy who can't speak for himself?* I was incensed. This just wasn't right. I needed to talk to his cycling friends. Maybe there was something I didn't know about the rules of the road. Maybe Tony was riding too fast and somehow the whole thing was his fault.

As I walked toward the elevator to go up to the NICU, two guys exited. Their black sweatshirts with the bright-green cycling team logo "Taleo" caught my eye like a beacon of friendship, Tony's teammates. They were exactly who I had hoped to see just an hour ago, my wish granted as if by magic. Here was my chance to find out the rules of the road for cyclists.

Warren and Scott introduced themselves to me. I didn't know many of Tony's cycling friends because Tony usually met them on a ride far from our house. Even though they had never met me either, I was certain they would want to help Tony. I relayed the conversation I had with the policeman and how he had determined Tony was at fault for riding too fast.

"Is there a different speed limit for a cyclist versus a car?" I asked.

"No. The speed limit is thirty-five miles per hour for cars *and* cyclists. He was probably riding around fifteen, maybe twenty-two miles per hour, tops. But in an intersection, he'd definitely slow down to five or ten miles per hour." Scott told me. Anger bubbled inside me as I thought again of what the cop said.

"We were supposed to ride with him that day, but Tony got hung up on a work call," Warren offered, looking more at the wall instead of me. "We were returning from our ride when we saw Tony and waved to him."

"Typical Tony. He goes above and beyond for his customers," I said, slightly irritated that work got in the way again.

"We think he was hit about a minute after we saw him," Warren continued. My eyes nearly popped out of my head.

"Cops don't like cyclists, especially highway patrol. They are biased," Scott informed me, almost as an apology rather than a statement of fact. *Geez. Really?*

"I gather cyclists don't like cops either." Dark humor seeped into my words, the morning's experience fresh in my head.

Now I knew I needed a lawyer to defend Tony against the cop's absurd and all-too-convenient claim. Tony was never careless on the road; I was sure of it.

The first thing I noticed when Tony and I said our hellos that morning was how groggy he seemed. Nurse Healy fiddled with the tubes to one of the machines helping Tony while she explained why he must rest. She confessed she had let him have too many visitors yesterday, and he was wiped. I felt a little guilty because I thought his friends would cheer him up, not wear him out. Plus, they *needed* to see him. I sat for a few minutes next to him, in a stiff plastic chair, no armrests. I was a good four feet away from the bed because there was so much medical equipment tracking his heartbeat, pulse, hydration, pain medication, and oxygen levels that I couldn't get very close unless I hurdled over the equipment into bed with him. He wanted to talk to me but his eyes kept flickering, straining to stay awake. *Poor guy. Sleep! It's better for you.*

Since I was losing my audience to a mind calmed by dreams or drugs or both, I flipped through the e-mails on my cell phone, the hairs on my arms rose as I read the following subject line: "If you need a lawyer."

"I know this isn't the best time to be thinking about a lawyer," the e-mail began. "Should you need one, my good friend can help. His number is . . ." I couldn't believe the timing. I didn't waste a minute slipping into the hallway to make that call.

I stood outside the big doors to the NICU, sort of my hospital office or telephone booth. I didn't care if one of those elderly ladies in a pink smock, with teased hair like cotton was parked at her desk and could hear everything I said. Those Cotton-Hair Volunteers were posted like sentries around the hospital, and they all dressed the same with the same puffy-white hairstyle. What choice did I have unless I took the five-minute walk, went down the elevator to the lobby, and outside the hospital? I didn't want to be gone that long. I left a message with the lawyer's wife, explaining the connection so she wouldn't be leery of me. After all, it was a Sunday, but I was anxious to set things straight with the police officer.

When I returned, Tony was awake and wanted to try to walk, to keep the blood flowing and his muscles working. I thought he was crazy but he was determined to heal fast and nothing was going to stop him, until he discovered how much it hurt. The fight-or-flight adrenaline had dissipated and now he felt the pain. "Excruciating" was written all over his face and manifested in his stiff, clunky movements. *Ugh.* My bones ached watching him. First he sat up, slowly moving his bed to a more upright position, his jaw was tight and lips pursed the whole time. Once he was upright, he swung his legs around, slid slowly off the bed until the grippers on his stocking feet touched the shiny white linoleum floor. And he shuffled away from the bed and back, grimacing with each slow step. His cyclist legs and determination were so strong that he willed himself through the six-foot round trip. He could *feel,* even if it hurt, and that was a good thing. The pain was proof that the nerves in his spine were intact and no wheelchair would be in his future. Even if he was hard to watch, I couldn't help but feel encouraged by Tony's stamina. He had dodged a deadly bullet and was very much alive.

The few steps of exercise tired him out, and he was ready to eat his lunch in bed. He added milk to his tea because he knew he needed calcium to heal and not because he liked it that way. I was worried for my husband and wanted him to get better, but I wasn't like Tony. I didn't see that there were things that could be done to help him recover outside of what the nurses and doctors did for him. I trusted that they were giving him the very best care.

My cell phone buzzed my stomach with a call; the phones were safely tucked inside my yoga pants again. I jumped out to my hallway office to take the call before a nurse reprimanded me for using my cell phone inside the NICU. The lawyer was calling back just hours after I'd left my message; his voice strong and caring.

"Thanks for returning my call," I said, almost out of breath.

"Is this a good time?" he asked right away.

"Unfortunately, I can't really talk right now. Can I call you back after three, when the nurses change shift?"

"Yeah, yeah! I'm just leaving the golf course. How about I pick you up, and we can grab coffee or something." He sounded so earnest and open to meeting me on his day off. I let out a deep sigh. *I can't believe he works on a Sunday!*

I stood on the walk in front of the hospital and waited, Tony's green diaper-bag-backpack slung over my shoulder. My eyes darted to the left and right behind my tortoise-shell Ray-Bans, looking from side to side because I didn't know which way the lawyer would come from nor did I know whom to look out for or what kind of car. A few minutes after three a car approached; I could tell by the quick-angled stop of the metallic gray sedan that this was my lawyer date. He poked his silvery head out the open window. "Francie?"

"Yes. Thanks for coming." There was no stuffy "*Miss Low*" or "*Pardon me*" in his greeting. I liked him immediately. Smiling, I got into the car, knowing I could trust him.

We sat outside a small café at a table for two, one in a sea of weathered, iron dining sets bolted to the concrete, looking out at the strip mall parking lot. Most people had already had their morning coffee, so the patio was all ours—plenty of privacy. We didn't need to be amped up on caffeine at three p.m. either, so instead we clutched icy cold bottles of water in our hands; the sun was softly shining.

My earlier interactions with Damon and the police officer were still fresh in my head, and the conversations provided exactly the right facts that a lawyer would need to know. What originally seemed like unannounced or rude visits at ten in the morning to drop off a bike or question me were like finding cash in your pocket you didn't know you'd had. I quickly rattled off how and where the accident occurred and that Tony was going to be issued a speeding ticket. I was completely freaked out about going broke to pay medical bills, but I managed to ask him if the ticket would affect auto insurance coverage, if Tony was at fault, and if medical insurance would cover everything.

My fears kept pouring out of me. Rarely did I ever know enough about Tony's work life, because he tried very hard to leave work at work, both to give himself a break and to avoid boring me with the details. In the last few months though, Tony had mentioned a very large business deal he could lose if he wasn't on the job, even though he put the opportunity together. I knew Tony's life and his livelihood were at stake because of his accident.

I was so relieved to sit with someone I could tell all my worries to, everything. I did not second-guess the trustworthiness of this man for a second; my usual gut check never flinched. I told him how I had just started a blog and that I was scared to use real names or say the wrong thing. I was terrified of being sued or making someone mad. I told him about all the things I thought he could fix.

He listened patiently, his demeanor so confident and sincere. His grayish-white hair gave him the appearance of someone much older than his actual age. I guessed he was older than me but not by much, because his kids were only a few years ahead of mine. The F-bombs he sprinkled throughout his answers made him seem tough and able to stand up for us. I could feel my stress start to melt away. He would be our White Knight, saving the day again and again in the weeks ahead.

"I doubt Tony is at fault. I'll drive by the intersection to be sure." The White Knight was wielding a shield, blocking us from our first dragon. "I'll also call the policeman and tell him to leave you alone. Don't let him talk to Tony, especially since he's medicated." I'd never considered what Tony might say if he talked to the police at that point. I was feeling protected already.

"Thank you!" I breathed easier, not having realized the equivalent of an elephant had been sitting on my chest. Now it was only half an elephant.

The lawyer talked of a potential lawsuit against the guy that ran Tony over. He'd look into it. I wasn't sure how I felt about such a strong action being taken toward a young man, especially someone who had cried out of remorse at the scene of the accident. He was young and the accident was just that, an accident. I wasn't ready to think about repercussions for anyone except maybe that pesky cop buzzing around. Tony's well-being, speeding ticket, and medical issues were enough to digest, too much for me, really. I looked out at the parking lot instead of my new friend, the only time I was a little squeamish about his word, "lawsuit." As I looked at the sun gleaming off the parked cars, my eye caught a familiar face, my friend Liz had arrived with a care package. She'd said she would stop by. I had told her I was meeting a lawyer at the sandwich shop near the hospital.

"Hi!" Liz said as she handed me a crinkly plastic grocery bag. I smiled up at her. "Boxers for Tony and some trashy magazines for you!"

"Thanks! You certainly know how to take care of your girlfriends," I said with a chuckle.

The one thing that didn't come with the hospital gown was an undergarment. Tony was flashing everyone, not that nurses cared, but visitors caught their breath and politely looked away, so I'd asked Liz if she could pick up a package or two of boxers. The magazines were thoughtful, but I was too distracted to read anything seriously, even movie star gossip. Books, my usual escape, were just words on a page floating in front of my eyes, the story lost on me. My brain was so numb I couldn't get excited about reading.

Liz left, but the impact of her gifts lingered, and the White Knight continued to protect me with more useful advice. His wife had recently been hospitalized, so he spoke with wisdom, like he was preparing a younger knight for battle.

"That friend that stopped by, that's the kind of friend you want around you. She didn't ask about your situation. She just dropped off things you might need," he informed me.

"Liz is considerate that way," I said, a little surprised he picked up so much about her in just a few minutes.

"She dressed in sporty clothes. You should dress that way too. Wear comfortable clothes and shoes. You never know when you might need to go for a walk to get away." He knew more than lawyer advice. I felt more and more at ease the longer I listened to him.

I drank in everything he said. I needed someone sure of himself to talk me through at least a handful of unknowns.

"So, you really think I can talk about whatever I want on the blog?" An acquaintance told me to only say positive things, and I wasn't sure if I should listen to the suggestion.

He spoke in an unwavering tone, "Just be yourself." A calm enveloped our table. *He is so wise!*

The White Knight's parting words resonated so deeply that I felt confident about what to say. I couldn't wait to share updates on the blog now.

I don't think he knew just how much peace he gave me in one afternoon visit. As promised, he called the officer to tell him to stop bothering me and to direct all questions to him. I could be my more normal self, caring for my family and not stressing about an inconsiderate and biased police officer. The White Knight was making things right, clearing a path for us to focus on getting Tony better. He was yet another angel looking after us.

CHAPTER 7

Unexpected Cheer

Two Days After the Accident,
Evening

LEAVING TONY AT THE HOSPITAL at night tore me up inside. He needed me, but the boys needed me too. Alex and TJ needed a sense of normalcy at home for at least part of the day so they wouldn't worry about their dad. And *I* needed the boys. They were a minibreak from the exhausting and ever-changing hospital woes. Over dinner at home, the boys shared stories about their adventures with other families, giving me a chuckle sometimes and also insight as to how they were coping.

"Mom! I ate at *Taco Bell*!" Alex said triumphantly in his excited ten-year-old voice.

"How was it?" I asked, trying to mask the revolt taking place in my stomach with the thought of a fast-food burrito oozing soupy refried beans. We never took our kids to Taco Bell.

"It was delicious, except for the quesadillas. I think they are *microwaved*." His eyebrows raised in horror.

TJ learned new card tricks—his favorite, "pick a card," where he guessed which card was picked out of a deck of fifty-two possibilities. He was very much a part of the family he stayed with over the first weekend, even getting caught in the middle of a battle between siblings. TJ found himself the human barrier, wedged between his friend and his friend's sister in the back seat of the car.

"It was so funny, Mom. I was like the Great Wall of China." TJ snickered at the silliness of it all. TJ applied his uncanny head for facts and love of world geography and culture to everything he did, even a sibling spat.

With one family, TJ hung out at the tennis courts drinking Jamba Juice during an open tennis tournament with pros, junior, and college players. At another boy's house he shot airsoft guns. Both of those activities were like the Taco Bell experience Alex had—a first. My mom-friends were doing much more than shuttling my boys to music lessons or sports practices. To this day, they are happy and thrilled to have had experiences they never would have had at our house.

Years later I asked the boys what they recalled about all of this, and TJ said, "I thought it was cool." The accident didn't seem so important. And for Alex, the initial impact stung, but after that he went on with swim practice and tennis clinics, never shedding another tear. "I just don't remember it being a big deal," Alex explained. *Mission accomplished,* I thought.

In the first few weeks, especially, it felt like angels surely must have hijacked the boys. They were so abnormally accommodating, it was almost scary. I was grateful they weren't fighting or being difficult if I asked them to unload the dishwasher, but it still seemed strange.

The comic relief surprised me too and lifted my spirits; the boys were doing just fine. I kept the upbeat momentum, telling the boys Dad was healing well and sleeping a ton. I didn't give very many details, because I didn't want them, especially Alex to overthink anything. He cried when he first heard about his dad, and he didn't even know if Tony had just skinned a knee or had broken several body parts. My updates to them were so positive that if an adult asked either boy about their dad, they said, "He's great. He's going to be OK!"

One of the first nights we had together at home, they kneeled at the family room coffee table drawing pictures for their dad. I couldn't remember the last time I saw them together with a pad of paper and a pile of markers. Tween voices sang along to "I'm the Man," by Joe Jackson, "Barbara Ann" by the Beach Boys and "Mexican Radio" by Wall of Voodoo, songs burned on a CD by Dad. Tony had influenced their musical tastes since they were born; he wasn't the "Twinkle, Twinkle" type, especially for long car rides.

Most nights while Tony was at the hospital, they watched the TV show *Everybody Hates Chris*, a comedy based loosely on the teenage years of comedian Chris Rock. I watched some of the episodes too, giggling from behind my laptop at the dining room table. Even though I faced the family room TV, I was more focused on posting to the blog. Tony's injuries were extensive and grotesque, and sometimes the medical care was downright frightening. The first couple of posts were awkward, because I worried about sparking anxiety attacks or laptops snapping shut. I had one friend tell me, "Say only positive things." Another friend told me, "We love you no matter what you say." The lawyer's "nonlawyer" advice settled my approach: just be yourself.

I sank deep into my mind to create funny or gentle updates, just like I did with the boys. I couldn't look at it any other way either, or I would fall to pieces. Humor and positivity were my best weapons against the dark side. I thought about ways I might tell a story at my childhood dinner table: make it funny. But sometimes there was no skirting the truth. If Tony's lung was full of muck, I said so; his cough was flat out gross and very, very painful. And if he said something snarky to a nurse, that came out too.

What I didn't expect was the number of virtual friends I would make from the blog. I wasn't a Facebook user in 2010, so I didn't get the allure of social media. Readers could post comments on the blog, and I felt the love and support from those messages. Some were encouraging to Tony, saying things like, "You'll get better fast!" "We're pulling for you!" Messages came for me too: "You're the best wife!" "Awesome post! I never expected to laugh." I never expected to laugh either or receive compliments. I didn't expect anyone to say anything. My stomach was light and bubbly instead of constricted for a change.

Other replies cracked me up. When I relayed stories about saving Tony from the nurses and questioning who was the "real" nurse in the situation, I got a surprising comment: "It's all going to work out. And I'm a *real* nurse." I literally laughed out loud. I couldn't believe she was following Tony's progress, let alone commenting. Just a month before Tony's accident, her husband had a heart attack on a ride and died at the side of the road. To me, she was "real." She was funny and had "real" heart.

In my first post, I talked about the doctor following Tony's case, "We were told by Dr. Truj . . ." I stopped. I didn't know the legalities around using someone's name without permission. So I made up names based on jobs or behaviors. The ER doctor we started with became El Doctor given his Spanish accent and his position. Fake names made the situation seem a little less serious even though their connection to us was very, very serious. What could have been an additional worry, a potential lawsuit over a blog post, turned out to be a bright spot.

As word of the blog circulated, the replies to my updates were like talking to a hundred Tonys, my best listener and advisor. A virtual conversation began. Tony's friends became my friends through the blog. Acquaintances became my friends too, people who just heard about us through the swimming pool, Tony's bike club, Boy Scouts, and tennis team. People we knew and loved and people we barely knew were concerned for us and that made me so happy.

Another gift from the blog was that it improved my state of mind. I wrote every day for the first three weeks, feeling the need to keep everyone in the loop. Sometimes I woke in the middle of the night or early in the morning with a burning story or thought. It was like I was starved and couldn't satiate my storytelling appetite fast enough. Then I would click "submit" and hope I didn't just freak someone out.

For some followers, the updates were read over breakfast while on vacation. Others found inspiration. A friend's son was heading to medical school. He tacked up a phrase on a bulletin board about a doctor we loved because he was so down to earth and dressed in casual clothes. And others would write back with, "OMG, I can fix your problem!" Even though I was trying to be myself, avoid scaring anyone, and dodge lawsuits, I worried after every post. Over time, I learned somebody out there would love me for what I wrote, and if they didn't, they kept quiet.

I never understood why journaling, a common recommendation by doctors, social workers, and therapists, was supposed to be a way of coping during times of trouble. Some of my friends kept notebooks about their feelings surrounding a loved one's injury and afterward, they never wanted to look back. They pitched their paper journals into the stinky trash bin or the coals of a crackling fire. Mine, a digital journal, stayed locked up in my computer. Like my friends, I didn't want to look back at my blog either, even if I had tried to be funny. But after two years, I did. Many friends asked how we got through the accident so I felt compelled to write about it to help others.

When I hit the save button for my first blog post, the floodgates of love were opened, surrounding us from every part of my life and Tony's, far and near. Blessings and guidance made me a better cheerleader for Tony and for the boys. I knew I wasn't doing this alone.

CHAPTER 8

The Power of Positivity

Four Days After the Accident

WHEN I ARRIVED AT THE HOSPITAL four days after the accident, I was surprised to find Tony in a private room inside the NICU, one with glass walls draped in taupe burlap curtains. It was a definite upgrade from the wall of white cotton-thin curtains in the NICU arena that barely provided any privacy.

I felt safer for Tony and for myself in that private room, at least I thought we were better off. Even the patient lying in a lump with two bored police officers on either side of him didn't scare me as much. The crazy thing was, that criminal wasn't really as much of a concern as guarding Tony from some of the staff.

"Keep the lights low and the TV off," instructed the new nurse of the day, Nurse Cathy. In the new room, the light and TV could be managed to suit Tony's needs and not an arena of patients. A very attentive but unemotional nurse had replaced the perky, southern-charmed Nurse Healy from the last two days, I assumed Tony needed more rest, so I didn't question why all the precautions were in place.

The good news for Tony now though was that a fan stood next to his bed to keep him cool. Since arriving he had been overheating while his body tried to fight off infection from his many injuries, so this was a luxurious upgrade from the arena where he wasn't afforded a fan. The good news for me was that the new quarters came with a private bathroom. "No lock on the door," Nurse Cathy warned me. The risk of someone bursting in on me was well worth the "exposure" if I could avoid leaving Tony or losing my cell phones.

I was also surprised, when I walked in, to find a visitor gazing over Tony as he slept. My friend Roger was a member of one of the PTA boards I'd served on in the past and he was a pastor at a local church. Somehow, he had finagled his way past the nurses. Pastors seemed to get a back-stage pass in traumatic situations, but I would have let him in anyway. Knowing somebody was watching over Tony in my absence was a comfort to me. Roger didn't stay long as he completed his mission to see and pray for Tony and he probably wanted some air after such a sight. Tony was not easy on the eyes if you didn't love him like I do.

If I were a stranger seeing Tony for the first time, chills would run down my spine. The beeping and gasping machines were disturbing enough but a bruised eye, padded neck collar and sling were too much. Watching Tony switch positions or simply reach for his water made even the faint-hearted wince. The battle wasn't over just because the cup was in his hand. His lips would blindly search for the straw, similar to a game of pin-the-tail on the donkey. One good eye, one good arm and a neck he could barely turn, was challenging. Any shift in his body was so painful he had to move very, very slowly. Even then, pain was written all over his face.

One of the few times Tony surrendered to help was at lunch. It was hard for him to eat anything from a bowl or plate since the neck collar prevented him from looking down at his lunch tray. To make matters worse, he had to use his left hand to eat because his dominant hand dangled in a sling. No amount of willpower could help Tony accomplish this monumental feat. Instead, Tony sat very still and let me help with the broth or pudding. I focused on feeding him or making him comfortable instead of lamenting over the broken parts stopping him from feeding himself. It's strange how all his big injuries, machines and wheezy breaths didn't rattle me. My heart swelled taking care of him in the hospital: anticipating ways to make him cozier, tucking the blankets close to his body to keep him warmer. That's the way I liked sleeping so I hoped Tony did too.

Even in Tony's broken state, he never stopped thinking like an athlete. Racing cyclists train to rise above pain whether climbing a long steep hill or just trying to keep up with the peloton, the main group of cyclists in a race. He wanted out of the hospital as soon as possible and he was willing to do anything to speed up the healing process, even if it hurt. His Swiss cheese like lung required strengthening. A healthy person might go for a run to pump air in and out of his chest. For Tony, the closest thing to cardio was blowing into a spirometer, a plastic tube attached to a fist-sized clear plastic box. Black lines marked the box like a measuring cup, the idea was to raise the tiny ball inside to reach the highest line. The task sounded easy, but the only problem was, his rib cage moved with each breath and with nine broken ribs this caused his busted body to scream with pain. Deeply inflating his lung over and over seemed more like a practice in withstanding torture than exercise. Tony proved over and over to be an expert at enduring extreme pain.

"Alive and fixable" became our mantra and our inspiration to keep a positive mindset. Tony *would* get better. I really believed that and so did Tony, and it showed. He demonstrated his strength and fortitude daily, leaving me in jaw dropping awe. Whether he was forcing himself to walk, stay awake to talk to me, or simply summoning up instructions for his work, he found a superpower deep down that allowed him to attain what he wanted. He was desperately holding on to any bit of control he could in order to maintain his fitness and get back on the bike as soon as possible. Tony wasn't afraid to challenge the nurses who got in his way.

I chuckled when he got into a feisty debate with the Nurse Cathy, a fact-to-fact battle. Her manner was emotionless and her thinking, black or white. One afternoon, Tony needed a chest X-ray and the Nurse Cathy wanted to put him on a gurney so he could be wheeled to radiology. As tough as Tony was, there was no way he was going to move from one bed to another if he could help it.

"Isn't the bed I'm in a gurney? It has wheels." Tony pointed out. Nurse Cathy stopped in her tracks. He had her cornered. I covered my mouth to hide my smirk.

Tony relished the moment for about five minutes until the male nurse assistants came to get him for his X-ray and put the kibosh on Tony's win to stay in his bed. Only a small gurney would fit in the X-ray room so it was either pay now or pay later. For me, seeing Tony push back gave me joy and a sense of calm that everything would be OK.

My presence gave him the peace and comfort he needed to rest properly. While he was in the NICU, I watched Tony sleep or I dozed off in the god-awful uncomfortable plastic office chairs provided for visitors. The bright-blue color made the chair *look* lively and inviting. But clearly no one was expected to stay long. My legs were stretched out in front of me and my head fell onto my chest, but I was at the ready if he needed anything. If Tony stirred even the slightest, my eyes flicked open like a light switch. As Tony's lung healed, he started coughing out the gunk in his chest, like a kid getting over a cold. I jumped from my chair to gently hold a pillow on his chest to smother the pain in his ribs when he had a coughing fit. Once he got the tickle out, he slept some more. I didn't mind his quiet company. In fact, I didn't mind being quiet. I never had the urge to pull out one of my trashy Hollywood gossip magazines to pass the time. Being close to Tony was soothing to me.

As much as we tried to make the best of a bad situation, creating a safe world filled with hope and gratefulness, we could easily be jerked back to reality by the simple reaction of a visitor seeing Tony for the first time. Their expressions revealed how Tony looked to others: a wrecked, lucky-to-be-alive man. Four days after the accident, The White Knight, our tough-guy, F-bomb slinging lawyer came to see him just after lunch. Tony was sitting in a chair, surrounded by pillows to prop up his back and arm. The White Knight witnessed one of the coughing dances and about melted into the floor, sinking back into his chair. His skin turned to ash and his breath seemed to stop. I wasn't sure who to care for first, Tony or the lawyer. I honestly thought our White Knight was going to pass out or throw up. He probably didn't remember a word that was said at this meeting; Tony's injuries were too distracting. It was the same thing that happened to the pastor during his visit; the pastor couldn't pray over Tony fast enough. *Was Tony that bad?* I was astonished to see visitors looking so stunned. Tony seemed pretty good to me but I think that's where the expression "love is blind" took on a whole new meaning. I loved him, for better or for worse.

I walked our lawyer out of the NICU through the ominous doors. Neither of us said anything along the way. After a brief goodbye, The White Knight took a few steps down the hall and turned to look at me.

"If you need anything. *Anything.* Let me know. I have two sons who can mow your lawn or take out your garbage. You let me know." The hallway suddenly seemed hollow and gray, with just the two of us looking at each other with great intensity. I was taken aback by his sincere offer.

"Thank you." I said quietly. I didn't know what else to say. I was still getting to know him and I don't think I ever felt someone care so much about helping my family.

As I walked back to sit with Tony, a young woman dressed in street clothes stopped me. I guessed she was another social worker, like the one from ER. I don't remember either of these ladies explaining their connection to us. No introduction of, "Hi. I'm Mary and I'm a counselor/social worker/therapist."

"How are you holding up?" she asked softly.

"Fine," I said warily. Wondering, *what does she want from me?*

"I wanted to pass along some pamphlets for you to read, in case you need some support." She nodded toward my husband's bed and brushed a tear from her eye.

"Thanks," I whispered, trying not to cry. *Crap! Don't take me down with you!* I thought. *Why do these social workers have to be so sad? And why do they just show up out of nowhere?* I stuffed the "dealing with grief" papers deep into my backpack and never, ever looked at them.

I know she was trying to help but it didn't feel like help to me. Again, someone saw our situation as dire and dark; their behavior baffled me. Somehow a powerful shield was protecting me from feeling down like the social workers. If I couldn't be upbeat around my husband, how the heck was he going to have any hope? I knew more than ever at that point how important it was to surround myself with positive people and positive thoughts.

My upbeat attitude was fueled by the kindness of others; the angels that started to appear in our life daily if not hourly. Just that morning, an angel showed up as I took a few extra minutes to cut up a papaya for Tony, the fruit, a source of comfort to him.

I hate cutting up produce, especially exotic fruit like pineapples, mangoes or papayas. Tony was the expert slicer. He was horrified any time a knife was in my hand, laughing to the point of tears at the results: pineapple with more brown freckles than my Irish skin or mangos so mushy a baby could eat my work. I stared at the fruit in my hand, wondering where to stick the knife first. I'd barely started on the papaya when the doorbell rang. My neighbor came to check on me.

"I didn't know if it was OK to come over. I don't know what to do in this kind of situation," she said apologetically. She shuffled her feet a little, not sure whether to stand there or walk into my house.

"I don't know what to do either. Come in. I'm cutting up some fruit for Tony before I go to the hospital," I said as we walked into the kitchen together.

She watched me as I awkwardly hacked into the soft golden-yellow skin of the papaya, flecks of pale orange split away; the oval ball lost its shape like a melting snowman.

"Here, let me do that," she said as she took the knife from me.

Before I knew it, my friend had sliced up the peachy-colored flesh into bite-sized chunks with ease. Papaya saved. My insides were warm with delight.

Opportune moments like the day's chance meeting with the pastor, the attorney and my neighbor helped me keep a positive attitude. Every worry inside my head was met with someone showing up to help as if they heard my request and responded immediately. Another community was forming on our behalf; angels were a pleasant surprise of the day, like finding a lucky penny on the sidewalk. I started to look forward to each day, my eyes peeled.

Positivity and humor were my morphine. I think that was why the blog to broadcast Tony updates was informative and entertaining. I didn't know it at the time but discovering things to laugh at or cheer about was a way of coping and steering clear of the dark side. And that was a big part of how I survived. Tony too.

CHAPTER 9

A Very Bad Day

Five Days After the Accident

TONY'S PAIN SPIKED OVERNIGHT. Who knows why? Maybe his body shook off the shock, unmasking the dagger-like stabs in his chest from nine broken ribs or maybe it was the newly inserted chest tube draining the muck from his punctured lung. Whatever the reason, it became very evident after four days in the NICU, the current protocol was not working. Pain management was hard to predict, and the amount of medication he was getting was in baby doses. An epidural was ordered.

I cringed. I knew what Tony would be facing: a lot of pain.

"Do you two have kids?" the doctor asked, as we stood around Tony's hospital bed. The lights were low and glowing to make for a more restful healing experience, but the effects were lost on the suffering patient.

"Yes. Two," I replied.

"So, you know about epidurals?" he asked delicately. The hum of the fan, cooling Tony's oven-like body was the only sound in the room for a long moment.

"Yes," I answered.

I looked at my Tony to see if he understood what this meant for him, his face blank. I don't think he remembered much from when our sons were born. He probably hadn't even peeked when I leaned over, bent at the waist, so the anesthesiologist could get the needle into my spine at just the right place. As the doctor explained the procedure, Tony's body caved slightly. Changing positions in his bed was excruciating, so the thought of contorting his upper body, disturbing nine broken ribs for even ten seconds was horrifying.

I did not want to stick around, but I didn't want Tony to feel abandoned either. My face scrunched with worry. With great relief, the doctor made the decision for me; he strongly advised me to leave the room.

I escaped into the hallway, just outside the ominous doors of NICU. Tony's agony hovered in my mind as I made a crucial call to his eye doctor. His eyeglasses prescription was five years out of date, and right now contacts were not an option. His right eye was still puffy and black from the laceration to his eyelid; the stitches still fresh.

But Tony was blind as a bat without his contacts. I kidded him about who would save us from an intruder in the middle of the night, since he couldn't see whom to fight or protect. He rarely wore his glasses, so for him any updates were a waste of money. He sure needed them now though. I was only too happy to make it happen as quickly as possible, something I thought I could control, since his excruciating state was in someone else's hands for the moment.

I didn't want to be too far away from Tony in case he needed me. One of those Cotton-Hair Volunteers sat at her desk a few feet away from where I made my call. I turned my back for a bit of privacy.

"Hi. I'm Tony Low's wife, and I was wondering if you could fax a prescription to LensCrafters. He's in the *hospital*." I hoped my over-pronunciation of "hospital" would be enough explanation and convey my desperation.

"It's against our policy to send out prescriptions without seeing the patient first. We need to measure his eyes with the frames to be sure the lenses are lined up properly," she replied in a firm voice.

"Impossible. He's in ICU." The *N* in NICU seemed to disappear whenever I spoke to other people. "He can't get out, and I don't know when he will get out." I heard my voice getting loud and scary. "He can't wear his contacts, and his eyeglasses are hopelessly out of date," I said nearly shouting into my cell phone. At that point, I really didn't care if the grandmotherly volunteer heard every word.

"Well . . . I'm not supposed to do this, but I guess we can this time," she said as if she was doing me a huge, huge favor.

"Thanks" I said, my tone terse. But in my head, I screamed, "Finally!"

I stepped back into Tony's room to see how he'd fared after the torturous procedure. At last, he was in a deep sleep. My mighty sweetheart had endured. To call him tough or brave didn't even begin to describe his fortitude. I didn't have to be there to know. Watching him reach for a tissue or even scratch his nose spoke volumes about how hard it was to move the tiniest bit; he hurt.

While he slept, I drove to LensCrafters, located at a mall about fifteen minutes from the hospital. I brought Tony's old frames for the new prescription. All I had to do was wait, hopefully for less than the advertised hour to complete an order. I sat on a bench outside the store, a little more relaxed; my mission was almost complete. I pulled a whole-wheat bagel with goat cheese and left-over roast chicken out of the dark green backpack I carried everywhere now. While I ate my lunch, I watched slow walking shoppers with multiple bags dangling from their arms. Most were moms and their kids buying back-to-school clothes. *Ugh. How am I going to get my kids ready for school?* I realized.

The eyeglasses were ready after just thirty minutes. I raced back to the hospital, pleased with the speedy outcome. I couldn't wait to give Tony his vision back.

I bounced into Tony's room, eyeglasses in hand so I could put them on his face and see him smile. My enthusiasm dropped like a fifty-pound rock. I was startled at my husband's condition. He was struggling in pain again, skin glistening with sweat. The fan that had kept him cool for the last few days was gone. What had happened to it? And why wasn't the epidural working? My eyes flitted up and down Tony's body, looking for clues. I tried to get answers from my husband; he spoke in a raspy voice, like someone pinned under a fallen tree. I sprinted to the nurses' station.

"Hi. Sorry to interrupt, but my husband isn't making any sense to me. He's in a lot of pain right now . . .and . . ." My words rushed out, abruptly stopped by the nurse's terse response.

"I'll get there in a minute." She replied through tight lips. Her neck turned bright red as she whipped around to put away a file she was holding. The tone of the message was an even greater barrier than the tall counter separating us. I had been dismissed.

I didn't want to push her too much, because there was no telling what she could do to my husband when I wasn't around. I backed off and quickly returned to Tony's bedside. My foot tapped rapidly against the shiny linoleum floor as I sat with my arms crossed in the stiff chair next to Tony. My eyes darted between him and the empty doorway, waiting for Angry Nurse to appear. *More* than a minute had passed.

"I'm going back out to ask what is going on," I whispered furiously, glaring at my watch. "This is RIDICULOUS!"

"Don't. Don't screw me. Don't screw me," Tony begged in a wheezy voice.

Defeated, I stayed in my chair, glaring harder and harder at the door. The fury inside of me was like a pot on the verge of boiling over.

After what seemed an eternity, Angry Nurse entered the room carrying a waterless shampoo cap used to wash a patient's hair. She dropped the plastic package on the end of the bed. I had asked her earlier in the morning about getting Tony's hair washed; five days seemed long enough to tolerate a greasy head.

Tony gasped out, "Nnnott *now*!"

"I tried to tell you he was in a lot of pain. A LOT." My words strained to contain my frustration, as if his sweaty, grimacing appearance was not enough of a broadcast.

Angry Nurse turned to look at the small screen on the epidural machine. "The epidural drip is off," she said in quiet disbelief. "It's been off for three hours."

"What?!?" I wanted to explode, but Tony's message of screwing him over stuck in my head.

"I'll get something to relieve the pain immediately, until the epidural takes hold again," she said.

Tony was barely settled in when two of his cycling friends came for a visit.

"Your timing is impeccable," Tony squeaked out. "The pain is at a ten."

I ushered his buddies into the waiting room to explain the drama of the day.

"I came back from LensCrafters to find him in a pool of sweat, sounding like Darth Vader during his last breaths, all wheezy and squeaky," I said as I dabbed my eyes. "Sorry for the tears."

"Hey. It's OK to cry," one of the friends said, empathetically. But I felt weird getting emotional in front of guys I barely knew. I was glad only a few tears had escaped.

As we continued talking and Tony's friends consoled me, the same Cotton-Hair Volunteer that was sitting outside of the NICU from the morning wandered into the room. She placed her hand on my shoulder. All three of us looked up at her in wonder.

"It's going to be OK. You're young. I see a lot of things, and I know it will be OK." Her tone was sweet and sincere. She must have seen and heard the emotional side of families' experiences in a way the medical staff rarely did, like watching a soap opera.

"That's how a nurse should be," I said as she walked away. "One who is kind and attentive and doesn't turn red when you talk to her." I choked back more tears as I looked at Tony's stunned buddies. "She probably packs needles too," I joked, trying to cheer us all up.

A few minutes with Tony's buddies pumped me back up to face Tony with a smile and not wet eyes. I was glad I didn't see Angry

Nurse on my way back in to the NICU. I might have violated Tony's rule to not screw him.

At this point, the only powers Tony had were his thoughts and the words he choked out to convey his will. Tony was rarely at the mercy of anyone until now. He was always the doer, the caretaker for our family and me. After two C-sections, I was forbidden to help much beyond feeding our newborns. Tony on the other hand, whirled around the house as if he were the Tasmanian Devil, mowing the lawn, changing diapers, and making us lunch. Tony was so vulnerable in the NICU, I had to do what I could to make him happy, even if it meant swallowing my pride around Angry Nurse.

I sat with Tony until his breathing slowed and he was fast asleep. I thought about how I could take control of a situation I knew nothing about, machines and meds. I had to do something.

The next day, I came in carrying a clipboard so I could document each dose of pain medication. I made a note of when it was administered and how much. Nobody was *ever* going to put my husband through agonizing pain again, not on my watch.

Word of the epidural mishap must have been passed around before I even arrived, because Nurse Cathy was back and didn't seem surprised by my unhappiness. She even tolerated my request for the pain medication schedule.

Tony did what he could too. As much as I worried about him at night when I wasn't there to keep him company, he seemed to find a friendly nurse to chat up and discuss his progress or concerns. He told one night nurse that he never wanted Angry Nurse on his case again. She stayed away except to check on a glitch with the epidural that for whatever reason only she knew how to repair. Her back was turned except for the split second she glanced over at us. Our bodies stiffened and our eyes narrowed as we watched her every move. I'm sure she felt our fury and mistrust.

In Angry Nurse's defense, maybe she had too many patients to watch that day or maybe something ticked her off to make her short-fused and forgetful. Regardless, I learned very quickly that my job was much bigger than feeding Tony soup or keeping him company. I had no idea how much I would become his protector, saving him from the experts supposedly there to save him; this was a warm-up for my role as Tony's in-the-flesh guardian angel.

CHAPTER 10

Bring in the Boys

Six Days After the Accident

"GOOD MORNING," I SAID QUIETLY, trying not to startle Tony as he gazed out at the oak-studded hills through the window of his new room. He'd moved out of the NICU and into the medical-surgical floor of the hospital, his condition was downgraded from critical.

"Hi," he said in a sleepy, relaxed voice. "Nice view, eh?"

"Yep. The same view I had waiting in the ER. I like it from up here better—more sky," I said lightheartedly. "Great you could have your own room." I poked around as if I was touring a new apartment, peaking into the private bathroom with a sink and a bathtub and a *locking* door. A desk was crammed into the corner with *two* of the familiar stiff chairs. I could use one of them to put my feet up. The last nurse in the NICU told us Tony was moving to the new wing of the hospital, the Cadillac.

"Yeah. I have real walls so it's quieter. I heard moans and groans in ICU, especially at night." The *N* in NICU didn't register for Tony either. Tony sounded a little more upbeat even though his hand moved slowly to pick up a cup of water with a bendy-straw from the table. It was on his left side, I noticed. It took the nurses in the NICU several days to get the table placed on the side of the bed with Tony's usable arm, the left. The nurses in the new digs seemed to be immediately aware of which arm was in a sling and which arm was reaching for a drink. I was happier already with the location change. His medical equipment, or the ball and chain as I endearingly referred to it, were still attached to him: the epidural, lung pump, IV, and catheter.

All this time, I assumed Tony was so full of injuries that he earned a private, quieter place to heal. But in truth, the privilege came down to one injury. Tony had had a concussion, a bad one. It made sense Tony was concussed. After all, the trailer rolled over his upper body, his neck and his head, cracking his helmet—the helmet that saved his life. I never put a label on his brain injury or really acknowledged that his brain was even injured. I didn't remember getting any description other than he might repeat himself in the ER because he'd hurt his head. Since there wasn't a bandage on his head or some sort of indication his brain wasn't right, it didn't occur to me to ask questions.

How was this major diagnosis never shared? Or maybe it was? Hospitals with busy doctors and nurses, a near-flattened husband, and me are not a good combination. Or as Tony liked to say, I am like a pinball machine: too much information and I start to tilt, shutting down, like the game. Once I weeded out the worst, death or paralysis, I concentrated on Tony's comfort more than anything, especially pain management. "Alive and fixable" stuck in my head, enabling me to remain in fix-it mode and keep up the cheery attitude for Tony and the boys.

A million questions spun in my head in addition to Tony's care. I was definitely on the verge of going on tilt. How would I pay the bills? Tony handled all the finances. How were the boys holding up? TJ got so tired with too much stimulation caused by all-day playdates; he was an introvert. Would insurance cover all the expenses? Sorting the medical bills would take hours. When was a good time to share the news with my extended family? Later was easier. Tony's family was up to speed and that was enough family involvement for me. Should Tony take a leave of absence or use vacation time? Tony worked in high-tech sales; what did his customers need to know and who should tell them?

With so much on my mind, I had to delegate responsibilities such as care for my kids and of course, letting Tony's medical staff look after him; that was their job. Although I was learning to keep at least one eye peeled with the doctors and nurses. I focused on what I thought I could control, like pain management, given the epidural fiasco. I let go of bringing more papaya or anything else he was used to eating daily. Hospital food had improved since the time I had delivered babies twelve years before. Besides, Tony wasn't complaining.

The first thing I did once I checked on Tony and inspected his new room was to introduce myself to the new nurse responsible for Tony's care. I pulled my clipboard and pen out of the green backpack and held them to my chest. I marched to the nurses' station a few feet outside Tony's door.

"Hi. I'm Tony Low's wife. Are you the nurse taking care of him today?" I asked with a big, bright smile.

"Yes, I am. I'm Priscilla," she replied with a polite, slight British accent, eyeing my clipboard.

"I was wondering if you could tell me when his last pain medication was administered and when he is scheduled to have his next dose. We had some problems in ICU, so I hope you don't mind." I said still smiling, hoping I sounded friendly and not intimidating.

"Mrs. Low," Priscilla began in a formal tone with a hint of let-me-tell-you-something-sister. "I tell all of my patients they must ask for their medication. Too much could lead to respiratory failure . . .blah, blah, bah." I stopped listening and dropped my clipboard to my side and out of her sight. She was going to manage me.

"Oh. OK. Good to know. Um, thanks." I slumped back to Tony's room in defeat, a little embarrassed and disappointed my clipboard tactic was futile.

I noticed a whiteboard hung above the desk. The nurses wrote the day of the week and the date so the patient could keep track of time. Later on, I saw new information below the date, the time of his last medication. I don't know if the meds schedule was for my benefit or if it was hospital protocol. Either way, Priscilla and I ended up getting along just fine.

Keeping track of all of Tony's ailments and how to ensure he was getting everything he needed was a challenge for someone not medically trained. I was trying to think like a nurse, like I did when my kids were sick, but Tony was definitely harder. As much as I was impatient with the inattentiveness of the nurses, I was beginning to empathize a little, much to my surprise.

What I also didn't expect was how the boys would help me gain more understanding of the medical situation when they finally came to visit. After spending most of the day with Tony, feeding him lunch and keeping him company, I went home for a quick dinner with the boys and to prepare them for their first visit. In the immediate days after the accident, our friends had started a dinner schedule. That night, my friend Dawn cooked for us, bringing one of the most memorable meals. We dined on fresh roasted chicken, destemmed strawberries (impressive to me, as the labor was above and beyond), and boutique bakery cupcakes thick with whipped butter cream frosting in several flavors. Every part of the meal was so thoughtful; I had no idea my friend was such a phenomenal cook. We saved a cupcake for Tony.

The mood was lighter during dinner, knowing Dad was well enough for a visit. The three of us climbed into the big white Toyota Sequoia and drove for twenty minutes to the hospital. The boys couldn't wait to see Dad and find out what was inside a hospital and what kind of room he had. I tried to set an honest expectation using a matter-of-fact tone, not woeful—exactly how I wanted doctors or friends to talk to me and what my psychologist friend had suggested.

"He is very weak, and his face isn't happy or sad. Smiling or frowning use too much energy. He can't walk very well or very far; he's really slow. He has machines connected to him to help him get better," I said as we drove out of our neighborhood.

"Is he getting better?" Alex asked.

"Yes! Dad is getting better every day. He's in a different part of the hospital where he can have visitors. That means he's stronger and doesn't need as much help." I was so glad to have cheery, honest news for the boys.

As we headed into the hospital parking lot, the boys stared up at the mirrored-window building in wonder. Part of the hospital was under construction; cranes balanced on the rooftop. Alex insisted on carrying my green backpack so he could look like the majority of people he saw walking through the automatic glass doors at the entrance. He was going to look professional, as if he had walked across a hospital campus a thousand times, an extra spring in his step. TJ proudly carried the cupcake to give to Dad. Both walked in front of me, wanting to be first to see all there was to see, almost like going to an amusement park.

When we entered the room, the excitement quickly dissipated. The boys quietly drank in every detail, their eyes hung on their dad, sitting upright in his big bed. The black-and-gray whiskers under his nose and in patches along his cheeks were new; Dad never had whiskers. The pale-gray nightgown with tiny, dark-gray dots, reminiscent of faded wallpaper looked strange on a dad that only wore blue-plaid flannel pajamas. After six days, his hair looked windblown, sticking up in places and smashed flat in others. His big, cushiony navy-blue neck collar with a white plastic frame and the navy-blue cloth sling that held his right shoulder close to his body looked uncomfortable. After a week, his eye looked as if nothing had happened to it—no signs of a stitched-up, boxer-like black eye. One less thing to digest.

Machines with tubes and wires framed the bed like haphazardly placed bookends. A pitcher of water and plastic breathing tools resembling toys rested on the bedside table with wheels. I wasn't sure if the boys would cry or stand stiff in fright. Neither happened. They both handled the visit with grace, listening intently to every word Tony spoke in a gentle whisper, partly because of the concussion—his brain was bruised—but also out of fatigue and pain. Talking took effort, rattling the rib cage and lungs if he used his normal speaking voice.

"This tube, it sucks out liquid from my lung like a vacuum cleaner. If I didn't have the machine, my lung would fill up like it would if I was drowning in a swimming pool. My right lung has holes in it, where the ribs poked through, popping it like a balloon." *Gads! Tony isn't hiding a thing. The boys* seem *to be doing OK with the graphic explanation.* I watched the boys closely; their eyes followed the tube to a silver-topped machine with a clear plastic base the size of a coffee maker. Tony continued, "Do you see the box with white pasty stuff in it? When the white stuff stops filling the box, my lung is better and I can go home." Tony explained the thoracic aspirator better than any doctor or nurse.

"When do the doctors expect you to go home," TJ asked in his serious voice, not a trace of emotion. *Thank goodness he wasn't freaked out by Tony's "professor" moment.*

"I don't know; a few more days I hope," Tony answered.

Tony's explanation helped me learn more about what the machines were doing too. Having the boys around allowed me to hear the message at a simpler and slower pace. I needed the information repeated as I'd probably missed a detail or two along the way.

Alex stood eye level to Tony's feet. He observed Tony's navy-blue calf-wraps, used to simulate blood pressure to prevent clots. Tony wasn't walking around enough to keep the blood flowing naturally.

Alex turned up his nose and said, "You smell like a footlocker!" I burst out laughing. Alex surprised us sometimes with his spot-on analogies, like the first time he ate a slice of vegan cake at a birthday party. "I didn't like the cake. It tasted like the ground," Alex said disappointedly.

"What do you know about footlockers, Alex?" Tony asked, kidding him. As far as we know, Alex knew nothing except how to use the word appropriately in a sentence. He must have read it in a book or heard it on a TV show. He was only ten years old.

"Why don't you guys show Dad what we brought for him," I suggested.

The boys eagerly pulled the chocolate cupcake from the box and gave it to Tony. He happily ate the confection, something he never would have done before the accident, as keeping weight down for racing was so important to him. Tony could eat regular food now, but it was odd to see him devour a dessert in just three bites, as if it were the first food he'd seen in weeks and not just a cyclist diet breaker. It was a joy to watch. I sat near the window on the narrow ledge meant for vases of flowers so the boys could sit in the *only two chairs* in the room, close to their Dad. Even banged up, Dad was a pleasure to be around. Deep down, his superpower or mystery inner strength was fueling his will to hold his sons' attention.

I was relieved that we could finally be together as a family. The boys had a way of blessing us with their innocence, making us laugh and reinforcing our belief to focus on the future. Now that the boys would see their dad for a short time every day, I felt a little better about leaving Tony alone at night.

Our visit lasted about an hour. Tony was tired and the boys were growing restless. We said our goodnights the best we could, the boys gripping their dad's good hand since they couldn't hug him or stand tall enough to give him a kiss on the cheek. The sky was growing dark by eight p.m. as we loaded the truck to go home. A heavy silence filled the air, each of us lost in thought about what we saw. I broke the quiet.

"TJ, you didn't say much during the visit. Didn't you have any questions?" I asked.

"Mom, I was trying not to say anything funny, like you told me, but I could only think of funny things. I decided not to say anything,"

TJ said. I stifled a chuckle. I was very proud of him and how he handled my direction.

"That was very thoughtful, TJ," I responded happily.

Making Tony laugh, even a little giggle, sent a jolt of pain through Tony's ribs. I half-kiddingly instructed the boys and any visitor: "Don't crack jokes because the ribs are cracked" or "Be fun, not funny."

"I wanna bring Dad another cupcake. He likes them a lot," said Alex. *Oh my gosh! The boys are so sweet.*

"Maybe you can help him with his dinner. He can't feed himself very well," I offered.

"Both of us?" asked TJ.

"Yes, both of you." My boys had never been so agreeable and helpful. I needed this kind of behavior right now. My heart was full of love and pride for my boys.

It's strange, but the hospital was going to hold a lot of memories for us. We think of Tony each time we drive past to this day. A piece of each of our hearts is still there.

CHAPTER 11

Family Time

Eight Days After the Accident

TONY'S NEW HOSPITAL HOME was an easy adjustment. I liked walking in and out as I pleased, without having to introduce myself via intercom for admittance: Visiting hours spanned the whole day without the "temporarily closed" hour for the change of staff. Only a handful of nurses were managing Tony, so we didn't have to start over as often in regard to pain management protocol or the bedside table placement. We also saw a lot more of the doctors caring for Tony than we ever did in the NICU, in particular, El Doctor, the first doctor we met in the ER and the one following Tony's case.

"You will stay in the sling for five more weeks. Don't move," El Doctor instructed in a rushed tone. No driving for Tony; *I will be his chauffer*, was my immediate thought. El Doctor and I looked over Tony, much like we did in the ER, only this time Tony was taking part in the conversation.

"Wow. Five more weeks," Tony repeated in a whisper. "What about the neck brace?"

"Wait for the neurosurgeon. He can tell you. Now, you need to get moving. No more lying around in bed all the time. Someone will help you walk in the halls." And with the last statement he was gone. *He's on his way! He can walk!*

El Doctor wasn't long on conversation partly because of his demanding patient schedule and partly because he was more of a science guy than a social butterfly. Tony talked to him long enough at one visit to find out he was a fellow cyclist. Anyone who cycles seriously will drop everything to talk up fancy bikes or favorite rides, even a busy physician. One of the nurses rode mountain bikes, so she and Tony talked about the numerous trails convenient to our home. The boys even noticed Tony's uncanny ability to ferret out the bike enthusiasts. Tony, ever-the salesman, engaged people in a way that made it seem as though he had known them all his life. Since Tony worked from home, I heard him laugh a lot while he was on the phone. I used to think it was all friends; it wasn't. Tony was a fun friend, coworker, husband, dad, and patient.

An occupational therapist turned out to be the "someone" to help walk Tony down the hallway of his floor, a young lady who barely looked old enough to drive. Tony was anxious to get back on his bike, but he had to learn to walk before he could ride. He shuffled fifty yards from his room, just past the nurses' station and back. Tony was attached to so much equipment it took two of us to take him out for exercise. The epidural and the lung machine were my responsibilities; I pushed the equipment from behind, careful to keep his slow but heroic pace. I really wanted to watch Tony take every one of his miracle steps and cheer him on with my smiling eyes, but I couldn't. The risk of tripping over wheels or jerking out any tubes from his body wasn't worth taking a long peek. Luckily for me, the occupational therapist led the way with the harder and less pleasant job, serving as Tony's human cane—holding him steady on one arm and scooting his catheter bag, the yellow stuff, with the other. My new job as equipment manager felt more useful and important than sitting by his bedside. Now we were getting somewhere, at least something we could physically see: a workout on what I called the *hospital Olympic track* to recovery.

Tony gained another freedom too. For the previous eight days, TV, cell phone, and books were off limits, but the door was opening a crack. The neurosurgeon modified the brain-injury protocol. Tony could flip through a magazine and turn on more lights. No more staring up at the dimly lit ceiling or the insides of his eyelids for hours on end. His neck brace stayed for two more weeks, however. Two more weeks of blindly stabbing at his lunch plate and gingerly walking with a guide didn't seem so bad if he could amp up the mind stimulation.

"You can begin small exercises to strengthen the brain," announced the friendly neurosurgeon. "Your brain is still very delicate, but you can play multitask games like Scrabble that involve spelling and math." *Scrabble would be good for all of us; family fun instead of family trauma,* I envisioned.

"Can I e-mail?" asked Tony. His laptop and phone were his lifelines before the accident.

"Maybe next week. Social e-mails only." *Geez. He never stops thinking of work.* I was glad the doctor was telling him to take a break, because he wouldn't listen to me.

"The guys will love playing games with you," I chimed in to remind him his boys really wanted to be with him and were far more important than work.

TJ and Alex were getting a job suited to their expertise: board games. *Monopoly* came to mind but the boys decided it was too long, much to my relief. All those plastic houses and hotels could easily find their way to the floor or get twisted up in the sheets. *The Allowance Game* was their recommendation, a simulated experience of buying and saving, using small bills and coins. How fast can a person make change from a buck? For me, a game of mental math was a challenge, and my brain wasn't injured, just flabby.

The boys were stepping up like grown-ups, finding a unique solution to help Dad's brain and keeping him well nourished. After a week in the hospital, Tony was strong enough to move to a large recliner for meals, surrounded by several pillows for added comfort and support. Since the neck brace wasn't going away, the boys could feed Tony. TJ was gentle. He tossed the salad with dressing and cut up the chicken breast in small bites. "This is the first time I've fed someone older than me," TJ comforted Tony.

"And this is the first time I've been fed by someone younger than me," Tony answered back. My heart was glowing. The whole room seemed to feel like I did, bathed in loving warmth and soft light.

Alex fed Tony mushroom soup. He carefully crammed the spoon into Tony's mouth, triggering a gag reflex a few times, but at least no mushrooms were lost. I cherished the interaction for different reasons from the boys. Witnessing Tony, the impatient perfectionist, succumb to the boys' clunky but tender care was precious. I contained my laughter to spare Tony's ribs.

Feeding Dad became a nightly routine for the next few days. The boys stood around the hospital dinner plate, anticipating the removal of the plate cover as if it were a birthday present. What was Dad eating tonight? All throughout the meal, Tony offered tastes to the boys.

"Would you like to try the ravioli?" Tony asked Alex, his little boy eyes admiring the tricolored ravioli in green, red, and white resembling the Italian flag.

"I'm good, Dad. You eat what you want first," Alex answered without hesitation. I couldn't have been more proud of his selflessness. When Tony was finished, the boys attacked the plate like big black crows to roadkill, more like they would at home. Stuffing and chocolate mousse were the biggest hits.

After dinner Tony hobbled to the bathroom to brush his teeth; I rolled the medical equipment behind him. The boys, armed with dripping washcloths, gave Dad a standing sponge bath, rubbing down his hairy legs. I don't think they liked the job very much given their grimaces and sloppy wipes. Tony wasn't his usual fresh, Irish Spring soap-scented self after a week of only sponge baths. I kind of wondered if scrubbing down a dad wasn't pushing his luck trying to make the boys feel helpful and included. Tony could do better washing himself, and he did.

Tony's brain wasn't completely defunct, despite the cautionary return to mental activity. He realized the midmonth bills were coming due. I was dreading this moment, and it came too soon. The last time I paid bills was in the early nineties, and I did it the old-fashioned way with checks, stamps, and envelopes. By 2005, Tony handled the finances, online only. My biggest fear of figuring out how to pay the bills electronically was allayed: TJ and Tony would do it together.

Thank goodness Tony's superpowers were at work again because I would not have known when the bills were due, how to pay them, or where to find the passwords. We took so many precautions to keep our accounts safe from hackers but never considered me being locked out too or that I might have to handle the bills alone.

We made a plan to pay the bills after a family dinner. Since the meals our friends made for us were already packaged for travel, we could grab the bag to eat picnic style at the hospital. Then we could hang out as if we were watching a movie together instead of googling up our AT&T bill. I hunted down the bills, grabbed the laptop, and packed the boys into the Sequoia. Gathering all the stuff and a big enough bag to carry it all took forever. I couldn't find the case for the family laptop; it always stayed home. We were easily thirty minutes behind.

The boys and I clamored into Tony's hospital room with bags of food, the laptop with the cord dangling halfway down my leg, and a stack of envelopes. Priscilla was giving Tony his pain medication when we arrived.

"He waited for you," she said flatly without looking at us, a reprimand. I felt like a little kid whose mother just twisted the knife of guilt. His dinner sat untouched on his bedside table, the warming lids still covering his now-cold food.

"Sorry, Tony," I said to him; I couldn't bear to look at Priscilla. "Sorting the bills took a little while." I felt bad enough we hadn't lived up to our promise to be there when his dinner arrived. I didn't like Priscilla adding to my guilt, an awkwardness forming between us.

"It's OK. I want to eat with my family." Tony did what Tony did best in his current state: remained calm. His hunger to be with his kids was more important to him than eating on time.

Priscilla left us to our family time. TJ cut up Tony's poached pink salmon into bite-sized pieces and Alex was the salad tosser, dressing the salad in pools of vinaigrette. After everyone was fed, Dad with assistance, we got down to work. TJ was set up in a corner with the desk facing the wide white screen. His little head of chocolate-colored hair brushed his shoulders as he looked to Tony for direction and then back to the laptop to follow through. Alex slouched in the chair next to TJ, staring up at the screen with great anticipation. Like me, neither had paid an online bill before. Their eyes were big with the anticipation of what it would be like to be inside the adult world. I perched myself at my usual station, the narrow shelf intended for vases of flowers.

Tony tried to be the mighty family patriarch, standing over TJ in his neck brace, sling, and wispy, faded cotton hospital gown, flashing boxers through the opening in the back. He grasped the rolling stand, holding his chest tube machine as if it were a royal scepter; the recent graduation from the catheter and epidural further enhanced his regalness.

But standing took strength, and his was zapped after just a few raspy commands to TJ. The box of cream-white liquid from his lung kept filling up like a rain barrel in a never-ending storm, so he continued his instructions from his bed.

He wasn't supposed to look at the computer screen anyway, per the neurosurgeon's rules for coming back from a concussion. Besides, hovering over TJ would have made TJ even more nervous. So, it was just as well he was forced to go back to his bed. Tony had to give direction from memory to a twelve-year-old boy whose only computer skills were Word documents and *Black Ops* on Xbox. Tony was ever the perfectionist, so I held my breath as the father-son moment Tony had wanted unfolded.

Tony asked TJ to copy and paste some numbers into a sidebar digital notebook to use later. I jotted the numbers down on paper, just in case the information got lost, because Tony's instructions were coming out faster than TJ could type, and sometimes the old-school way was quicker.

"Now TJ, log out of that program—don't close it. Always log out so you don't leave a back door open for someone to come in," Tony instructed.

"But I don't see where to log out. It doesn't say that anywhere." TJ was scanning the screen and getting a little frustrated.

"It's a tab; it's in there. Probably at the top," Tony explained, calm and patient as ever.

I looked over TJ's shoulder, "Here it is—'sign off,'" I said, and pointed to the screen.

"Now, TJ, paste that number in and click 'OK,'" Tony commanded.

TJ was getting flustered trying to figure out what to cut and where to paste, Tony's idea of efficiency. I sensed a teary argument brewing, so I stepped in again to show TJ my handwritten number. In a flash, TJ typed in the digits before Tony ever realized we'd done it the old-fashioned way.

"Dad, I don't see an 'OK' button." I sucked in a breath, scared this might be the moment Tony ran out of patience.

"It's in there, just look around." I hoped TJ was listening. *Come on TJ, you can find it.*

"All I see is the button that says 'Yes.'" TJ's voice was rising. I felt bad for him, but before I could help, Tony responded.

"TJ, what does 'OK' mean?" A little giggle escaped me. The tension lifted in a poof.

CHAPTER 12

Preparing for Home

Eleven Days After the Accident

TONY COULD GO HOME! I was elated, feeling as if I was walking on sunshine. At last, after eleven days in the hospital, his chest was not spewing out fluid like a fire hose. If all went well with the tube removal and his chest X-ray showed an inflated lung and no liquid, he was FREE! If the X-ray didn't look good, the tube would be reinserted and the hospital stay would continue. We really hoped El Doctor was right: Tony was ready.

"*Exactly* how does the chest tube come out?" Tony asked El Doctor, bracing himself for horrific news. He wanted the play-by-play to suit his engineering mind.

"We pull the chest tube out. PIP! I slap my hand on the chest real fast, POP! And I pull the thread tight," El Doctor answered cheerily, his sound effects like a bowl of crackling cereal. The process certainly seemed quick and easy to me. A pip and a pop and it was over.

"Will I get extra painkillers?" Tony imagined how unbearable the extraction was going to be.

"No. It's fast." Tony wasn't so sure though. He anxiously anticipated breathing freely again. The long tube draining the muck from his lung was like a giant sword lodged in his chest. The gnawing pain was a constant reminder of the intrusion.

I arrived at the hospital minutes after the extraction. I spotted El Doctor in the hallway. He was looking over paperwork at a small counter, a tiny cubby two sizes too small for such a big man.

"How's the patient?" I called out to him.

"He's sooo hawpy!" El Doctor called back in a drawn out Spanish accent. "The tube is out."

"That's GREAT!" I said with a little chuckle. He might not have been a master conversationalist, but he was peppy.

I bounced into the room, happy-stepping my way to where Priscilla was hovering over Tony. The nasty tube and box full of white pasty goo, the pus from his lung, were gone. Where I expected to see Tony full of smiles, his lips were sucked in tight. His eyes were filled with tears, but not tears of joy per El Doctor—tears of agony, per the nurse.

"He is crying," Priscilla announced. She looked like she might cry too. "Removing the tube hurts a lot. I gave him extra pain relief so he might be a little dizzy." It took a lot to bring Tony to tears of pain. In fact, I'd never seen him cry, ever.

My bubbly excited mood was extinguished faster than a kid blowing out candles on a birthday cake. Gads! Every time we turned around, Tony's threshold for pain was pushed higher and higher. I was glad I wasn't there or I might have lost my breakfast or slapped El Doctor's shoulder. "What the heck?!?"

El Doctor did not mention pain. Where were the pips and pops that sounded so fun and easy? Had we known, Tony and I would have looked at this moment with dread instead of pure liberation. Going home sure did come at a hefty price. The long tube felt like a slow-motion sword coming out of Tony's chest, an agonizing ten seconds.

For best results, Tony had to be fully aware during the barbaric procedure. If Tony were on meds, he might not hold his breath long enough or he could flinch. Priscilla tried to negotiate a pre-procedural painkiller, but El Doctor wouldn't have it. Thank goodness for Priscilla's readiness, just seconds afterward. Fortunately, the chest X-ray post-removal was clear, or the tortuous tube would have been re-inserted.

The hardest part was out of the way, but we still had a few more steps to accomplish before being released. Tony and I had to learn home care, so another teenaged-looking occupational therapist taught us how to get Tony dressed. We grew uneasy when she showed us how to pull a T-shirt over his head, around the thick neck collar and into the sleeves with a dislocated shoulder. To try that feat in reverse was not going to happen.

"I will cut the T-shirt off before pulling it back over my head," Tony said half-jokingly.

"Well that would be too expensive," the naïve occupational therapist said, pointing out the flaw in our plan. Tony and I both rolled our eyes. We were more and more ready to go home with each passing minute. Life would be hard at home but easier than navigating around people who just didn't understand us.

Our friends seemed to know how to help us. My blog post describing the "dress rehearsal" fiasco elicited ideas from someone with a history of broken ribs and collarbone after a mountain bike tumble, an angel with real-life experience.

"Snap-up cowboy shirts and V-neck T-shirts will fix your problem," she offered in her comments to my blog post. She also got us thinking about how Tony would sleep at home, because there was no way he could get up from a lying down position with nine broken ribs. She suggested a Lazy-Boy or hospital bed. Her advice couldn't have been better timed. We still had the hospital staff's attention. I would ask El Doctor. My plans were coming together: to have a well-appointed, patient-ready home with everything from furniture to clothing, as if I was preparing for a newborn.

Surprisingly, one of those social workers that showed up randomly into our lives was the ticket to getting a hospital bed at home. She leaned back casually in one of the plastic chairs near Tony's feet, holding a yellow legal pad in her lap. Her upbeat manner was authentic and reassuring, no sniffling or "there, there . . ." First, she spoke at great length with Tony to see if he was mentally ready to leave, brushing her slightly gray hair behind her ear as she waited for an answer to her burning question.

"How do you feel about what happened?" she asked.

"It wasn't my time," Tony told her without hesitation. He had stumbled onto a message we'd hear over and over again with each physician we met, even years after the accident: "Someone was looking after you. It wasn't your time."

"All I can think about is my next ride," Tony continued. He was preaching to the choir. This woman was a cyclist too. From her assessment, Tony was not harboring any woulda', coulda', shoulda' or woe-is-me ways of thinking; he was ready to go home and put his hospital experience behind him.

El Doctor interrupted the conversation. "Hello. You are set to go home tomorrow. The lung is good." *Thank God,* I thought as I clasped my hands in praise. We had dodged another bullet, or a "sword" in this situation. Tony was really going home! I seized the moment.

"Do you think we could get a hospital bed at home? You know, rent one. With nine broken ribs, getting out of a regular bed will be impossible," I reasoned.

"No," was his quick answer. "The bed will become a crutch." El Doctor's tough-love, automatic response landed like a stake in the ground.

"He's an *athlete,*" said our new friend, Miss Cyclist Social Worker. "He is *not* going to be lazy about his recovery. He wants to *ride* again." I loved her so much in that moment.

"OK, but not for long," El Doctor said, relenting. I had never been so appreciative of a social worker in the hospital until then. This kind of advocate was my cup of tea, tough and sporty, no melodramatic tears. I checked one more thing off my to-do list.

Tony's return was becoming real. Shopping, one of my strongest talents, was my top priority. I scheduled my outings around visitors so Tony could have alone time with his friends—talk like a guy. I found stretchy V-neck tees from the Gap in black, gray, and white. *Do I get a large to make sure the opening is big enough to stretch around the neck brace, or medium, Tony's normal size?* I bought both, just in case. Target had Western snap-down shirts, stylish in 2010, the short-sleeved version on sale. Tony was going to look swank!

While I pushed a cart around Target, my cell phone rang, the caller ID flashing our lawyer's name. I picked up the call, slowing as if I were pulling over in traffic instead of a wide aisle in the bath department.

"Hi Francie! How's Tony?" the White Knight boomed. He seemed like he missed us. I hadn't talked to him in a few weeks.

"Great! He's going home tomorrow!" I matched his enthusiasm.

"Good, good! I was hoping he was feeling better. I'd like to set up a meeting if you think Tony will be strong enough to talk," he asked hopefully.

My stomach twisted into a knot thinking about how difficult it would be to move Tony around, for both of us. "Tony can talk, but I'm not sure he'll be ready to go to an office," I replied reluctantly.

"Oh no. I'll come to you with my team," he was quick to offer. "How about a Sunday, say two weeks from now?" The White Knight was always thinking about how to help us. Once again, he was giving up his weekend time.

"Wow! Thank you. It's a date," I agreed happily.

I quickly shifted gears back to prepping Tony for home. In early August, cheap towels and washcloths were abundant in stores—preparation for the college bound. Guilt-free shopping was my best friend. I grabbed the biggest jug of bleach on the shelf since I picked out white for anything that would touch his body. My guard was up; no potential contaminants were going to get by me. Tony slept with scads of pillows all around him to prop up his legs for blood flow and hold his dislocated shoulder level. I picked a mix of sizes, standard and king—six total. My shopping cart was an overstuffed linen closet, minus the sheets, because I didn't know what size to buy for a hospital bed.

I crammed boxes of waterproof bandages and medical tape in between the pillows in the cart, wherever there was room. The hole left from the blasted chest tube was stitched up, but Tony couldn't get it wet in the shower. The razor aisle was my last stop. Tony did not miss shaving, the upside of being in the hospital for almost two weeks. The whiskers were growing in along his jowls and under his nose. I didn't know they could do that; Tony never tried for facial hair. I had to find an electric razor to trim his growing beard, and mustache. *What do I know about razors except that they are pink or purple and work great on legs?*

"Excuse me," I said to a young man restocking the shelves with shaving cream. He stood up from his crouched position. "I need to find an electric razor."

"We have several models over here," the Target employee said as he walked a few steps down the aisle. "What are you looking for?"

"My husband got into an accident and has a neck brace. I think I need one that can move easily inside the brace, like a vacuum cleaner under a couch. You know what I mean? What do you recommend?"

The young man puffed up, proud to know more than someone much older than him. A Remington cordless electric razor joined the pillows and washcloths in my cart.

I wished that young man had known something about hospital sheets too, since I was already in the store. I wasn't sure who to ask at the hospital to get an answer. I just figured someone would let me know eventually, hopefully before the bed arrived at our home, at approximately who-knew-when. That's how it worked—nothing was spelled out.

We were at the beginning of a slow breakup with the hospital. We got what we needed from each other; El Doctor being the first to cut ties with us. Tony was stitched up enough to go home, the neck brace and sling holding him steady. The social worker checked Tony off as emotionally sound.

We had one more hurdle to get over before Tony was fit for life outside the hospital. The occupational therapist trained us on walking. It wasn't so much how to walk, as it was how I could protect Tony. Much like a gentleman during the Victorian era, I walked on the side closest to the street, to shield him from cars or inadvertently stepping off the curb. We practiced stairs, placing both feet on a step before moving up to the next one, as if he were three years old again. I stood close to him, providing balance and looking out for rocks or cracks he couldn't see himself, as the neck brace prevented him from seeing his feet or anything in front of him.

Tony's last night in the hospital was filled with joy and anticipation. He was going home! As if the day couldn't get any better, two of Tony's friends made a quick visit on their way home from a long bike ride up Mount Diablo and back down, one of Tony's favorite rides. Dressed in their cycling kits and helmets, they hovered over Tony's bed sheepishly giggling, like they were up to no good.

"This is what you are going to look like real soon!" They said like a couple of twelve-year-old boys.

Tony tried not to laugh with them; his ribs still hurt. He grinned from ear to ear. He was so "hawpy."

When I think back to the delicate state Tony was in after he was discharged, I shudder at the responsibility the system placed on me, a nonmedical person. But even if it was risky, we were ecstatic Tony was going home. Getting our family life and privacy back were worth putting up with the challenge. After all, we did have a couple of things on our side. The hefty amount of "on-the-job" nurse training I inadvertently received at the hospital would undoubtedly come in handy. If all else failed, Tony was drenched in miracles. The greatest one of all:

He was alive and fixable.

CHAPTER 13

Mom Angels

Thirteen Days After the Accident

HOW LONG DOES IT TAKE to check a patient out of a hospital? All day, apparently. Tony and I waited and waited in his hospital room for El Doctor to sign off on the exit papers. Which seemed silly since he told us the day before Tony was good to go, but I suppose something could have changed overnight. It didn't. By morning, Tony was even more ready to go, but there weren't any patients clamoring for his bed, so no rush to get him out. We did not see El Doctor until three p.m. for the final assessment. Hence, Tony was "blessed" with two more hospital meals, breakfast and lunch.

The wait was a masked gift: an opportunity for my mom-friends to help me out with my long, long to-do list. They came out of nowhere to ask what jobs they could check off for me. My pals were truly a godsend, pun intended, because they were surely heaven-sent with their sea of help. How did they know this particular day, of all days, I would need an army of angels? They relieved the pressure of me trying to do it all, a bad habit of mine, and probably of most moms.

While Tony and I "dined" to pass the time at the hospital, my friends rushed around preparing for Tony's arrival as if given royal orders for an esteemed guest. The biggest job was getting the house patient-ready. The sky rained pools of mom angels on that day.

"How can I help?" my friend Suzanne e-mailed me.

"Can you please buy two sets of twin, extra-long sheets in white for the hospital bed due to arrive any minute?" I messaged back. I found it ironic that nobody at the hospital knew what size sheets fit a hospital bed. Unfortunately, what should have been an obvious answer was not confirmed until we were checking out of the hospital.

Suzanne is Chinese like my husband and thinks like him: Buy the best possible sheets for the best possible price. I could not have asked for that kind of thoughtful service.

I left a key under the mat for anyone needing to stop by, so my friend Cheri took advantage of the open-door policy and readied the house as if it were her own. She brought a bouquet of bright yellow sunflowers for cheer. Then she proceeded to the garden to deadhead my roses, knowing I wouldn't get to the gardening for a while. Flowers are one of my favorite things so I felt like her angelic touch was a special welcoming, just for me. My home felt so peaceful when I arrived with Tony.

Even my friend Cheri noticed how good fortune happened to drop in at just the right time. She beamed and chuckled, recounting the happenings of the day to me.

"Hello. Low residence," Cheri greeted a caller on our home phone. Cheri was full service, dropping her dishcloth on the kitchen counter to answer the phone.

"Hi. I'm Francie's friend Lora. I was calling to see if I could stop by with some vegetables from my garden. Do you know what they need?"

"Funny, I asked Francie what I could get from the store, and she said veggies!"

I could not make this up! The two worked out a list, considering our empty refrigerator bins and the healing powers of the vegetables. The giant basket Lora packed had red ripe tomatoes, rich in antioxidants to reduce swelling and boost the immune system.

Emerald-green zucchini, golden crooknecks. and purple-and-white-striped eggplants were full of vitamins, potassium, and fiber to help build Tony's strength. Lora included a beautiful bunch of fresh basil mixed with another bouquet of giant golden sunflowers in a mason jar of water, back-to-the-farm fashion.

When Alex saw the pristine and colorful looking veggies, he thought they were plastic, until he picked up an eggplant from the basket.

"This is real?!?" Alex said, wide-eyed. The eggplants we bought at the store were boring dark-purple, not marked with cool white stripes like the organic kind from Lora's garden.

Everyone was fulfilling our needs, stamping their gifts in their own way. When all these coincidences occurred time after time, I couldn't help but feel grateful and happy and loved. I never felt alone, and I think that was key to keeping an upbeat attitude for my family and me. I felt empowered. My girlfriends did everything I knew needed to be done but better. Every day had been a surprise visit by angels, but today every hour had a surprise.

Even that morning, before I picked up Tony, Annie, my lane buddy from my six a.m. Masters swim class had something heaven-sent to tell me. "As my mother would say," and she looked deep into my eyes to be sure I was paying attention. She made a melodramatic sign of the cross over herself, gently reminding me to ask for divine help in a way that made me smile and motivated me to action. We were in the ladies' locker room, surrounded by our other swim buddies who were drying off after a shower or in various stages of getting dressed. They were oblivious to our intense discussion.

Annie said exactly what my own Catholic mom would have said to me in a way to guilt me into doing what she wanted, sweet and sing-songy. "You should pray. You might need that little extra."

As I left, I turned to say goodbye to my friend, my hair wet and my red duffle bag heavy on my wrist like a handbag. And from halfway across the locker room, Annie looked hard at me again, making two quick signs of the cross to further drive home her message. She really meant what she was pantomiming. A very prominent angel was watching over me—my mom. I could feel her spirit stirring in my heart.

The funny thing was, I felt like my prayers were answered before I asked or even knew what to ask. I couldn't believe how a short thought of "I need sheets" or "the lawn needs mowing" could turn into reality. I needed to say prayers for sure but not necessarily requests, but rather, prayers of thanksgiving. Coming home from the hospital was particularly bountiful with my mom-friends bringing gift after gift.

When we finally pulled in front of our house, a banner for Tony was waiting. A long span of brown butcher paper taped to the porch with the message, "Welcome Home Dad!" in neon-blue, green, and yellow paint greeted Tony. The boys and I had made it the day before. He couldn't see it until we walked arm-in-arm to the door because turning his head from inside the car was stiff and awkward, the neck brace holding him tight.

"Wow! Was I gone that long?" he said with a gigantic smile. "I am honored." He recognized the pomp and circumstance we gave TJ when he came home from fifth-grade camp.

Cheri met us at our front door like family.

"Welcome home!" she cheered. Cheri knew how to brighten any moment. I was so happy to be home, grinning from ear to ear at Cheri's sunshiny presence.

I held on to Tony's arm and guided him to the office couch now parked in our living room. I planned to put the hospital bed in Tony's office and figured an extra piece of furniture in the living room was an appropriate home. Two ex-football player dads from the neighborhood helped me move the couch the night before. Tony sat down slowly, leaning slightly into the arm of the couch as he stretched his legs across the cushions. He dozed immediately. The drive from the hospital had been exhausting.

No sooner had Tony settled into a nap, then a big white truck with "Medical Supplies" stamped on the side, pulled in front of the house with a rumble. The bed had finally arrived. Neighbors couldn't help but notice something was wrong at our house. Unless you had kids, belonged to the neighborhood pool, or were a good friend with papaya slicing skills, there was no way to know what was going on with our family. I started to get e-mails of concern almost immediately.

"Wow, I thought Tony went on a trip when I saw the banner. Then I saw the medical supply truck and thought, 'uh oh,'" one neighbor messaged.

The truck drivers quickly moved a brand-new, still-in-plastic mattress and bed into our home and vamoosed. Cheri and I rolled the bed around Tony's office three times, trying to figure out the best use of space and functionality for Tony. As I learned in the hospital, Tony needed access to water, snacks, and meds on his left side. The best place for the bed was perpendicular to the wall so he could look out the window and have access to the bright red bedside table that used to belong to TJ. Cheri, a former opera singer, considered how Tony might call for help. She brought from her home a variety of small musical instruments to ring or shake depending on Tony's need. A tinkling bell might mean water, and a maraca rattle could mean meds, or a tap on a tiny drum might be a call for a pillow fluff. We settled on a bell. If I heard anything, I'd come running no matter the jingle or thump.

I thought of one last thing to complete the room: the fire truck nightlight from Alex's room. Tony might need to see where he was going if he got up on his own in the middle of the night. Alex wouldn't mind if it was for his dad.

Suzanne arrived with the sheets, shortly after Cheri and I agreed on the ideal spot to place the new bed. And not long after that, another friend arrived with the boys; she had entertained them the whole day. The four of us huddled together talking logistics for the boys and how Tony being home would change our needs. School registration was the next week so one of my friends offered to stand in line for me; I wasn't ready to explain to new people about our situation. Just the thought of repeating the accident story weighed on my stomach and zapped my energy. Tony was sort of top news in the community, so of course people were curious if the stories were true.

It felt normal to talk about the accident with my gaggle of friends. I loved the camaraderie, as if we were discussing a volunteer project instead of something serious and sad. This kind of talk was exactly what I wanted—no pity, just problem solving with my friends.

Every time I mentioned to Tony about an angel helping us, he'd say, "Oh, we have to give them a bottle of wine!"

"We'd need cases and cases if we gave a bottle of wine to every person who helped us!" I countered. Now he could see and *hear* for himself. While he appreciated the support and seeing me in my element, the chattering banged on his soft brain. He was ready for the angel parade to go.

Our last angel of the day came with dinner: fajitas, churros, and peanut butter cups. When I was out buying pain medicine for Tony the day before, I saw a package of peanut butter cups while I was waiting in line. I didn't want to lose my place so I passed on my temptation. Now here was the treat, as if I asked my friend specifically.

Things were going to get better. Moving from the hospital to home, where we could do what we wanted when we wanted, was like moving out of your parents' house for the first time. We were free! And we had an army of angels to help us get through.

I was so warmed by the day's events, tiny gifts filled with love and joy. I felt immense comfort and a huge sense of belonging, fueling my confidence for our next frontier. We could do this!

CHAPTER 14

Daddy Daycare

Thirteen and Fourteen Days After the Accident

WHAT A RELIEF IT WAS to look after Tony in our own home. Our responsibilities grew compared to the hospital, but it was with great joy that every member of the family found a personal way to take part in making Tony comfy and safe. Alex helped me with the sheets for the hospital bed but not before he took it for a spin first. He laid his wriggly, golden-brown ten-year-old body right smack in the middle, arms down and belly button up. He squirmed with anticipation as his head and chest slowly rose up and then down again with a press of a button on the remote control. Not quite a roller-coaster ride, but it was pretty fun since it was free and inside our house. I was sure Tony was going to love his new bed too.

Tony was more than ready for sleeping at home with his family and getting a real shower. Twelve days in the hospital with only sponge baths and dry shampoo left Tony feeling like he was sealed in a sticky second skin. He smelled like a ripe hospital too, so I was just as anxious to scrub off all the grimy flecks related to that fateful day and send them down the drain.

I dressed in running clothes to help him with his shower. An ironic choice since I gave up running a few years before and swam for exercise instead, but a swimsuit was harder to put on and seemed like overkill. The shower was pretty roomy, and it was fairly easy to stay out of the line of fire from the showerhead, if for any reason I needed to hop in with Tony.

Tony was outfitted with a plastic shower-model neck collar. It was an ugly dark-peach color, matching a skin tone that exists only in a box of crayons. It seemed to me that a brilliant hue to mirror a beach towel or pool noodle would have been more practical and fun. Besides, it wasn't as though Tony was going to host a party in the shower, and he felt self-conscious about his appearance, especially at forty-five years old. Why try to camouflage something you want to be completely aware of in the first place?

I taped a small sheet of plastic over the chest incision that had held his chest tube, the only thing he couldn't get wet. He was ready to take the plunge. I poured shampoo into his left hand three times to scrub off the shampoo-cap residue from the hospital. Tony closed his eyes and swirled the soapy suds around and around his head with his left arm. I gently pulled a warm washcloth back and forth under his bad arm as he was forbidden to move it. Not that he could budge any direction in the slightest, even a tiny, tiny bit on his own. He was as helpless as a newborn.

Tony stepped gingerly out of the shower onto the white bath mat where I dried him off ever so carefully with the new Target towels. We needed all of them, as some served as seat covers for the cold marble tub deck. Tony sat perfectly still while I aimed the nozzle of my salon-quality hair dryer at his injured underarm, just a sliver of space for the soft air to pass and far less intrusive than a fluffy towel—no frizz. When I blow-dried his hair, the warm and gentle breeze made him smile. He closed his eyes and tilted his head back like a dog with his head hanging out a car window, trying to capture every wisp of air.

After dressing him in cotton jammie bottoms and a Hanes muscle shirt with a super-stretchy neck to get around a fat neck collar, he was ready for bed. Just like the times I laid my babies down to sleep, I felt immense comfort putting him to bed all squeaky clean on crisp, fresh sheets. Tucking him in was like a pillow-arranging dance, placing four or five pillows at just the right spot behind his head, under his knees and at his sides. He liked to rest his arm at stomach level so he wouldn't pull his shoulder. He was packed in for the night like a priceless porcelain doll being shipped around the globe.

With his painkillers, crackers, water, and musical instruments at his bedside, he was ready to close his eyes. Something about being home helped him fall into a deep sleep, only waking to go to the bathroom at two a.m. and take his meds at four-thirty a.m. My mom ears heard him both times from my bed two rooms away. I got up to make sure he was OK, but it was a quick enough check that I could easily go back to sleep. After all the practice in the dark of the night at the hospital without me, he was managing his needs really well.

The next morning, TJ took a turn at caring for Tony. We dressed dad in his new lightweight sweat pants and a stretchy V-neck tee, just enough for a mid-August day. TJ put on the new sling we were given before we left the hospital, black with several long straps and coated in Velcro. Tony referred to it as the Octopus. The night before, I had been too tired to get a handle on it after Tony's shower so it was a crisscrossed, uneven mess. I had planned to read the directions in the morning, but I'm not so gifted in the 3-D puzzle department. TJ figured out where all the straps were supposed to go, neatly securing Tony's arm into place. By age twelve, TJ had tons of experience building complex Lego creations. The Octopus was a piece of cake compared to a four-thousand-piece Lego Victorian grocery and cafe.

TJ's gift for precision spurred Tony to ask for one more favor. After far too many self-inflicted scratches from his long and jagged nails, he looked to TJ to help him out.

"Can you please trim my fingernails?" Tony asked in a low and slow voice. Manicures were not really a priority in the hospital, and I'm not sure how or when anyone gets around to it. Meds were difficult enough for the staff to manage.

"Yeah," TJ replied, deadpan.

I thought this was a bold request on Tony's part, but since he was on painkillers, I figured it was probably OK. I dug up the nail clippers and handed them to TJ. He sat on the edge of the hospital bed his head down and his long chocolate hair falling around his face like a veil. He took Tony's leathery fingers one by one into his pudgy hand. Snip. Snip. Snip. TJ actually did a nice job.

Once Tony was all spiffed up, Alex took him for an afternoon stroll outside. Since the accident, Tony had not stepped outdoors except to get into the car or walk up to the house. I wasn't home when the two ventured out together, or I probably would have put a stop to it. Alex hadn't been trained by an occupational therapist like I had. He didn't know to take the side closest to the street or to be Tony's eyes so he wouldn't trip over a twig or pebble. The hospital physical therapist said the biggest challenge with Tony would be slowing him down. He'd already asked her about doing stomach crunches. Are you kidding me? This was the same guy who demanded a hospital bed to avoid the intense stabbing pain in his ribs when he rolled in and out of it. I guess he was hoping for an agony-free way to save his hard-earned rippled abs while he healed.

Since this was Tony's first time out, he couldn't walk very far. Tony teetered more than walked because it hurt. Alex, normally a squirrelly, jumpy boy, was very patient. He stayed with his dad one tiny step at a time, past our neighbor's house and back. That was it. Driveway to driveway, and Tony was wiped. Alex escorted him home and into bed, a favorite hangout spot for a nap. Alex, the snuggler, often laid next to Tony in the hospital bed whenever he could, touching his dad ever so slightly, leg to leg and arm to arm, just being. Both of them were content, looking out the window or dozing like two peas in a pod; their big brown eyes, broad noses, and brilliant smiles were almost identical despite a thirty-five-year age difference. Alex had hoped his dad could spend some time hanging out before going back to work. He got his wish.

In the evenings, the entire family played games. The top pick was a card game called *Killer Bunnies* where players collected carrots and killed off opponents' bunnies. It might sound like a sick game, but it's hilarious, fun, and unpredictable to the bitter end. Quality family time had been rare before the accident, but now it was becoming commonplace, more the way Tony and I grew up, before electronic games, cell phones, and hundreds of TV channels.

The accident changed Tony's eating habits too, activating a sweet tooth I didn't know he had. As a cyclist, he avoided anything with sugar, and that included many of my favorites like chocolate chip cookies, wine, bread, pasta, and even straight chocolate. The heavier the rider the more "baggage" there was to carry up the hill. Now he *wanted* to eat the taboo foods. He claimed if he craved sweets then his body probably needed it. He sure must have "needed" a sugar bomb on our way home from the hospital because he asked to stop at a Japanese frozen yogurt shop called Yoppi's. He piled on chocolate chunks, Boba poppers, almonds, granola, bananas, and strawberries on top of a mountain of creamy vanilla yogurt—seven bucks worth. He ate the *whole* thing. After all he'd been through, he deserved buckets and buckets of sugar bombs.

In times of illness or injury, I think you regress back to childhood, craving the comfort foods your mom gave you like grape juice and cherry-flavored Jell-O. I didn't hesitate when Tony asked me to pick up the retro treats at the store. Alex, the expert Jell-O maker, was more than pleased to boil water and stir up some old-fashioned happiness.

Caring for Tony was a family pleasure. Everyone contributed in the most unassuming ways: Alex the teddy bear, bed tester, and Jell-O chef; TJ the manicurist, sling and clothing outfitter; and me, the mom and manager. We did everything in our own time, just like we liked it, no nurses.

CHAPTER 15

Scary Office

Two Weeks After the Accident

I COUNTED OUT THE PAIN PILLS the hospital had issued. The featherweight bottle didn't feel as though the meager contents could carry the hefty load of Tony's misery through the weekend. We were so excited to go home, neither of us thought to check if we had enough meds. At 11:15 a.m. on a Friday, I left a message with a nurse at Tony's primary care office, requesting a refill. While I waited for a call back, I busied myself in the bedroom closet, organizing a shelf at eye level so Tony could find his clothes without looking down or bending over. I categorized his staple wardrobe into stacks: the new, stretchy Gap tees, sweats, socks, and jammies.

At 3:40 p.m., I realized I had accomplished *a lot*, so much that I began to wonder if the doctor's office had forgotten to call me back. I gave the nurse or doctor the benefit of the doubt by checking with the pharmacy first. Maybe they'd called it in and just didn't call to let me know. Nope. It wasn't there. I called the office for an update.

I had remained pretty calm throughout all of our trials and tribulations surrounding this accident. My work experience in customer service and sales taught me the benefit of speaking kindly and collaboratively so I could get what I wanted. I could easily maintain my cool with a simple phone call, so I thought.

"Hi, this is Tony Low's wife. I called earlier about getting a prescription refilled for my husband. I haven't heard back and just wondered where we might find the glitch. Can you help me?" I asked hopefully.

After *ten minutes* on hold, the receptionist relayed this message: "The nurse's assistant says we can't call in prescriptions like this unless we see the patient first."

I could not count to ten at this moment. All my professional etiquette flew completely out of my head. Fireworks ensued.

"WHAT DO YOU MEAN YOU CAN'T FILL THE PRESCRIPTION? HE WAS JUST DISCHARGED FROM THE HOSPITAL TWO DAYS AGO! WHY DIDN'T YOU TELL ME THIS AT 11:15 A.M. WHEN I CALLED THE FIRST TIME? WHY ARE YOU WAITING UNTIL THE ELEVENTH HOUR ON A FRIDAY AFTERNOON!?! THIS DOES NOT WORK FOR ME. WHO DO I NEED TO TALK TO? THIS IS NOT GOING TO HAPPEN!!!!!"

After *another* ten minutes of eternal hold, the office manager got on the phone and was basically calm and honest about the situation. Somebody had dropped the ball, and nobody would have noticed had I not called back.

"Doctors cannot fill prescriptions for narcotics unless the patient is seen first," she explained. "State law." Then she suggested calling the hospital to see if El Doctor, the doctor who issued the prescription at the hospital could help. I was not about to hang up with this lady until I got an easier way of calling her back.

"I'M NOT GOING THROUGH THAT SYSTEM AGAIN. I NEED A BACK-DOOR PHONE NUMBER SO I AM NOT LEFT ON ETERNAL HOLD!"

"I'll give you my direct line," offered the office manager.

Of course, not even El Doctor would issue more pills unless we saw him first. And if he wasn't available to see us, we'd be starting all over again in the ER, as if Tony had never stayed at the hospital. I was discovering the frustrating side effects of narcotics, the ones not included in the prescription disclosures: refills extremely difficult, may cause blood pressure to spike if attempted. So, we were back to the primary care office.

After talking with the office manager, she told us she would get everything ready so when we arrived, we could walk right in, no waiting or paperwork. This was the best I could negotiate even after I explained the great risk we were taking putting Tony back in the car. The doctor's orders were clear: Avoid car rides. Concussions are exacerbated the second time around, especially if the first one has not healed. In just twenty-four hours, between getting Tony home from the hospital and driving for drugs, we were finding it very difficult to follow the doctor's crystal-clear command. Hence, I loaded him up in the back seat like a toddler and drove like a white-knuckled granny all the way to the appointment.

The office manager lived up to her promise; we were able to walk past the chairs in the waiting room, past the nurse's desk, and down the hall to an examination room. Evidently, it must have been family day at the doctor's office as the physician's kids were lurking about, and the doctor shooed them out of the way. Since it was late on a Friday afternoon, maybe the family had planned to go to dinner straight from the office? I could only guess. The kids cleared out quickly. Seeing a hobbling man in a neck brace and arm sling was more frightening than getting away from a highly contagious illness.

The nurse who led us into the examination room stood at her computer while Tony tried to sit. We explained his collection of injuries.

"I'm not touching him," she said staring at her computer. I did not take offense to skipping a blood pressure or temperature check. I was sure nothing had changed in the last twenty-four hours.

The doctor arrived shortly after the nurse's abbreviated patient assessment. If there was an express lane in a medical office, we were in it, and I was very happy, as Tony was so very weak and dazed.

The physician was a partner in the practice, someone Tony had never met, not that Tony knew his regular physician much better. He couldn't even remember his doctor's name when he was asked for it in the hospital; he made one up. All of his medical information was sent to a doctor we didn't know, and we never heard from his office regarding the mistake. Now we found ourselves briefing a complete stranger on Tony's injuries, because he didn't have any files. We explained to him about how we wouldn't even be there except we didn't have enough pain pills.

"You wouldn't be joshing me, would you?" he asked, looking at me, then Tony, then back to me. Addicts came in all kinds of packages, which was news to Tony and me. We didn't think we gave off the air of a junkies. The nurse seemed to believe our story, not wanting to even look at Tony for fear she might break something with her eyes. I presented my case since Tony's appearance alone was not convincing.

I held up my hand and started counting out how many pills we needed on my fingers, the doctor's eyes following along. At two pills every four hours we needed at least twenty-four more pills to get through the weekend. Here I was telling the doctor what to prescribe, facilitated by a *kindergarten* counting lesson. Unbelievable. I set aside my disgust and took the prescription. And thus, Scary Office was born.

We returned to Scary Office a week later to have Tony's stitches removed from the chest tube extraction and to get a prescription for physical therapy, the only instructions listed on the discharge papers from the hospital. As much as we feared going back to Scary Office, we did not have the luxury of shopping around for something better. We were just trying to cope at home.

In all fairness, Scary Office was equally nervous around us, possibly nicknaming Tony, Scary Patient. His collection of injuries were frightening to everyone and probably seen by very few. And when you add in his bodyguard wife, who was not afraid to yell at anyone over the phone, we put people on edge. We were greeted with extreme gentleness and politeness the second time around. We were hard to forget.

An older, more experienced nurse showed us to an examination room and wanted to start with taking Tony's blood pressure.

"*Don't* touch anything on the right side. Everything on the right side is broken," I quickly piped up before she could make a move. For some reason, it was an autopilot maneuver to reach for the right side of any patient, even in a sling. I witnessed over and over again the disregard of Tony's injuries while changing the hospital bed sheets and the lack of pain management leaving him wheezing in agony. I was not going to stand for anyone mishandling my man. Everything was too fresh; my guard was up. Way up.

As the nurse read through the file, she double-checked with us to confirm she was reading it correctly.

"Wait. You broke *nine* ribs?" she asked as she typed into her computer.

"You punctured the lung?" Type. Type.

"Oh, and fractured the vertebrae!" Type. Type.

"Wow. And you had your shoulder reduced?" Type. Type. Type. Reduced meant the shoulder had been put back into place. Tony came into the ER on a stretcher doing a permanent queen's wave, the arm stretched high above his head as if acknowledging adoring his fans.

The nurse continued with her questions. "So, what exactly are you here for? It's hard to tell from the discharge plan."

If a medical person can't glean much from the written document, how the heck was a lay-person supposed to know? My blood was boiling.

"Tony had a chest tube removed, and it's time to take out the stitches. It's been a week." I spoke on Tony's behalf, the bodyguard in me.

"Yes. You are right. They need to come out," she replied.

Then I couldn't help but ask, "So, does the doctor know how to take out stitches?" We had a specialist for everything in the hospital, so it seemed like an intelligent question. I got an eye roll from both Tony and the nurse.

"Yes, he can take the stitches out. He can put them in too," she said with a hint of sarcasm. "Tony should take off his sling and shirt," she directed.

"I'll help with that. I'm kind of an expert now," I said. She was all too relieved to let me take over; she wasn't touching anything, just like the nurse we had during our last visit to the Scary Office.

Tony sat at the end of the examining table while the nurse removed the bandage and we inspected the incision. The dark purple markings looked like a Chinese character about the size of a nickel, sort of a tattoo made from scar tissue. I don't know which character the scar represented, but I hoped for "long life."

At last, the mystery doctor arrived, the doctor Tony alluded to in the hospital but whose name he couldn't recall. Neither Tony nor the doctor recognized each other as Tony had only come in once or twice for a sore throat or brief physical. As he moved toward Tony to check out his chest, I stopped him.

"Careful! His whole right side is injured," I piped up again.

"I know. I read the report," the doctor replied in a matter-of-fact tone. "OK, now lie back, and I'll remove the stitches," he requested. I could not believe my ears.

"No," Tony and I said in firm but calm stereo. He stayed seated in an upright position.

These doctors and nurses didn't get it. I thought he had read the report. He might have read it, but he still didn't get it. Broken ribs—even just one, not *nine*—equate to extreme pain especially getting up or down from a horizontal position. Laughing, sneezing, or coughing were luxuries. To me, this should have been medical school 101. My blood boiled again. I kind of wondered if my blood pressure shouldn't be taken at these appointments too.

The stitches came out without incident, not even a tear or yelp. The doctor issued a prescription for physical therapy. And then I almost fainted with the next question from the doctor: "Do you have enough pain medication?"

I have to admit, it was nice to be asked if he could do anything more for us, especially pain management. This offer alone almost made up for all the inconveniences and screwups by office staff.

Despite the niceties at the end of the appointment, Tony decided to find a new primary care physician he loved and would call his friend. Now they talk about a lot more than just Tony's ailments and won't stop until the office manager cuts off the conversation for the sake of the next patient. We learned any red flags during minor appointments will be magnified 100 percent during a crisis. It was worth the effort to shop around for the right fit, like a favorite pair of jeans worn over and over again for their loving comfort.

And just in case, I have the awesome doctor's contact info in my cell phone so I can double-check Tony's responses during a concussion. I hope I never have to use it.

CHAPTER 16

The Elusive Normal Living

Fourteen and Fifteen Days
After the Accident

OF COURSE, THE SECOND NIGHT Tony was home, I didn't sleep well. As much as I tried to slip into a dreamlike state, part of my brain was on alert, listening for a jingle or a rattle from Tony. Instead of Tony calling for me, I startled myself awake in a panic. Earlier in the day, I was notified our credit card number had been stolen. I had called to cancel the card. But it suddenly occurred to me, the call seemed too easy.

"Wait a minute! Did I just give all my personal information to cancel our card to a crook?" I practically screamed the thought in my head.

At one thirty in the morning, I flew out of bed. My bare feet pitter-pattered across the hardwood floor to the family room, the farthest room away from my sleeping family. In my thin summer PJs, I stood shivering near a softly lit lamp, the big white Sony mobile phone pressed to my ear.

"How do I know you really work for the credit card company?" I interrogated.

"You called me—the number that's on the back of the card." The patient young man answered. He had a point.

I reluctantly divulged my stolen number, zip code, and some crazy fact about my mother that only I would know. All of that to confirm my number had really been stolen and I had not compromised my identity earlier in the day to some criminal.

Home was supposed to be safe. Yet I couldn't stop protecting my family, even while I slept. Or tried to sleep. After two weeks of medical staff letting us down, and a policeman fishing around for reasons to blame my husband for getting himself run over, I trusted no one. The stolen credit card number only added to my suspicions of any outsiders. In one of my blog posts, I half-joked to any potential visitor coming to our home: no admittance without valid ID. My antenna for danger was on high alert. I was kidding about the ID, but part of me wasn't. Getting back to normal was going to take time.

After my middle of the night freak-out, I plodded back to bed. I slept deeply for a few hours, only to be awakened again.

"My chest hurts. I think it could be a heart attack," Tony said in a sleepy voice at four a.m. on our first Saturday morning home. "Do we have any aspirin?" He stood at the foot of my bed as if he were one of the boys. Somehow, I hadn't heard him shuffle in from his new bedroom in the office.

"Let me look," I croaked in my morning voice.

I jerked out of bed to search through our medicine cabinet. Nothing. I checked the medical kit in my car and found a small package with an expiration date of 2005, five years out of date. It would have to do. Who took aspirin these days anyway?

The pain was different, not due to broken ribs or a punctured lung. Tony did not have key symptoms of a heart attack like an elephant sitting on his chest or numbing down his left arm. I wasn't too anxious to return to the ER, but just in case, I text messaged a friend, a cardiac nurse at a more sane hour of six a.m. She wouldn't mind in a potential emergency.

"Tony is having chest pain. Do you think it's a heart attack?" I tapped into my phone.

"It's probably from the chest tube. He'll be fine." she replied. That made sense. Having a tube slightly smaller than the diameter of a dime ripped out of your chest was bound to have repercussions. And as my friend predicted, nothing happened. *Thank God!* I thought. I was thanking God a bunch, almost daily.

We had barely been home two days, anticipating a calmer time together, like we were used to living. I thought I'd planned for every need, between towels, sheets, bandages, and clothing. But pain management was challenging even at home, between the prescribed drugs we begged for at the Scary Office just twelve hours before, and now, simple aspirin. And of all people, *I* was the nurse in charge.

Since Tony's pain wasn't a serious matter, I could still take Alex to the biggest championship swim event of the season, a two-day affair. TJ would be Tony's caregiver for the weekend. Should anything happen, the swim meet was only a twenty-minute drive away, so I could get home quickly to help.

County, as the swim meet is referred to, is one of the biggest recreational swim meets in the country. Over one thousand swimmers participate, ages five to eighteen, from all over the northern East Bay suburbs, where the climate is warmer than San Francisco. Swimming is a very big deal here, almost like football is to Texas. Whether you have a swimmer or not, the whole community knows it's a championship-swim weekend because parents paint the windows of their cars in team colors with "Swim Fast," "Rock the Blocks," or "Eat My Bubbles!" It's been this way for over fifty years; that's how embedded swimming is into the culture, and that's why I didn't want Alex to miss this meet, *the* meet.

Despite the importance of the event, leaving Tony behind tugged at my insides. *I hope I'm making the right decision.* A sliver of doubt crept into my mind. At the same time, Alex needed me to be there. He's a hardworking, competitive kid with a tender heart. I didn't want him to worry about his dad or feel cheated that I couldn't see him swim. Tony and I both believed everything would be OK eventually, and we wanted our kids to feel the same way. Tony was comfortable and capable enough without me for the day. I went, even though I was torn over what used to be an easy decision.

It's not like hanging at a pool for two days, all day, was a vacation. Swim meets were tiring, even if I wasn't swimming. I wanted to be a normal swim mom, watching my kid race. After two weeks of pawning my kids off to friends, I was ready to take my mom job back. I wanted to experience the fun kind of adrenaline rush from a race and not the survival mode of the past two weeks.

And as much as I tried, I can't say the conversations I had with other swim parents were easy. What do you say to someone whose husband was nearly killed three weeks before? The interactions were even more awkward than at the last swim meet, just a day after the accident. Back then, people hugged me or offered to bring food. But at this meet, I wasn't sure if they were afraid to upset me or to come across as nosy. I wasn't sure I knew what to say either. I made a feeble attempt at keeping the discussion light.

"Can you believe it, I drove to the wrong pool today?!?" I laughed, trying to chat up whomever stood next to me. We stared at the bright-blue water from the edge of the pool, waiting for the race to begin.

"Really? Did you forget?" replied a swim parent, taking her eyes of the water for a split second to look at me.

"Well, momentarily. I'm a bit brain dead from sleep interruptions. Heck, I even forgot to bring a towel today! Ha, ha, ha. Luckily there are plenty of towels for Alex to borrow at a swim meet. Right?"

Light chuckle. And then we went back to staring at the pool again, waiting in silence for our sons to swim. I didn't know what else to say, and she didn't either.

At the time, it seemed an appropriate exchange, but perhaps it was more of a window into life at our house and the toll it was taking. I didn't elaborate on why I was awakened in the middle of the night and nobody asked. It was very unlike me to be so absentminded, and my swim team friends knew it. *Who forgets to bring a towel to a swim meet?* I tried to talk about anything but Tony, to sound *normal* and approachable, even if my behavior was off.

I was glad I went. Backstroke was Alex's best event. I never tired of watching him. His dark-tanned body pushed off the pool wall with his feet, arching his back to plunge into the water, sort of a backward dive. Skinny straight arms whipped around and around like a tiny windmill propelling him faster and faster. I breathed a little easier when he flip-turned successfully into an arrow-like streamline for his second lap, arms outstretched into a point until he surfaced and the windmill took over again. His lithe little body glided into an eighth-place finish out of thirty swimmers, dropping almost three seconds from his preliminary time.

"Go, Alex, go! Go, Alex, go!" I had screamed for the entire two laps, 35.65 seconds. He couldn't hear a single cheer; I knew it. But I liked to believe he felt my enthusiasm, as if our spirits were connected. I had nothing to do with his success as he swam; I just felt better, like a football fan cheering for a favorite team. Regardless of the outcome, it was worth the perceived stares and awkward chats to see Alex swim.

While I was at the meet, thoughts of Tony's well-being flitted in and out of my head. I knew Tony was in good hands even if his main caregiver was just a kid. TJ was cool as a cucumber, my flatliner. Sometimes he was so emotionless you couldn't tell if he was bothered by anything. His maturity and vocabulary belied his twelve years; he conversed better with adults than other kids his age. He came home once from a brutal loss in a tennis match exclaiming, "I am not meant for sports! I am going to be a stoic banker!"

TJ knew his way around the kitchen, having watched plenty of food TV. Garnishes were his favorite part of cooking, so I knew whatever he made for Tony would be beautifully plated with a sprig of cilantro or dried bay leaf.

The second day of the meet, our friend Gil brought a lunch for Tony. Gil and his wife Kim are like an uncle and aunt to our kids.

They knew tragedy, having been in a car accident five years earlier, both suffering serious injury. Their positive attitude and belief in sharing their story with anyone served as a model for Tony and me. Kim stayed home to let Tony and Gil have their time together.

I had thought our friends' presence that afternoon could be a little insurance in case TJ needed assistance. However, TJ looked after Gil too. Apparently, Gil did not know how to load a dishwasher.

"Just so you know, for next time, we load the dishwasher differently," our parenting words respectfully echoed back through TJ.

I was glad he retained the teachable moment tone of my voice instead of the exasperated, "DO AS I SAY OR ELSE!" He was the perfect host according to our friends. TJ got out dishes for the lunch and put beers in the refrigerator for the guys who were coming by to cut our lawn.

"You should be proud," Gil reported.

And I was proud. I was proud of both my boys for stepping up to care for Tony and keeping an upbeat attitude, as if they were far older. Alex kept a positive mind and swam his heart out. TJ genuinely enjoyed the respect and responsibility he was given. I rather hoped the boys' helping mode would stick long term. But more importantly, Tony seemed to be perking up in just a short time, our togetherness at home like fertilizer. Normal was within our grasp.

CHAPTER 17

Date Interrupted

Eighteen Days After the Accident

AND ON THE FOURTH DAY HOME, we rested. The stress of getting Tony settled and Alex's two-day swim meet exhausted us. Since it was still summer break and we had nowhere to be the first Monday home, the entire family slept in late. The last to rise were Tony and TJ. The ability for Tony to sleep solidly for so many hours meant the pain wasn't waking him up, so his need for meds was diminishing. Sleep has incredible healing powers, allowing the body to regenerate overnight. If it weren't for the neck brace and sling, Tony's bright eyes and relaxed stature made him look as if nothing had happened.

Lucky me, I had Tony all to myself on our day of rest. Sort of an all-day date, something we rarely did before the accident because we both had errands or workouts or sporting events for the kids. After breakfast, the boys left to hang out with their friends, for fun, not because they needed a place to go while I was at the hospital. With our day laid out before us, Tony and I thought a walk in the sunshine would be a great way to begin. But first, Tony needed breakfast, a shower, blow dry, and a clothing change. By noon, we approached the front door and in walked lunch, literally.

His friend Sal dropped by with his favorite Morucci's Deli sandwich, just for Tony. As a former New Yorker, Sal hoped his idea of comfort food would comfort his injured friend, even if it came from a California deli. The juicy pastrami sandwich was as close as he could get to the real deal from the Big Apple. I'm not sure Sal or Tony would look at it that way but from my perspective, the message emanating from the brown paper bag was love disguised as a sandwich. After twenty minutes of chatting in the entryway of our home, Sal departed, and we headed into the great outdoors for our walk, at last.

My first trip with Tony out on the open road was a little bit more precarious than the hospital hallway. Loose rocks or giant cracks in the road or sidewalk were a little too frequent, making me a nervous wreck. I was so scared he could slip off the curb even with me as his guardrail. I don't know how Alex would have managed if Tony had fallen or if it would even have occurred to Alex to save his dad. We chatted a little, not really getting into our fantastic date as much as I would have thought, and not just because of the road hazards.

All the medical armor was attracting attention. Some people waved or shouted "atta boy." It wasn't every day you saw someone with a fat neck brace and blue cloth sling walking slowly down the sidewalk with his wife holding her arms out to catch him if he fell. One guy screeched to a stop and jumped out to talk. I barely knew the man, but seeing Tony made him want to share war-wound battle stories. He had been in all sorts of crazy accidents, breaking or straining more body parts than Tony, but probably not all at once like Tony. Ironically, both guys pumped the other up saying the other guy's injuries were worse than their own. Seeing Tony bond with someone and make a positive out of the situation inspired hope for a better day.

We continued on, walking past a few houses when an elderly neighbor, Roy, interrupted our conversation. He slowed down in his car long enough to call out, "I know there's a story behind this one! Heh, heh."

Since we walked at a snail's pace, Roy passed us again, on his way back from a short trip out to the grocery store or Ace Hardware, the only nearby options. Curiosity got the better of him so he parked abruptly alongside our driveway, blocking anyone from going in or out. Tony used to attract conversations in the driveway while he washed our cars. Now people were stopping while he walked, his injuries broadcast like a billboard announcement to the neighborhood that one of their own was down. Unfortunately, it can take a tragedy to get neighbors talking to each other and not just the ones I knew well. We didn't mind the quizzical looks or cheers; we were grateful for their concern.

Roy got out of his car all smiles, zipping around the trunk as fast has his senior legs could get him to where Tony and I stood near the street. I knew he was expecting a silly story of a tumble off the roof or getting tackled by his boys or something. Roy is a character, rewarding candy to the neighborhood kids for repeating back the words, "Dow Jones Industrial Average."

Tony explained in short order how he earned his medical adornments. "I was basically steamrolled by a trailer while riding my bike."

"Wow! You just never think a young guy is going to be wearing something like this. Unbelievable!" The guy chuckled and shook his head. If he was horrified, he hid it well. I was relieved to see someone take Tony's situation lightly.

I realized at this point we never really knew how people were going to react to Tony and his story. I'm so darn honest I just tell it like it is, but for some it was startling, causing them to look away from me with shivers and quiet "ewws." Others were like Roy, just going with the flow and laughing it off in a "holy shit" kind of way. I found it to be similar to the premise of the book *Life of Pi*. There are two ways to tell a story: all truth or sugar coated. I found it best to play down the injuries until I got a better read of the person. The upside, smoothing over the details kept the pity-factor down, something that made *me* groan and look away.

By evening, we found ourselves alone for dinner; the boys stayed on with their friends. One of my mom-friends dropped off a meal, so it felt as if we were on a dinner date. The last date we had at home took an act of God to happen. I booked a sitter with a driver's license to take the boys out so we could have the house to ourselves. I worked for weeks on a goofy love song to play on the guitar, singing along to profess my gushing love in celebration of seventeen years of marriage. Singing "Anyone Else but You" to my soul mate made for a special evening back then, but somehow this night meant even more to us.

I made the most of our romantic time, setting the table outside on our back patio in the cool of the summer evening, the sun slowly fading. Freshly mowed grass and trimmed bushes by the gardening angels made for a peaceful setting. Cloth napkins were not too fancy for this special moment, even if I had to unearth them from deep inside the linen closet. Deep-purple grape juice in a wine glass for Tony and real wine for me made our taco salad seem exotic. We didn't even have to talk, just taking in the quiet and each other's presence was fulfilling. As we sat together, basking in our good fortune, the doorbell rang.

"I'm sure that's Darla stopping by. She called earlier to let me know," I said to Tony as I stood up to answer the door.

"Do we know her?" asked Tony.

"She's the one that was struck by a car while running a tag-team marathon six months ago."

Tony's eyes lit up. "Didn't you make dinner for her family?"

"Yes! I'll be right back." I dashed through the kitchen to the front door. Darla, tall and lean stood in her summer dress and sandals, perfectly healthy and holding a brown paper grocery bag. I guessed it was Darla—we had never met. Earlier in the year, my heart went out to her and her family when I received the e-mail message through our Boy Scout troop requesting support. I felt I had to make dinner for her even if I didn't know her. I wanted to reach out. Ironically, tragedy was what bonded us from both sides.

"Hi. Thanks for letting me come," she said stepping inside and handing me a bag. "Two tubs of potato salad, as promised. And a little wine." She had begged to bring something, anything. I sensed her intense compassion over the phone, so I desperately wanted to say yes to something.

On the phone, Darla had offered to share leftovers from a thank-you party she hosted for all the neighbors and friends who helped her and her family, a party we would have attended had the circumstances been different. Instead, she brought the party to us, suggesting potato salad and wine, since we were set for gifts of dinners for weeks.

Darla quizzed me on favorite wines and where I found them. I used to work in a wine store right after college so her questions didn't surprise me. Lots of friends asked for recommendations. When I looked in the bag, my heart melted.

Inside were two large tubs of potato salad, a treat for the boys—Tony too—and a surprise: an ice-cold bottle of my favorite wine, Honig Sauvignon Blanc.

"You shopped special for this one Darla! Thank you!"

We walked to the patio so Darla could meet Tony, partly out of courtesy and partly a need to connect. I think for her own closure, she wanted to see Tony and deliver her true gift to us, an angel-inspired message.

"This is what you will look like really soon. The neck brace will go away, and you will be excited to look down to tie your own shoes. I cried when I lost my neck brace forever. I ran eight miles two days ago. You will get there but not as fast as you like; it's the athlete in us."

I nicknamed her the Angel of Things-to-Come, describing our future to us. We needed to hear it just as much as Darla wanted to tell us. Our all-day date wasn't really meant for our togetherness, as much as it was to feel loved and supported by our community. The interruptions were the real gift.

CHAPTER 18

What About the Money?

One Month After the Accident

WHILE TONY AND I BATTLED the medical world head-on, the legal and financial challenges were catching up. I'd already had a few run-ins with the medical insurance company where I learned how idiotic the payment process was for the patient and how brilliant for business.

In an emergency situation, a patient does not choose any of his doctors. At our hospital, Tony was seen by a number of physicians, and not all of them were in our network. He was penalized for using out-of-network physicians, radiologists for example. Only 50 percent of their bills were paid by insurance. Tony had chest X-rays every day for almost two weeks to check the fluid in his lungs. Anyone could see how the bills were going to build up. The invoices arrived by the stack in our mailbox, one chest X-ray reading per envelope.

Some services were unidentifiable. We received one bill for two hundred forty dollars, no itemization or doctor name. What costs two hundred forty dollars? A sheet? Breakfast? An IV? I couldn't imagine the insurance company was going to pay for a mystery service. The medical bills were far more complicated than I had expected, and I was starting with the smaller ticket items. The hospital bed and pharmaceuticals came later and were the most frightening numbers. A small house in Arkansas was about the same price as an ICU bed in a California hospital. The meds were tracked dose by dose as if moving bullion, golden brick by golden brick. Before the nurse gave Tony his little paper cup of pills, she scanned a number into a computer. Over the course of almost two weeks in the hospital, Tony had racked up a mint of expenses. And the hospital stay was only the beginning.

My greatest fear was drowning in a sea of bills, possibly losing the house. My friend Kimberly promised she wouldn't let that happen. "We'll just have a bake sale or something."

"That's a lot of cookies," I said with a giggle. The loving intent was there and made me feel, once again, I wasn't in this alone. My friends were looking after me.

"You know, it might take as many as three phone calls to the insurance company to get them to pay," advised my friend Gil. "That's how it works." He knew, from the horrific car accident he and his wife were in years before.

I knew this too from my experience trying to get payment for a service for my second newborn. I spent a year calling until the agent finally gave up and paid the claim. There was no explanation for the delay, more of an "all right already." No wonder why I had to dig in my heels, for Tony. His situation would be a much harder and longer fight. The numbers were steep.

For my first battle of wills, I set myself up at the dining room table, *my* home office. I had worked in an X-ray billing department during college, so I knew a lot about the process of dealing with insurance companies. The job involved lots of documented calls and dates and follow-ups, tedious but necessary tasks. I armed myself with plenty of pens, a calculator, and file folders labeled new, pending, and paid. I was ready to attack the towering stack of invoices.

The first blockade was the tiny, tiny font on the back of the insurance card; it was nearly impossible to read. My eyes squinted as I punched the numbers into my Sony wireless home phone. I clicked my pen into action while I waited for someone to answer my call.

"Hello, this is Candy. How may I help you today?" asked the very cheery customer service rep.

"Hi. This is Francie. We have several hospital expenses covered at just 50 percent. How can we correct this?" I politely asked.

"Oh, right. You can file a grievance and a decision will be rendered in thirty days," the young representative chirped.

"Well, I will be calling you every day. I have *a lot* of grievances," I replied with a joyful edge.

"Oh, you can save them up and call them in all at once," Candy happily offered. *Geez*, I thought. I was not happy about adding that to my list of responsibilities.

The more I talked with Candy, the more I learned. Nonpayment was quite normal. A system and staff were in place to sort out claims, and somehow the insurance companies still made money. Getting Tony back to normal at a fair price was going to be the ultimate challenge, like a marathon versus a hundred-yard dash.

Managing Tony's medical care and insurance claims were overwhelming enough, but what about the ticket Tony was issued for getting himself run over? Surely some kind of compensation was due for the "damage" done to Tony. If the injuries from the accident didn't crush us, the insurance companies and legal system would. We needed some expert help.

The first to reach out to us was a buddy from Tony's racing team, Carlos. After a visit to the hospital, Carlos was intent to right the wrong done to his good friend. He had connections to law enforcement even though he worked in construction. He called me at home to introduce himself and report his findings.

"Hey. This is Carlos, Tony's friend from the team. How ya doing?" he jumped in right away, his thick Brooklyn accent a bit intimidating at first.

"I'm doing OK. Tony, not so much," I answered as I cradled the phone on my shoulder while folding laundry.

"Ya, I know. I saw him today at the hospital."

"How did you get in? It's family only." I asked.

"I told 'em I was his brutha from anutha mutha." Carlos was hard to refuse.

It could have very likely been true, the brothers story. They are both dark skinned with black hair. Tony's look is so universal he could be Mexican, Puerto Rican, South American, Hawaiian, Filipino, Japanese, or simply Chinese, his true heritage. Since visiting was limited to family, his buddies were coming up with all sorts of connections. If they were white like me, they claimed to be a brother-in-law. And now I knew if they were dark like my husband, they were blood.

Carlos had made some calls to his police buddies. "Nobody is sayin' nothin'," he said as if we were investigating a crime. We kind of were. His parting words were the most tender of all.

"You take care of those babies. It will be all right." I loved Carlos. He had our back like nobody else. His tough accent made me feel safe now.

What Carlos couldn't do, our lawyer, the White Knight, could. He took a crack at sorting out who was at fault for Tony's mangled state.

A direct conversation between the White Knight and the ticketing officer changed things for Tony. From a cyclist's perspective, the officer's take was expected: a cyclist is guilty until proven innocent. Somehow our lawyer helped the officer recognize the flaw in his judgment and the ticket was reversed: Tony was not speeding nor was he to blame for getting squashed into the pavement.

"The young guy who ran over Tony, he's officially at fault," the White Knight explained to me over the phone when he called to confirm our Sunday appointment.

"Oh, thank God," I said with relief.

"My team is working on compensation. Is Tony OK to meet? At your house of course," he reminded me. The White Knight was ultrasensitive to Tony's fragile condition. I appreciated his concern. A month after the accident, Tony remained in a delicate state; no car rides permitted unless absolutely necessary.

Since the meeting was later in the day, my Sunday morning was free. I decided to go to church. Something inside pulled me to go, probably my Catholic upbringing. I had not been in weeks, and I usually went just about every Sunday. I always felt better afterward, calmer and worry-free, a soft glow of protection surrounding my mind and my heart. I called it a spiritual workout, and it was just as important to me as a lap in the pool or spin on a bike.

I threw on my favorite full skirt in black-and-white gingham and a black cap-sleeved T-shirt. The outfit made me feel like Sophia Loren in an Italian film, the fifties-style skirt flared out like an umbrella if I spun around. This was the most dressed up I had been in a month, and it was nice.

After church, I kicked off my cork wedge sandals to quickly straighten up the house before the lawyers came. When the doorbell rang, I couldn't find my sandals anywhere. I couldn't even find a random pair of flip-flops tossed in a corner. We'd worked so hard to clear the clutter so Tony wouldn't trip on anything.

I answered the door in my bare feet. My pedicure was fresh, thankfully, as a friend took me out for a couple of hours for pampering. Still, I felt my toes sort of curl up and try to hide.

"I'm sorry, I can't find my shoes," I meekly stated, my cheeks flaming. The lawyers didn't care. I felt ill-prepared, so unlike my former-sales-executive self. Ugh. Three professionally dressed men walked into my dining room and sat at one end of the table while Tony in his sling and neck brace sat on the other, smiling and cordial.

"Is he always so happy?" asked the White Knight, looking at Tony. "He must close his bedroom door at night and cry."

"Nope. Never," Tony replied, still smiling.

"Surprising, but true," I said as I put down a pitcher of water and sat at the end of the table.

The White Knight introduced the two young gentlemen with him as lawyers specializing in insurance claims and maybe something else. I tried to concentrate as I monitored everyone's water glasses and hid my feet deep under the table and out of sight. When the conversation turned to the accident, my heart picked up speed, and my eyes were laser focused on the White Knight and his every word.

"The driver of the truck that hit Tony, does not own the truck. He borrowed it from a relative. Neither of them, own a home; they rent," our lawyer informed us. Deep inside, I was relieved. Both Tony and I felt uncomfortable with possibly taking so much away from a young guy just starting out in the world. I remember early on I prayed for whatever was fair. I was stressed over what our financial future might look like, but I also didn't want to destroy someone else's future in the process of saving ours.

Tony and I both came from meager childhoods. We knew how hard it was to get ahead under normal circumstances. The guy who ran over Tony was only twenty-eight and was probably trying to scratch out a living just to pay the rent or save up for a house for his own family. He would never achieve his dreams if we drove him into bankruptcy. Suing felt like going after someone with an atomic bomb when a simple negotiation would do. Our guts ached at the thought of what seemed to us greedy and harsh. Tony's plight was going to be long and expensive, but somehow, we couldn't take more than we needed.

"Can you give Randall here all the insurance statements you've received to date?" the White Knight asked at the close of our meeting. I couldn't tell by the tilt of his head which one was Randall, but that didn't matter.

I swiftly scooped up the neatly categorized file folders of medical invoices and held out the fat stack to both the young lawyers sitting at my table. I was elated when the bundle left my hands. To take something so ominous off my plate was beyond liberating. I forgot all about my bare feet and the empty water glasses.

The White Knight and his team handled it all. They negotiated with the auto and health insurance companies. We never met the young guy nor did we ever exchange words with the pesky police officer again. And much to my relief, I never had to file another grievance with cheery Candy from the claims department.

Thankfully, we kept our house and our bank accounts remained intact.

Tony's recovery would get our full attention.

CHAPTER 19

Big Changes for Tony

Five Weeks After the Accident

BEFORE WE KNEW IT, Tony was back to work five weeks after the accident. It was his idea. He felt strong enough to sit at his computer to type e-mails for short bursts of time. With the help of an adjustable armrest and pillows, Tony propped up his bad arm to reach the keyboard, typing as if nothing had happened. Basic messages he pounded out with ease. Rarely-used symbols like + or *{}* were out of the question, as the neck brace barred him from looking down, the same problem he had with a dinner plate.

The new workday began around nine a.m., when Tony rolled his battered body from his hospital bed. He whipped up a mean, left-handed scramble for breakfast before hitting his office by ten a.m. The commute was quick, just a short shuffle from his hospital bed to his desk, an advantage we hadn't considered when turning his office into a convalescent space. In high-tech sales, all Tony really needed was a laptop and a phone to reach his customers. But by about noon his head felt compressed from the talking and typing. His damaged brain was filled with constant static like a poorly tuned radio station, the static barely noticeable until he grew tired.

Then the volume suddenly blasted like an old-time TV turning fuzzy white and buzzing in the wee morning hours when broadcasts shut down. He was ready for a nap, and relief was only a few reverse-commute steps away to the awesome hospital bed.

Getting to this day wasn't easy. Tony awoke most mornings in a sopping twisted mess. The painkillers made him sweat, and his boxers spun up tight around his thighs. The daily routine included washing Tony's hair, sheets, and neck pads—everything was soaking wet. He didn't like the groggy foggy feeling in his head either. The pain was almost more appealing, *almost.* Eventually, Tony's superpowers triumphed over the pain. His inner strength in combination with a lot of help from ibuprofen, Tony was able to drop the supermeds, no regrets.

As for the rest of the house, we did our part to make Tony's life easier. The boys, with great effort, attempted to put away their things instead of dropping backpacks, racquets, jackets, and shoes at the front door or in front of the couch. Tony couldn't see his feet or two feet in front of him because of the neck brace. If anything was left out, all I had to do was yell, "ALEX! TJ! WHAT DO YOU SEE THAT YOUR DAD CANNOT?!?"

The boys knew without even looking exactly what I was referring to. Breaking bad habits was hard, but if your dad was affected, suddenly there was motivation to do what your mom had asked over and over for years: Pick up your stuff! The one upside for the guys, the toilet seat stayed up in the main bathroom, for Tony's benefit and to the boys' delight. For me, I just didn't go in there, especially at night.

Tony's work wasn't pushing him to go back a month after getting smashed up. In fact, the Boss, was really understanding, and HR encouraged an extended leave of absence. When Tony was late to turn in his sales forecast that fateful Friday, the Boss had called his cell to check up. For some reason, the young guy who hit Tony was holding Tony's phone at the accident scene. Maybe everyone was busy helping the paramedics by pushing debris out of the way or picking up valuable items that might be lost. Maybe he just wanted to be useful. What was even stranger than holding the phone was the fact that he answered it.

"Hey, Tony," said the Boss casually.

"Uh. This isn't Tony. I think I ran him over," confessed the driver. He was probably in shock, feeling horrible for Tony and the situation. Damon, our paramedic friend said the guy was remorseful and teary-eyed.

That phone call explained why HR contacted me hours after the accident, trying to get all the paperwork in order before I even knew what was wrong with Tony. The Boss was one of the first to know, even *before* the Wife.

I had no idea what was said after the initial exchange but the Boss did tell Tony he would never forget the screams and howls of pain radiating out loudly enough to be picked up by a cell phone. No wonder the Boss was so sympathetic.

No matter how much pain surged through Tony's body, he could not stay away from work any longer. Even under normal circumstance, vacations were not really vacations, as he's always spent an hour or two a day communicating with customers. An unfortunate accident wasn't going to keep him from his job either. He was in the middle of a really big deal and didn't want anyone taking it over in his absence. Tony might have been slow to move, but his work brain was active enough to know how to save his job and his paycheck.

Even in the hospital he was working, with me as his messenger.

"So, your office wants your accounts handled by another guy, not the one you said," I relayed to Tony.

"I'M TELLING you, I want my engineer," he sternly relayed back. He was in control despite being in ICU and newly concussed. I don't know where this second-self came from, but it was operating in the background and showed up when business was at hand either for work or paying the bills. We were both very, very lucky the second-self was there and catching the things I couldn't. An undercover angel was doing inexplicably good things.

When I was carrying around Tony's cell phone for the first two weeks after the accident, his phone rang often. I picked up his calls to spread the word Tony was "out of the office." I distinctly remember the most important call, the guys behind the BIG DEAL.

"Hello," I answered from the back seat of my Sequoia parked in a dark parking garage at the hospital. I took naps there during staff changeovers, when I couldn't be with Tony.

"Ahh. We are looking for Tony. He's supposed to be on a conference call with us right now. Is there something wrong," asked Tony's client.

"Tony was in a bike accident. He'll be OK. I'm not sure when he'll be back to work though." I carefully worded my response. I didn't want them to know the seriousness of Tony's injuries. I stayed vague and positive.

"Tell him we wish him the best," said one of the guys hesitantly, not sure what to say.

"OK. And thank you so much for supporting my husband and our family."

"Man. We are just doing our job," one of the guys said, kind of uncomfortable with the hero status I'd laid on him.

If it seems surprising Tony was back to work after five weeks, you don't know Tony. He has an internal strength and stamina matched by very few. Before the accident, he never required much sleep, stayed up late to finish work projects, and woke by dawn to ride his bike before work. He rode with a pack of competitive cyclists in similar circumstances who all were trying to fit in a spin around the workday. He wore a headlamp for safety, looking a bit like a stormtrooper from *Star Wars* with his aerodynamic helmet and head-to-toe team uniform of bright-green, black, and white. Team members were required to wear the team garb whenever they rode, part of the payback for sponsors with company names plastered across the jerseys.

Equally surprising, was the fact that I, the Wife and his bodyguard, would allow him to work so soon after the accident. However, Tony erred on the side of caution, especially anything that could bring harm to his family or finances. After seventeen years of marriage, I trusted his instincts. The bossy superpower that surfaced from Tony, early on in ICU, only reinforced my gut feeling that Tony knew what work he could handle, and I couldn't change his mind. After all, it was a low-risk decision given the fact the hospital bed was just three feet away. If he'd had to drive or if I'd needed to drive him, he would not have been back nearly as early.

Meanwhile, little by little, Tony's eyes grew brighter and brighter. "Today he is normal," I'd sigh in relief. Then the next day I'd think, now he's really normal. Then the next, next day, I'd think *now* he's *really* normal. In his healing state, of course, he wasn't ready for too much physically, so the sparkle in his eye made him seem like a shiny ornament: pretty to look at but not very functional.

His pain was up and down, still. He could not even poke his right toe out of bed until a dose of Tylenol or Advil seeped into his system. Just like any middle-aged athlete, Tony was creaky getting out of bed, but times one hundred, because of his healing bones. And just when it seemed safe to take a deep breath, his Darth Vader voice would come back, the one we first heard in the hospital. His raspiness was like a megaphone for his pain. On those days, he was slower to rise and longer to shower.

His whiskers were growing in patches. He didn't have the energy nor the need to shave. But after four weeks, the neck brace became too itchy. He did his best to maneuver the electric shaver along his jowls, his left hand crammed inside the brace. It was a good time to tackle shaving with TJ too. As a young teen, he was getting a fine-haired mustache, and I was scared to death to teach him how to shave.

Tony shivered when I told him how I would go about taking off the faint shadowy strip. I had suggested TJ swipe horizontally, swoosh. My method guaranteed a ripped upper lip. Short, downward strokes was the correct way, a tedious process in my naïve opinion. Tony said he didn't die in the accident because it wasn't his time. I interpreted his statement to mean he had a grand purpose to fulfill, one big job. It was the little things like teaching his son safe shaving skills that added up to the bigger plan, being a dad. I was thankful he could complete this sweet and tender job, or surely, I would have scarred TJ for life.

Tony's professional and family life was slowly ramping up, but what Tony wanted more than anything was to get back on his bike. We were hopeful the thumbs-up would come very soon from the neurosurgeon, a doc we *liked* from day one at the hospital. With great effort and determination, we climbed the flight of stairs to his second-floor office like toddlers, placing both feet on a stair before moving to the next one, me holding Tony's arm for balance. The pesky neck brace couldn't be dismissed soon enough.

"I don't see you getting on a bike for at least nine months," the neurosurgeon told us at the first follow-up appointment.

Gasp! I literally choked on the neurosurgeon's words.

I lived vicariously through Tony, so this news was crushing to me too. Cycling was contagious even if I didn't ride. For years I heard about rigorous workouts in the great outdoors or how much fun it was carpooling to a race with a teammate. Meeting Tony's cycling buddies *showed* me how much his community gave him joy and a sense of belonging. He desperately missed all of it, and I wanted him to have it back.

All along we had been focused on the mantra "Alive and Fixable." The fixable part was not going to be anywhere near the three months mentioned in the ER.

Healing would be a long and painful process. Pain was exactly what precluded him from riding sooner. The neurosurgeon reminded us that the hooks on the spine broke off, useless except for being a *real* pain-in-the-neck. Some neck injuries could ache for years.

We did get some good news though: the neurosurgeon said Tony could start taking the neck brace off, before his neck muscles forgot how to do their job. YES! The theory was similar to the African ladies with stacks of necklaces. Their heads would flop over without the support of their coils. Brace-free meant Tony could see a little bit more on his dinner plate and walk upstairs like a grown-up. When the boys first saw him, they thought his neck looked longer. Probably because Tony sat more erect and the stretchy V-neck tee enhanced the long look. To me, he was just plain cute. We could see his new beard with a tiny white patch right in the middle of his chin, a little kiss from a snow-angel, I liked to think.

The other good news, he could ride in a car as often as he wished, as long as he was comfortable—no more lockdown. As a precaution, he rode in the back seat, since the chance of bonking his head on the windshield during a crash was very low from way back there. I felt like I was Hoke Colburn in *Driving Miss Daisy*. As Tony's chauffer, I loaded him into the car first, strapping him in on the left side to avoid bumping the injured shoulder. Since he was directly behind me, our conversations took place through the rearview mirror. It wasn't perfect, but at least we could get out of the house a little more.

Our spirits were easily lifted with each mini victory, like the ones from the neurosurgeon: unlimited car rides and eliminating the neck collar. I think it was harder for our friends and neighbors to digest the unfortunate incident; they didn't recognize the highs, the big changes. That's why we got comments such as, "Look at you two? You're not mad or sad?" Or, "Is Tony always so positive?" Our eyes would drift down, scanning our bodies to see if there was something about us that could explain our rosy attitude. We could only shrug.

And then once in a while we'd get a reaction from a kind and elderly neighbor that cracked us up with its colorful honesty. Beau walked the neighborhood, bare-chested, pumping his five-pound weights from his shoulders to the sky. He stopped Tony and me on our walk to get the scoop, his 1970s Burt Reynolds sunglasses sparkling in the sun, his weights resting by his sides.

Tony described the accident and injuries in a few sentences. "Ribs . . .neck . . .shoulder . . ."

Beau didn't flinch, exposing only his southern roots. "Shee-it."

At some point, you have to throw up your hands and make the best of what happened. It helped that we were never angry with the guy who ran Tony over; it was an accident. Forgiveness freed our energies to focus on getting better, celebrating each step forward to a normal life, even going back to work. It made all the difference . . . and guys like Beau that kept it real and funny.

CHAPTER 20

Food Angels

Six Weeks After the Accident

FOR WEEKS, TONY AND I WONDERED about starting physical therapy. We wondered if he shouldn't go to an orthopedic surgeon for his shoulder too. Nothing was spelled out on the discharge plan.

The hospital docs did what they needed to do, and we were very, very grateful. They saved his life. But once the most obvious injuries were under control, they scooted us out the door and went on to the next emergency situation. We were left to fend for ourselves. Over and over, Tony and I thought, if we were not resourceful people, what would happen to us? We scratched our heads, thinking there had to be more to the discharge plan than a vague suggestion of physical therapy and instructions to remove stitches after a week.

"It's like the hospital turned us out to the wolves," I whined to Tony.

We didn't get much direction from Scary Office either, only a prescription for physical therapy to use after a few more weeks of healing. But where did we begin exactly? Do we just call *any* physical therapist? Why wait? Tony had had knee surgery years before where delaying physical therapy was a disaster. Too much scar tissue was allowed to build up, to the point that many of the earlier PT sessions were spent breaking up cemented muscles and tissue, an excruciatingly painful and tear-filled process. We knew the protocol for physical therapy had changed since the eighties—sooner rather than later was best. For the time being, we only discussed and wondered what to do next. The answer would come.

As usual, we seemed to find solutions in the most unlikely places and often by accident. E-mails from people who wanted to bring food to us continued. Not everyone knew about the dinner sign-up list a friend was keeping for us, so they offered directly to help. The list was full for weeks, but we hated to turn anyone away. We were learning over and over that it was therapeutic for both sides. As it turned out, another food angel was about to deliver us much more than just a meal.

Before leaving the hospital, an angel with real life experience, Wendy, gave us recommendations for surviving at home. The CaringBridge blog was interactive, allowing followers to comment; that's how we got her tips. She had injured just about everything in her body; most recently she'd broken three ribs mountain biking. She knew what she was talking about when she said, "Hold your nose when you think you will sneeze." Or "ring a bell in case it hurts too much to call out."

Wendy told us how to dress Tony too. I would not have known to buy snap-up shirts or V-neck tees or even thought of how Tony would sleep at home. We never would have asked El Doctor for a hospital bed if she hadn't told us how hard it was to sleep in a regular bed or on a couch with broken ribs. Wendy was mighty envious when she heard about Tony's good fortune. All her advice was a gift.

Now, Wendy was back. Bringing food was very important to her, another payback urge like Darla, the runner who brought potato salad, had had. "No" was not an acceptable answer. We agreed lunch would be helpful. I hate making sandwiches for school lunches or for Tony and me to this day.

If it were up to me, I would have brought a few deli sandwiches. Wendy, however, was half a fearless tomboy and half Martha Stewart. Along with a yummy pasta salad in a cute, decorative metal bowl with snap-on lid, she carried in a color-coordinated bundle of superhealing foods. A red bandana lined a basketball-sized wicker basket filled with personalized red-and-white labeled jars of honey, jam, and granola. Rounding out the remedies: healing tea, vitamin C drink-mix and Greek yogurt full of healthy cultures, calcium, and fat to put some weight on Tony. We just so happened to be looking for a new yogurt, without sugar.

Wendy brushed her long, wavy blonde hair away from her sparkling blue eyes after setting down the basket of goodies on our kitchen counter with both hands. She looked like a modern-day cowgirl in her burnt-orange floral top, loosely tucked into faded blue jeans with a distressed brown leather belt. The three of us, Tony, Wendy and I stood around the stuffed basket, admiring the bounty.

"Wendy! This is so much more than lunch." I said, my voice bursting with joy and gratefulness.

"This is my kind of food. So healthy! Thank you!" Tony said with a gigantic smile and saucer-wide eyes, like a kid getting the biggest present ever.

"My pleasure. I got tons of help after falling off my mountain bike. I wanted to pay it forward." Wendy smiled back; her cherub-like cheeks flashed pink.

Wendy rained blessing upon blessing upon us. We poured out our worries regarding next steps. Doesn't Tony need physical therapy? Shouldn't he see a specialist like an orthopedic surgeon? It just seemed wrong to stay locked up in a sling and then one day take it off and all would be normal. Our instincts were correct.

Through all her injuries, Wendy had amassed a physical therapist, orthopedic surgeon, and an internist. We could drop Scary Office! Her list was tried and true and meant we could leapfrog over the less helpful doctors. The icing on the cake: each one was sports oriented and *expected* the patient would get back on a bike. More often than not, we had physicians and nurses who treated Tony's cycling accident as his doing. They shook their heads as if to say, "Well, if you are going to play with fire . . ." I had to sit on my hands to keep from strangling physicians offering those tainted words of advice.

"Which doctor do we call first?" I asked.

"All of them at once. Don't let them tell you to wait two weeks. In fact, I'll text message them all to expect you." *She has a text messaging relationship with her doctors?* They sounded like real people with real hearts.

Once again, food helped us learn things and connect with our community. We needed Wendy more than we could have imagined. Tony's shoulder might have stayed locked up forever, or the path forward could have been a lot bumpier without her. The angels that spoke the loudest, like Wendy, the Angel with Real-Life-Experience and Darla, the Angel of Things-to-Come, never stopped knocking. They were willing to bring anything just to see Tony; those were the angels we could not afford to refuse.

The quieter angels from the dinner sign-up list continued to stream into our home with heartwarming meals and treats. We were so pampered and showered with love—a sure-fire influence on our healing and feelings of empowerment. We were not alone. However, Tony was growing more self-sufficient and our need for outside assistance not as dire. Maybe it was time to take care of ourselves? But after our experience with the desperate angels, we worried about hurting someone's feelings if we turned them away.

My restless mind and tender heart were instantly stilled. I will never forget a mom-friend from Alex's old playgroup who dropped off grilled skirt steak. Once again, I stood with our guest around the kitchen counter while she unpacked her bag of warm food.

"Thank you! Thank you for taking care of us." I couldn't stop. "We appreciate your kindness," I said as I drew my hand to my heart. She turned the charitable act around on me.

"Thank *you* for letting me help your family."

Goose bumps shot up all over my skin. Through the accident, I was learning how people felt the need to reach out, but I didn't think of it as me, the recipient, doing any big favors. I've made tons of dinners for other people so I know it's hard to fit it into the schedule, but in the end, I felt good knowing I brought cheer and relief to someone. But to actually see someone grateful for the opportunity to help, stirred me to the core.

Tony and I might have felt abandoned by the medical system, but our community was overwhelming. I did not cry at Tony's situation or the impact on my family. We didn't have time for moping. However, all the help we received, *that* moved me to tears every time. We felt so protected. Our horrible situation never felt horrible, because so many wanted to help us. For the first time in my life, I was realizing how many ways love could be packaged.

Not having grown up in a particularly ooey-gooey family that was full of "I love yous" every time we left the house or hung up the phone, I don't think I could have defined love. We were raised to be very independent. I remind my kids how lucky they are that every meal is made for them, breakfast, lunch, and dinner. When I was old enough to spread jam on bread, I made my own breakfast and lunch. My mom had no idea I ate peanut butter and honey sandwiches and a vanilla-frosted Zinger every day at school. Somehow, I stayed thin, and my teeth didn't rot.

To have so many people dote on us made my heart melt. Food is a way to share a piece of someone's heart. Anything dropped at our door was a reflection of that person, something they loved and wanted us to share in its special meaning. I really believed that. So, imagine our surprise when FedEx delivered all the way from New York City: Crack Pie. The dessert is a sweet and salty cookie-crust pie coming from a famous takeout milk bar called Momofuku. If food mirrored someone's heart, I really wanted to meet this guy, Tony's business associate, a cool and giving soul.

Knowing what we know now, if anyone asks how we survived, we say our community made all the difference. Accepting helpers into our lives no doubt contributed to the emotional healing, like a subtle cheerleader.

"You can do this!" they cried through the casseroles and cookies.

With so many offers to help from our friends, it was easier for our families to understand why we didn't need anyone to fly out from Colorado or up from L.A. to rescue us. My family was a little miffed I didn't let on about the accident until I was sure Tony would be fine, but eventually everyone settled on the positives—he was better, and we had plenty of hands to lighten the load. Tony eased his family's concerns with phone calls and texts, especially calls to his mom.

Because of our experience, I am more determined to help someone who is hurting. Even for just a minor thing, I will take over soup or cookies. To me, no matter how big or small the injury, relief is key, not judgment. A gift does not have to be earned. I did just that for an elderly couple down the street; both were feeling poorly. I think my visit meant more to them as I stayed an hour just chatting. The food was the admission ticket to a great conversation. They were so grateful for our help, they invited Tony and me out to dinner at their favorite Italian restaurant.

Who would have thought, one of the biggest lessons we learned would define love for us? Love is as simple as sending a Crack Pie, potato salad, skirt steak, basket of remedies, or mowing a lawn. Love is caring. Although not everyone is comfortable calling it an act of love, it is.

CHAPTER 21

The New Arsenal

Seven Weeks After the Accident

AS OFTEN AS WE ENCOUNTERED bump after bump in our journey, angels with impeccable timing seemed to smooth out our path. We got an appointment with the orthopedic surgeon (Ortho Guy) the same day we called. The wait could have been anywhere from two to six weeks. Maybe Wendy's referral message helped, or there was a last-minute cancellation by another patient. Regardless, the appointment angels were working in our favor.

Tony and I sat side-by-side looking around the tiny examination room. We learned from the framed certificates and photos hanging on the walls that the doctor played baseball in college and was a physician for a professional baseball team. All encouraging facts, validating what Wendy had told us: He was a sports-minded doctor. We were getting a very good feeling while we waited, and it was only going to get better.

When Ortho Guy walked into the room, we made quick introductions, walked him through the tragedy and laundry list of injuries. Instead of grimacing in horror or looking down his nose in judgment, his face lit up.

"Hey. I know this story. I've been hearing about it for weeks. Were you on the E-Ride the Thursday morning before the accident?" asked Ortho Guy, adjusting his frameless glasses to get a better look at Tony. His voice was friendly but his presentation was formal. His crisp white lab coat and neatly trimmed strawberry-blonde hair reminded us he was still a professional even if he rode a bike with Tony and his friends.

"Yes! You know Ethan?" Tony replied with quiet elation, his ribs were still sensitive to vocal outbursts.

"Friend of a friend, actually." Ethan had started an early morning cycling group; hence the name "E-Ride." Word of the organized group was getting out, so the numbers were growing even without a direct connection to Ethan.

Wow! Ortho Guy was a fellow cyclist, practically a neighbor, and a recommended physician. Our world was getting smaller and smaller with each angel encounter. Since E-Rides started in the wee-dark hours of five a.m. and all the riders dressed similarly in helmets and cycling uniforms, nobody really knew who was in the paceline, the string of riders where each took a turn on the front. Most of the guys crammed the ride in before work, so introductions were made on the fly, greeting only the one or two guys riding in front of or behind you.

At last, we found someone who could understand us, giving us peace of mind for the first time in weeks. Ortho Guy confirmed our suspicions: Tony needed an orthopedic doctor. In fact, one should have been following all along during his stay in the hospital. How was this overlooked? Once again, we were lucky to have another angel looking out for us, sending us to the exact person Tony needed to see first.

We learned Tony's healing was not all that simple. We expected Ortho Guy to prescribe a more thorough physical therapy protocol and a better-defined prognosis. To El Doctor or anyone, Tony looked like he had a simple dislocation that would heal up quickly.

To a more discerning eye, like Ortho Guy, much was wrong, and he didn't know why. He performed an almost primitive-looking test. He broke a wooden Q-tip in half and gently poked the jagged end here and there around Tony's shoulder and scapula. We learned Tony had dull sensations in some areas but not in others. And for some unexplainable reason, Tony's shoulder was still hurting even after four weeks.

Ortho Guy made all these assessments without grabbing Tony's injured body or asking him to lie down in impossible positions. We were already off to a great start even though we'd discovered more unknowns rather than answers. An MRI would tell us a lot about what was going on underneath his skin. Was there nerve or rotator cuff damage? Was the shoulder properly relocated? If not, Tony would have to relive his ER experience and have his shoulder manipulated into place. Most likely he would be under anesthesia, but it meant he would start the healing clock over again. We never expected to hear this kind of diagnosis.

As Ortho Guy delivered this information, he looked hard at both of us, or at least me. I learned this was his way of watching me process the facts and allowing me time to ask questions. Unbelievable! We could have someone sensitive enough to ensure understanding and not rush us out the door. Ortho Guy didn't offer any predictions either. He didn't say Tony would be on a bike in no time or Tony will never ride a bike. He just didn't know enough about Tony's injury and how it was healing to say anything.

A few days later we found ourselves in the physical therapy office. We met PT Man (physical therapy man) in the waiting area.

"Hi. Wendy told me about you. Come on back," he said in a quiet but firm voice. We followed the six-foot-two skinny frame with the straightest back I had ever seen to an examination table. He pulled a white curtain to create a thin wall of privacy, as if we were back in ICU. I recoiled at the sight, like seeing a ghost; I quickly moved my eyes back to PT Man.

Tony sat on the table facing PT Man, who was seated on a swivel chair with impeccable posture, holding a clipboard. Tony was like a little kid, going wherever he was told, waiting patiently to see what happened next. I stood near Tony, looking down on PT Man's silvery hair and then locked eyes with him.

"All right. Tony is very delicate," I started to warn him. I stopped short of giving him more cautionary guidance because PT Man kind of rolled his hazel eyes at me.

"I've got it. I can handle it," he said with gentle assurance. I don't know what it was that made me trust him with Tony, but I walked back to the waiting room while the two stayed behind in the examination space, *without me*. Maybe it was because Tony was doing better at managing himself and this member of our medical team came highly recommended. I felt a gentle tug on my heartstrings as a piece of me cut loose, like the first time I let my child go back with the dentist by himself. Tony and I had been so close for weeks, and I was reluctant to let him out of my sight.

From the waiting room, I could peek over the half wall separating the two spaces. The physical therapy area was one large room with eight cushioned examination tables around the perimeter. Against another wall were exercise balls, stretchy bands, stationary bikes, and weights, like a communal doctor's office and public gym in one place. My eyes bounced from the *People* magazine I was reading to PT Man and Tony. I'm sure PT Man felt my eyes burning into him. If he was unnerved, he didn't show it. He was probably used to an overly loving helicopter-spouse lurking in the wings. I finally got to a point where no Hollywood gossip article could hold my attention. I invited myself to sit next to Tony while he iced down from the stretching PT Man had done with him.

While we waited, we were introduced to PT Man's business partner, also a physical therapist. Tony became an instant celebrity because of his cycling hobby and his extensive injuries, the worst they had ever seen. Both partners rode bikes and PT Man rode with

Ortho Guy sometimes. Tony's accident could happen to any cyclist, maybe one of them, and they knew it.

"You are going to feel a lot of love here, Tony," PT Man offered.

We were so relieved, especially Tony. He had guys who respected him, his injuries, and his sport. He'd found his people. No "Tsk! Tsk!" under anyone's breath. We felt like we were in a world of people who understood our situation and wanted to be our friends. And more importantly, the new team wanted to help Tony recover, become a whole person and a cyclist. Now we knew why Wendy could be text-buddies with her doctors.

The last member to join Tony's arsenal of docs was the primary care physician. We were going about this in reverse order, but it was working out well. Usually a primary care physician will direct you to the specialist. But we were anxious to talk to an expert, especially Ortho Guy, as we had waited long enough locked up in a sling with too many questions swimming in our heads. Luckily our insurance company did not fight us on our upside-down path.

Our new primary doc was completely the opposite of our prior experiences. We knew in a few short minutes he was a triathlete and he was very, very smart. We had filled out zillions of medical forms by now and there was always a list of about twenty-five things we could thankfully answer no to, like heart disease, cancer, shortness of breath, etc. Filling out the form in this office was a group effort. The New Doc sat on a stool with his thick wave of brown hair peeking out like a mountaintop from behind the clipboard he was holding close to his young face. He literally *ran* us through the medical history list verbally. Dang. I was so impressed, and we were just getting started.

"You are really fast! I don't think I could recite the alphabet nearly as quickly." I couldn't resist paying him a compliment.

"Thanks. I can say the alphabet backwards too," he said amused. He proved it too.

Using his eyes and fingertips, he scanned Tony's injured areas so closely he could almost kiss the back, scapula, and neck. He was ever so gentle. Afterward, he recommended taking an even closer look at the vertebrae, the spine. He approved of all the experts in the arsenal, but in his opinion one more specialist was missing. We were seeing two "hardware" guys, an orthopedic surgeon and a physical therapist, but we didn't have anyone for the software—the nerves.

He believed we needed to examine the neck, as it could be the reason Tony did not have feeling in his shoulder and arm. Nerves run like rivers all over the body, some are outside of the spine and some are inside the spinal cord. If the nerves were damaged on the outside, he could heal and gain back tickling or scratching sensations. But if the nerves were damaged from inside, the spinal cord, Tony might not be so lucky. I imagine that was the case with someone paralyzed by a horrible crash or fall.

Luckily for us, the New Doc studied neurology, so he knew how to connect all the dots in a way nobody else could. Tony would be tested to see which nerves were firing or *not* firing. From there, we would figure out next steps.

We were entering a new and complicated phase that would take a medical team to decipher. We shuddered to think where we might have ended up if Wendy hadn't floated into our lives, sharing her real-life experiences and arsenal of athletic specialists. Tony might have stayed locked in his sling longer or skipped a specialist, unable to even change a light bulb in the ceiling because his shoulder was glued to his torso. Instead, our capable team of specialists gave us hope.

CHAPTER 22

Living and Healing

Seven Weeks After the Accident

"I'LL HAVE THE NUMBER ONE with pepper jack instead of provolone," Tony said as he looked to me to place his sandwich order.

We were both reading over the menu in front of the deli case at Morucci's in Walnut Creek. There wasn't one reason why he couldn't relay what he wanted to the deli clerk. A few seconds passed before it occurred to me, *he* could order his own sandwich. He never lost his voice or his hearing. I'm amazed at how quickly we'd both adapted to me managing everything. Not that I minded, but like the sling and neck brace, he was slowly weaning his dependency from me too.

Without his neck and shoulder supports, it was easier to see how much damage and loss of muscle strength Tony had sustained. His movements resembled old movie characters. The slow, slow mechanical turns of his neck were similar to an old-fashioned clunky robot in a black and white film. He sluggishly picked up a dropped napkin or pen from the ground, a monumental accomplishment. Without the sling, Tony looked normal, as if he had never been in an accident. On closer inspection, his arm was held close to his body with a slightly limp wrist, as if he were the gothic character Igor. As he gained strength, PT Man encouraged him to swing his arm while he walked so he could get movement back. Visions of John Travolta in *Saturday Night Fever* rocked in my head.

This cast of characters stayed with us for about a month. While we waited, an MRI turned up a torn rotator cuff, capsule, and possible nerve damage. Surgery was likely, but Ortho Guy wanted Tony to strengthen his shoulder even more through physical therapy to help ensure a more positive outcome. Only time would tell if Tony gained enough muscle mass and, more importantly, increased movement to "win" a ticket to the operating room. It was kind of weird to wish for surgery, but if surgery was possible then getting on the bike again was possible too. Ortho Guy was not offering predictions. His lips were zipped.

The possibility of never cycling over rolling hills or with his cycling buddies made Tony work as hard as possible on his physical therapy. He did not want his lack of motivation to be the reason his shoulder would not return to full function. Tony went to his physical therapy appointments three times per week learning all kinds of stretching exercises. Using a golf club, an eight iron, he pushed the club head into his right hand to force the shoulder into an external rotation, opening away from his body. A lot of scar tissue and muscle tightness had built up over the previous month. Tony thought it was because he was a superhealer, and maybe he was special. We did learn darker-skinned people are more prone to thicker scar tissue called keloid scarring. That explained why Tony had a fat, wormy looking scar on his knee from surgery years ago. My scars were barely visible on my pale Irish skin.

PT Man suggested wiping down a table several times a day too. I rather liked this exercise as he could conveniently help after meals: breakfast, lunch, and dinner. His friend Kevin teasingly told Tony, "Wax on! Wax off!" from the *Karate Kid*. The same concept worked well for washing a car too. With help from the boys, they had an activity to do together. Tony is car obsessed, going to car shows and meticulously washing his own car. What used to be a fanatical hobby was now a workout too, and it helped him reach his goal of riding again.

Those days, we all worked around the house without any grumbling. The boys really stepped up to take a turn at the dishes or folding clothes. For me, I never felt fatigued or frustrated at the never-ending caretaker role. I've had countless volunteer jobs where at one point or another I grew restless and crabby. Helping Tony was a pleasure, so there was no reason to be resentful.

Tony on the other hand felt terribly guilty for slowing our family down. He wasn't outwardly apologetic or depressed, but I think we gave him yet another reason to work harder than ever at his physical therapy. He wanted to hang out with the family like we used to, taking a day trip somewhere. Since he was getting stronger, he could tolerate a short day-trip to one of our favorite destinations.

On a Sunday afternoon, I drove the family to Carmel while Tony rode in the front seat, reclining as if he were on an airplane. He slept most of the way, thank goodness. I was happy he could nap but also happy he couldn't offer any driving tips. Usually Tony was behind the wheel, and on the rare times he rode shotgun, I got an earful of "watch outs," startling me to the point of extreme annoyance.

In downtown Carmel, we picked up sandwiches at our go-to deli, Bruno's Market. After another fifteen minutes of driving, we arrived at our destination, a little alcove on a hidden and near-empty beach. Tony sat in a beach chair, and we gathered on the blanket at his feet. We ate thick turkey sandwiches on Dutch crunch rolls and shared bags of Hawaiian Sweet Maui Onion and Salt and Pepper Kettle chips. When the winds were right, we unrolled the no-fuss miniature kites complete with string and handles. As long as there was a strong gust, anyone could fly the kite-for-dummies, exactly the way I liked it. Tony stayed in his chair, happy to watch our successful launches into the sky, the opposite of his old energy-of-a-teenager self.

On vacations, Tony was the guy seizing the day; he didn't want to miss anything. Tony relished boogie-boarding in the waves like a kid, while I, on the other hand, would be found napping in the warmth of the sandy beach, my face enveloped in shade from a floppy sun hat—my kind of vacation. We complemented each other: Tony dragging me out of my comfort zone and me reeling him in for relaxation.

At low tide, the boys and I climbed around the exposed rocks, looking into tide pools at sea anemone, hermit crabs, and starfish. Once again, Tony stayed in his spectator seat, yards away from the surf. Negotiating bumpy and slippery surfaces was far too risky. A fall would be as good as crashing on his bike, injuring an already injured brain and shoulder. Besides, looking down made Tony dizzy. It was a little sad to see him sitting underneath blankets of towels, the corners flapping against the chilly sea winds. He looked like a frail grandpa instead of a middle-aged dad. Normally he was the one with the boys, venturing closer and closer to the surf, making me a nervous wreck as I stood close to shore. I was afraid of the crashing waves sucking up one of my sweet boys or my darling husband.

At least we were out of the house, even if I had to be at the ready to retract a son from ferocious, pulling waves. I wasn't sure I could do that. The danger wasn't as bad as I imagined, or Tony would never have allowed any of us out on the rocks to explore, protecting us from harm even from his chair. Oceans scare me, even though I am a strong swimmer. I grew up in the mountains not at the beach. I am hopelessly cautious near the seashore.

We ended the day at the Village Corner California Bistro, where Alex could get spaghetti with red sauce and TJ a plate of lobster and crab pasta. I never tired of linguine and clams, while Tony is forever a fan of grilled lamb. The day was short and sweet, as Tony grew tired and needed to get back home. He slept soundly on the way back, his lungs filled with sea air and tiny grains of sand lightly dusted his charcoal hair. He pushed himself for his family, exhausted but satisfied we'd gotten out of the house.

Weekends were our time to slow down, not unlike before the accident. They just meant more to us, because we had stayed home for so many weeks and we cherished our outings. Seeing Tony strong enough to enjoy regular life again felt triumphant and priceless.

Not long after Carmel we were treated to an entire Saturday alone, while our boys went to college football games. Alex watched Cal play at home in Berkeley while TJ went to Stanford in Palo Alto, rival colleges in the area. TJ laughed at a "Cal" sign planted upside down in front of the Stanford Stadium. The rivalry runs so deep they don't even have to play each other to take a dig.

Our all-day date wasn't super fancy. We spent most of it at a sporting goods store looking at baseball bats for Alex. He outgrew his from the spring and was going to play fall ball. Home Depot was close by so we stopped in to get a "female" part of the hose. Tony might not have been fully recovered, but he could fix little things around the house, like the hose he used to wash the car. And while we were in the neighborhood, Tony showed me his secret lunch spot he took the boys to but never me. I was entering the boys club, which included an authentic Mexican restaurant where the food was excellent and super cheap. For $5.83 we had chicken tamales and sodas. I treated.

All of those activities wiped Tony out, plus his ribs hurt. He needed to get horizontal and give his brain a break too. I wanted him well rested as we had planned a dinner date later that evening, something we hadn't done in a while. He wore his stretchy V-neck tee in black, his dressiest look for now. It would be months before his hipster dress shirts in trendy floral prints or white linen would leave the hangers for a date again. Normally we drove thirty minutes to Oakland or Berkeley to dine at the foodie restaurants rarely found near us. Artisan Bistro in our hometown met our foodie palate pretty well, so it was a nice outing and not too far away.

As we ate fresh garden tomatoes with goat cheese, we talked about how the accident showed each of us more about our character than we knew existed. Both of us were surprised at how mentally strong we became in a time of adversity. Tony had a hidden inner power that kept him alert in the hospital, allowing him to keep an eye on work, our bills, and his healing. I held our family together, staying upbeat so nobody worried about Tony, including Tony. We saw things in each other at new depths, like caring and appreciation. Tony was helpless. As tough as he was, he could not look after himself. "How would I take care of myself without you?" he'd ask me. We always appreciated a birthday cake or Valentine chocolates, but the moment was fleeting and not nearly as piercing as leaning on someone for absolutely everything after a serious accident.

Our time together was changing too. I had to admit I liked the fact Tony worked far fewer hours, finishing at five instead of his usual six thirty p.m. He was too tired to push it any further. In the old days he broke for dinner and went back at nine p.m. to finish up. Working from home was a double-edged sword. He didn't have a commute, but he was never very far from cranking out another spreadsheet or e-mail.

Neither of us liked the schedule, but his job demanded it. The long hours were a big reason we didn't try for a third child. At the time we made the decision, Tony was traveling and the boys were four and two years old. Without family nearby to help, the boys were solely my responsibility. I was finally convinced; two was enough.

Being forced to slow down gave us an opportunity to focus on our family and on the two of us. So often, we worked independently for the good of the family. Tony was the breadwinner, and I was everything else. Tony helped with the kids, a lot but like most moms, I organized schedules, carpools, music lessons, sports, and social calendars. I was tired of being on my own so much.

I was not glad for the accident or the hell Tony was going through just to function every day. But I did enjoy the quiet of just being together as a couple and a family. Unfortunately, to break out of the frenzy something big had to happen, and that's what happened to us. We were not going to parties or inviting people over for dinner. Instead, we ate at home and played games with the kids. What mattered the most was exactly where we spent our time, together.

CHAPTER 23

Doctor Dates and the Frankenstein Lab

Eight Weeks After the Accident

AS TONY'S CHAUFFEUR, I accompanied Tony to all of his medical appointments. I didn't mind, because I wanted to hear the assessments and updates in person. With so many physician and specialist visits packed into a week—four or five—we started calling them doctor dates. I don't think we ever had that much togetherness, ever. Not even in the early days when we were gaga for each other.

The best date was with the neurosurgeon. We learned Tony's neck was healing really well. The ridges that snapped off the vertebrae were lodged in muscles in his neck, so we didn't need to worry about any pieces floating into his lungs or wandering down to his big toe. As long as Tony wasn't in pain, the renegade fragments could stay. The X-ray proved it: no surgery needed. Even better, the neurosurgeon did not believe any nerves in the neck were nonfunctioning, nor would his neck stop him from riding a bike again.

We knew Tony was stronger based on the short walk to the neurosurgeon's office from the parking lot. He climbed the two short flights of stairs all on his own, minus me, his human cane. Graduating from the neck brace made it possible to see each step and the strength gained from physical therapy gave him the confidence to be more like his old self, albeit a little slow. Tony's progress meant we could remove the neurosurgeon from our dating circuit.

As soon as Tony dropped one doctor, he picked up another. He needed a nerve specialist to determine why his shoulder was not functioning. We respected the new doctor, as he seemed so forthcoming with information and quite jovial, almost excessive. He accentuated each statement with a cheery lilt implying a "by golly" or "really swell." The happy-go-lucky cadence coupled with his curly red hair and light sprinkle of freckles across his nose, made me think of Howdy Doody. Thus, he became Dr. Happy, at least for the moment. We didn't find out until months later that Dr. Happy wasn't always so happy.

Right away, Dr. Happy involved me in his analysis, pointing out places on Tony's body where clearly something wasn't right. His right scapula drooped like a sad, sad smiley face instead of being taut like an uberathlete. His clavicle protruded as if he hadn't eaten in months, a stick figure of a man. Muscle atrophy was to blame as opposed to a bad relocation; El Doctor had gotten his shoulder back into the right place. After eight weeks of being out of commission, it was no surprise Tony was shrinking up. But were the nerves to blame or just inactivity? Dr. Happy aimed to find out.

Fast-forward a week, and the results from an MRI on the neck indicated the nerves were fine, just as the neurosurgeon suspected. Now it was time to check the functionality of the nerves in Tony's arm and shoulder. Dr. Happy could run the tests himself, in his own office. His examination room was outfitted with a cushy table, a few chairs, and a tray of medical instruments. The only light came from an X-ray light box, emitting an eerie pale-blue glow. The doctor's shadow on the wall was like a mad scientist, hunched over his victim in Frankenstein's lab. Four of us entered the lab, Tony, me, Dr. Happy, and his lovely Igor assistant, Shirley.

Before beginning the Nerve Conduction Velocity test (NCV), Tony's arm was dotted with two-inch needles like a live voodoo doll channeling someone's demise. No yelps of pain slipped out of Tony, despite the tortuous look. Electrical wires lay across each needle, stuck to Tony's skin using simple blue painter's tape, as if jury-rigged by the real Frankenstein. Then the doctor threw the switch, firing up each needle with a zap. If the nerve was hot or active, the sound of crackling Rice Krispies played through the computer's speaker. If the nerve was inactive or possibly dead, it was like listening to a soft wind blowing into a cell phone. We heard both.

The happy-go-lucky doctor morphed into his clinical side.

Without a trace of cheer in his voice, he said, "I tell ya, it looks better than I thought it would. However, the axillary nerve in the shoulder is not working. I can't say if it will come back. I can't say it will never come back. I can't even give percentages." The axillary nerve controls the deltoid, triceps, and elbow extension. That is a lot of responsibility for one nerve. This explained why he couldn't raise his arm above his head or reach across the dinner table for the bowl of mashed potatoes. The news was the darkest prognosis to date. All hope evaporated from me like a deflated balloon, my jaw and shoulders slackened.

For the first time, a visible disappointment crossed Tony's face. His initial response: "I guess I won't be throwing a ball." Ironically, even though the procedure hadn't hurt, the results did.

We spent the day absorbing the information, considering what this really meant.

Fortunately, we were on a doctor-date dating streak. The same day we got the bad news, Tony had a physical therapy appointment. PT Man was hopeful. He thought something was firing, because Tony definitely had some triceps activity. He even believed Tony could ride again, someday.

A few days later, our next doctor date was with Ortho Guy. We explained all of our findings. He had guessed from the beginning the axillary nerve was the heart of the problem. He believed Tony had some hope of regaining activity in the nerves as nerves do regenerate, but *slowly*, one millimeter per day or one inch per month. Growth starts all the way from the neck to the shoulder and could take a year! No extra vitamins, steroids, or Miracle-Gro could speed up the growth. I'd asked.

The nerve was stretched out, not cut or severed, so the casing with all the nerve endings was still intact and could provide the proper path for the nerves to grow. If Tony's nerve had not been damaged, he would have been preparing for rotator cuff surgery right away instead of waiting six long weeks for the nerve to grow. Ortho Guy said he had a rugby player with a similar injury, and he could still play rugby, just a little differently. The glimmer of hope he provided boosted our spirits.

Coincidently, Tony and I arrived at the same never-gonna-happen conclusion: he would not serve tennis balls. Tony doesn't really play tennis, so it was kind of funny we'd eliminated the same activity, the *only* activity at this point. We couldn't fathom him giving up anything else. How could a dad skip throwing a football or baseball around with his boys? This was the same dad that asked mom to check with the pediatrician to see what we could do to enhance hand-eye coordination with our three-month-old. We hoped and prayed nothing else would make the can't-do list.

So, back to PT, PT, PT, PT, PT, PT, PT, PT, PT, PT, PT, PT, PT, PT, PT filling his days to increase and maintain movement in preparation for those nerves to reach their destination and start firing again. Hopefully a bike trainer would work its way into the day. But with PT and work, it wasn't as much a matter of ability as it was hours in a day. Tony still slept a lot, so he couldn't pull his usual Tony and skip the sleep for a spin on the bike.

We hoped and prayed more than ever that the nerve would grow back. REVIVE. REVIVE. REVIVE.

CHAPTER 24

Driving, Eating, and Football

Three Months After the Accident

PT.PT.PT.PT.PT.PT.PT.PT.PT.PT.PT.PT.PT.PT.PT.PT.PT.PT.PT.PT.
PT.PT.PT.PT.PT.PT.PT.PT.PT.PT.PT.PT.PT.PT.PT.PT.PT.PT.PT.PT.
PT.PT.PT.PT.PT.PT.PT.PT.PT.PT.PT.PT.PT.PT.PT.PT.PT.PT.PT.PT.
PT.PT.PT.PT.PT.PT.PT.PT.PT.PT.PT.PT.PT.PT.PT.PT.PT.PT.PT.PT.
PT.PT.PT.PT.PT.PT.PT.PT.PT.PT.PT.PT.PT.PT.PT.PT.PT.PT.PT.PT.
PT.PT.PT.PT.PT.PT.PT.PT.PT.PT.PT.PT.PT.PT.PT.PT.PT.PT.PT.PT.
PT.PT.PT.PT.PT.PT.PT.PT.PT.PT.PT.PT.PT.PT.PT.PT.PT.PT.PT.PT.
PT.PT.PT.PT.PT.PT.PT.PT.PT.PT.PT.PT.PT.PT.PT.PT.

This was the life of PT: dizzying, painful, monotonous, and endless. If PT were a journal, Tony would fill up the entire book with just two letters, P and T, sprinkling each page with perspiration and tears. Tony being Tony, he kept his nose to the PT grindstone, his only hope of regaining use of his arm again and getting back on the bike.

The bedroom/office morphed into a gym and was accessible anytime—"24-Hour Rehab," if we'd hung a name on the door. Tony called it the torture chamber. I agreed with the creepy name, as animal-like grunts permeated the walls as he pushed past screaming muscles, willing his shoulder to normalcy. My body winced as I scurried down the hall on my way to the washing machine, cradling my laundry basket of dirty clothes like a shield against the "wild animal" behind the office door. I *really* didn't want to know what was going on in there.

The quieter exercises took place on the controversial bed-turned-workout bench, the one El Doctor had predicted would transform Tony into a couch potato. Tony lay on the bed at an incline, moving the golf club right to left and left to right above his head. The goal was always in sight: his red-and-white time-trial bike, the one that had survived the accident better than Tony, was locked into a bike stand, like a bright-red bull's-eye.

I could almost hear him talking to his target, his grunts so ominous I wondered if I should go in to rescue him. It was as if he was saying, "I'm going to ride you if it kills me."

As each muscle sprang back to life with the help of stretchy bands and a golf club, PT Man layered on yet another exercise to wake up the muscles in other parts of Tony's shoulder. A new exercise was like adding another line of PT.PT.PT.PT.PT.PT.PT.PT.—extending his time at PT appointments and in the torture chamber. Tony faced each exercise like a champ, pushing his pain and fatigue level to an eleven on a ten-point scale—impressing PT Man with his mighty will to overcome mighty injuries. To say PT Man had never seen anything like Tony was an understatement.

One of the new exercises, a seesaw motion, could easily be simulated using a pulley machine. Tony was all too happy to take a trip to Orchard Supply Hardware by himself in his Toyota Camry. Driving was a new privilege, so Tony got behind the wheel any chance he got. He came back grinning.

"I think I met one of those angels you talk about," he said in a low and quiet voice. He didn't want to admit it out loud, like a typical male asking for directions.

"OKaaaay . . ." I said with a suspicious tilt of my head.

"Well, I didn't want the OSH clerk to think I was actually building a torture chamber by asking for a rope and pulleys. So, I told him about my hurt shoulder."

"Did he freak out?" I asked.

"I didn't tell him *how* I hurt my shoulder. He didn't ask. Instead, the clerk lifted up his shirtsleeve to show me a long scar on the back of his arm. He told me when he was injured, all he used was a rope over a door to make a seesaw motion." Tony grinned again and held up a four-foot piece of twisted white cotton as thick as a licorice whip.

I smiled back, happy for his solution and amused he saw this man as an angel, just like I would.

Tony's tenacity was paying off in tiny steps. His forearm moved forward a few inches with intense concentration, sort of a first plateau to reaching the top of his Mount Everest. For a full extension, he used his left arm to stretch the right arm farther, placing his right hand on his target, the shifter in his car, for example.

Driving gave Tony a sense of control and happiness no amount of therapy could bring back. After a road test with me to make sure he hadn't forgotten how to drive, Tony felt safe to entertain the boys on his own.

"I'm taking the boys out for KFC and the candy store," Tony announced while holding the front door open, bouncing on his toes. I could see the boys in the distance as they clamored into the car. "I get shotgun!" "No, I do!" No hint of an invitation to me was in Tony's words.

"You're OK to shift?" I asked, for reassurance. I was not quite ready to let Tony fly on his own, even if I *had* OK'd him to get behind the wheel.

"I'm fine. The boys can help me shift. They'll love it!" And with that, Tony was practically running to the car too, his still-fragile state holding him back from a springy, childlike sprint.

Part of me wanted to high five his progress, and the other wanted to motivate him even further with cheers of, "Come on! Go! Go!

Go!" like I did for Alex in a swim race. But just like Alex in the pool, my cheers didn't make him go faster any more than Tony's shoulder muscles extended farther. Both my son and Tony's muscles were deaf to my words of encouragement.

Tony was coming alive. Whether he was sitting at his desk or lying in the hospital bed doing PT, I stopped to give him a big smooch. I couldn't help it, in the same way I couldn't help kissing my baby's chubby cheeks. He was ALIVE! At first, he seemed still in a daze, but eventually he was excited to see me too, whenever I made a smooch-stop.

Bit by bit, as Tony's energy increased, he reeled in time with the boys any way he could. A favorite pastime was taking the boys with him to get his hair cut, all the way to San Francisco, an hour away. He'd been going to the same place since 1990, when we lived in our apartment in the City. After twenty years, Tony was not about to give up his Vietnamese stylists who knew how to cut his "twelve-gauge wire" hair, Tony's way to describe his impossibly thick strands.

Tony wasn't quite ready to navigate the Bay Area highways on his own. I drove, much to the chagrin of the boys.

"What? Mom is going?" TJ whined.

"Does Dad really need a haircut? He has a lot of bald spots," Alex argued.

The answers were yes and yes.

We parked our car in a garage near Chestnut Street and walked two blocks to Tony's appointment. I followed the boys down their familiar path, stopping first to pick out a bag of chips at the minimart near the Haircut Store. The boys named stores for what was in them, because Mike's Pharmacy didn't make sense when you were only four years old, but the Medicine Store—the name said everything a kid needed to know. The names stuck, even years later.

Tony sat under a plastic cape while the stylist's razor-sharp scissors moved in rapid snips. The boys crunched on Cheetos or Cool Ranch Doritos, swinging their legs back and forth on the big chairs in the waiting area six feet away. I skipped the chips and just read a

People magazine. Fortunately, there were a lot of back issues, as I'd already read the latest and hottest movie star news waiting at all the doctor appointments we'd had over the last few months.

After the haircut, we headed to lunch but not to a Dim Sum Store, as I would have thought.

"Where is lunch?" I asked.

"Get Lost Dim Sum," Tony smirked. The boys broke into hysterics in the back seat.

"What?" I giggled too, not sure if I was the butt of a joke.

"The first time we ate there, we got lost trying to find it . . ." TJ spurted out in between snickers. "So . . .so . . .Alex . . ." TJ couldn't finish.

"I named it GET LOST DIM SUM!" Alex shouted before falling into fits of laughter with TJ. I was certainly missing out on some fun times before the accident.

We knew before dim sum, eating for Tony was challenging. He couldn't eat with his right hand. A fork full of food could almost make it to his lips, but it was just far enough away he couldn't make up the difference by bending his head down to slurp off the morsels. He had no choice but to work on his lefty skills. As his technique improved the piles of dirty laundry went down.

But in a Chinese restaurant, Tony faced an even bigger topsy-turvy feat: chopsticks. He could have succumbed to the Western way of eating but his Chinese pride wouldn't have it. He had to teach himself how to use chopsticks with his left hand, following the instructions he'd given all of us over the years: don't hold the chopsticks too close to the tip, and, squeeze with the thumb on one side and the middle and ring finger together on the other, like a lobster.

Tony did a pretty good job with only a few casualties. He even managed to help Alex clean his plate. After Alex stripped the noodle off the shrimp dumpling, his favorite part, Tony awkwardly pinched the leftover shrimp between his chopsticks, slowly bringing the bite to his mouth, like balancing an egg on a spoon in a carnival race. He was mastering another skill, one wobbly bite at a time.

Life was extra special now, and we were living it up in a way. Tony looked for significant things to do to make up for the time lost in the hospital and healing at home. I also thought Tony was making up for all the time he poured into earning a living for his family before the accident, instead of being with his family. Tough choices come with living in a beautiful and cosmopolitan area like Northern California.

We went to a Monday-night San Francisco 49ers game, unusual for us because professional sporting events were so expensive. But TJ had never been to a pro football game, and Tony wanted him to have the experience. We sat behind the end zone with the New Orleans Saints fans, the only tickets available to a non-season-ticket holder. I thought the Saints fans were more entertaining than the game. They were full of creative cheers and enthusiasm.

"Who dat? Who dat? Who dat say dey gonna beat dem Saints?" they called out as the team entered the field.

"Brees-sus Christ!" came a cheer for their quarterback, Drew Brees. I looked at Tony; we both snickered. It was really hard to cheer for our home team with so much Saints' energy surrounding us. Every time the Saints scored, a number of fans broke out a golden parasol. Cheering at a live game can make anyone a fan of the local team, but the Saints fans made me want to switch.

Tony, despite his bruised brain, remembered to bring a camera for our first family football game. We would not have any photo albums if it were not for his interest in photography. I always got too caught up in whatever adventure we were on to think of documenting our fun.

When he pulled out his big professional camera, trying to hold it with both hands like he used to do, he realized it was impossible. He couldn't hold up the right side, let alone hit the shutter with his right index finger.

We didn't know what roadblocks were out there until we ventured into more activities. Eating he could improvise and use his opposite hand. Washing his hair or putting on a belt, one hand worked. But two-handed activities never occurred to us until we were in the moment. We also empathized with the lefties in the world.

"I think we should start a movement," I joked with Tony.

"What's that?" he asked.

"Lefties Have Rights," I said, feeling as clever as the Saints fans around us, with their mascot and quarterback word twists.

In defeat, Tony passed the digital camera to TJ to let him take photos of whatever he wanted. We didn't really pay attention to what TJ was photographing because we were there to watch the game and sometimes the Saints fans. Tony checked out the shots in the car as we exited the parking lot.

"TJ! Why did you take a picture of the trash blowing onto the field?"

"Oh, I only took three pictures. I just thought it was funny."

Hooray for digital cameras! Delete. Delete. Delete.

CHAPTER 25

Giving Back

Four Months After the Accident

THE ACCIDENT HAD SHAKEN TONY out of his frenetic life of work, cycling, and family. As he came out of the injury fog, he felt as if he had been away for months. He missed the boys terribly and desperately wanted to make up for lost time. Once Tony was well enough to cook again, he stuffed the boys with food like his own mother had for him. It was as if I had starved them over the last four months and Tony needed to right things due to his absence. He made extravagant breakfasts for the boys, on *school days*. He was so happy to be with them and take care of them; he didn't care if it was Tuesday or Saturday. In fact, a school day was more important because he wanted his boys "brain ready."

He didn't mind if Alex jarred him out of a deep sleep when he jumped on the bed at seven thirty in the morning shouting, "Dad! Dad! You gotta get up! It's seven thirty!"

Even at age ten, Alex knew how much time it took to make a breakfast croissant or panini, stuffed with scrambled eggs, bacon, and cheese. He wasn't going to miss a fantastic meal, and Tony wasn't going to deny him either. Tony was grateful for his excited and jumpy alarm clock. We were both a lot happier making sacrifices for our family, because we came so close to not being able to help each other ever again.

Tony had come a long way from the splat on the pavement to the chef in the kitchen. As circumstances became less dire, we began to reflect on the progress Tony had made and how we got to this point. Angels of many talents could take credit for keeping our family whole, and we wanted to do something special for them. Nobody had expected to hear from us again let alone arrive with gifts of gratitude. But bringing Tony back to life could not go unrecognized; Tony became obsessed with thank-yous.

He started at the hospital, delivering boxes of chocolates to the nurses' stations. None of the nurses who looked after Tony were around, not even Priscilla, but the ones on duty were so appreciative of the gesture. For his medical arsenal, PT Man, Ortho Guy, and the New Doc—all avid athletes—Tony dropped off sporting goods gift cards. Cyclists can always use jerseys, bike tubes, or water bottles. They were surprised and touched. I have to imagine doctors and nurses rarely get any kind of accolade.

Surprisingly, I made the appreciation cut too. Tony gave me a Kindle because I read at least two books per month, my bedside table stacked with wobbly pillars of paperbacks. He even went so far as getting me a black cover with a pop-up light so I could read traditional books at three a.m., when he slept and I couldn't. Before the lighted cover, I'd balanced a small flashlight on my shoulder so I could hold the book open with my hands. If I squirmed or batted a tiny moth away, the flashlight sometimes rolled toward Tony, a sudden bump to the head that probably felt like an interrogation spotlight right in the eyeball. I loved my gift of guilt-free reading and newly spacious nightstand.

To all of us helpers, we were just doing the right thing to get Tony better; our efforts did not seem like a burden. But it meant the world to Tony. He was morphing into a Wendy the mountain biker or Darla the marathon runner, who beat down our door to give back after angels came to their rescue. Tony's heart swelled with warmth and appreciation, especially for the life-saving efforts of the first-responders. I was right there with him on this one.

If it weren't for Damon and the paramedic team, Tony might not have ever lived to thank all the others who helped him. At the time of the accident, Damon's crew was headed to a special training session. They weren't supposed to be taking the emergency call that came in for an injured cyclist. But, the firemen couldn't bear to pass off the responsibility to another station when they were only a few minutes away. To Tony and me, the miracle moment was the beginning of a cascade of uncanny events.

Because we knew Damon, it was as if we were dropped into the hands of family. His quick thinking meant Tony was sent to the best hospital in the area and closest to our home. Damon was able to grab Tony's bike for safekeeping. And most importantly, our compassionate fireman friend could pick out my name from the list of contacts in Tony's cell phone and called me immediately. I couldn't help but think angels were beckoned at the moment of impact, like parachutes of kindness and comfort.

Both Tony and I put our heads and hearts together to find the perfect thank-you. We thought paramedics might like some dinner, a break from cooking at the station. I checked with Damon's wife, and my friend, about what we should bring. Her answer was simple: "Meat. Lots of meat."

We ordered take out from Back Forty, Texas BBQ Roadhouse: beef brisket, barbecue chicken, and slabs of pork ribs. There was enough to feed two fire stations of firemen; we could not contain our gratitude. TJ baked a batch of his magnificent chocolate chip cookies. I'm a baker, and even I don't know what TJ does to make his cookies so much better than mine. Maybe it's the fact that he dumps in all the ingredients at once instead of a few at a time. Or maybe because he rolls the dough into perfectly shaped balls before baking, so they melt into perfect circles in the oven. TJ had some secret to his recipe that was secret even to him, and they are delicious. To a fireman, the cookies were fabulous just because a twelve-year-old made them especially for the station crew.

We parked to the side of the station as the road out front was streaked with speeding cars and no sidewalks. The whole family piled out of the Sequoia, Alex and TJ too; the waft of horse stables filled our noses.

"Pee-eew," cried Alex, pinching his nose. TJ snickered at Alex.

"Poor firemen," I said to Tony as I swatted away a horde of flies.

"No kidding. I don't know how they stand it," Tony agreed. We walked quickly to the entrance, our arms filled with paper bags of barbecue, slightly masking the nasty smell. We needed all four of us to carry the mountains of food; TJ carried his coveted plate of cookies.

Damon greeted us at the door. His eyes were brimming with honor, and I couldn't help but notice he looked stronger and more heroic in his navy-blue uniform as compared to the dad uniform he wore on the Little League fields. He escorted us back to the kitchen so we could put down our bags. Most of the crew that saved Tony's life was on duty, waiting with welcoming smiles in the common room. They were excited to have guests. And we were relieved and elated they were there to receive us. We knew at any moment the evening could be broken up by an emergency call, and possibly before we arrived. What would we do with all of that meat? Thankfully, no call came during the hour of our visit.

Damon was a gracious host, proudly giving us a tour of the station. The boys wanted to start with the trucks; it had been a few years since they had toured a fire station. We had to pass through a hallway from the firehouse to the garage, a giant yellowed map of the area, filling the wall like wallpaper. We made our way into the garage, our sneakers squeaked as we walked on the highly polished concrete and then looked inside and out of each vehicle. Seeing the long fire engine reminded me of TJ's fourth birthday, when we toured the neighborhood fire station with twelve of his best preschool friends. The next truck on the tour was not a good memory.

An eerie feeling welled up from my bones to my skin at the sight of the boxy ambulance that transported Tony from the street to the ER. I remembered the shiny red side panel and flashing red lights I followed to the hospital, by coincidence or miracle, I don't know. I could only remember a quiet somber ride as I drove behind the ambulance—no sirens. I'd watched cars glide out of the way like a parting wave to make room for the emergency vehicle. Everything had moved like a bad dream, slow and thick; even the air was heavy.

How many lives had been saved in this very vehicle? Of course, the ambulance was in pristine condition inside and out. It's not like we saw fabric shards from Tony's bright-green bike jersey or a bloody bandage. I couldn't look long enough to spot anything anyway. My imagination was enough to make me shiver.

"Hey, Damon, let's take a picture," said Tony. I gave my phone to TJ because I just couldn't look inside. Tony and Damon crouched around the gurney wrapped in clean sheets; an oxygen mask rested on top. The thumbs-up and big smiles belied the event that took place the last time they were in that compartment together.

We continued on with the tour, looking at engines the boys recalled easily from their old picture books.

"Alex, remember when we sprayed water from the firehose at my birthday party?" TJ asked Alex.

"Yeah. Kind of. It was heavy," Alex replied.

Damon led us back to the common area. Worn-out recliner chairs and couches were in the center room of the firehouse, a cavernous space with a concrete floor. A big-screen television doubled as art, hung on a wall facing the chairs. Décor was scarce. We sat with the station crew at the long dining table. I was seated next to the only woman in the station. She wasn't at the accident, but she wanted to hear our story.

"What were you thinking when you got the call?" she asked me. Her face was fresh, and her dark hair was pulled back into a ponytail. She wore the same navy uniform as her male peers: button-down short-sleeve shirt and chino pants. I knew exactly what to say, the scene was a pristine memory.

"From the minute I heard an unfamiliar voice coming from Tony's cell phone, I knew it was bad," I answered. My face grimaced, and I stared at the shiny concrete floor.

"What happened?" she continued.

"I swear Damon said Tony was hit by a bike," I replied. All eyes were on me. Jaws dropped.

"I'm pretty sure I told you he was hit *on* his bike," Damon corrected me.

"Well, the message was scrambled, because I kept thinking, how bad could the damage be if he was hit by a bike?" I swear this misinterpretation kept me sane so I could drive to the hospital safely. I knew Damon wasn't giving me the whole story from the hesitancy in his voice in describing Tony's injuries. Even so, I never once thought Tony was on the brink of death or had extreme injuries. Not even when the ER doctor cautiously described Tony's condition and suggested he stay in ICU, *just for observation*. I focused on the final outcome: He was fixable.

It wasn't until months and years later I came to understand more. Damon and I were at a fundraiser barbecue, when he described how close Tony was to heaven.

"When I first saw Tony, his body was curling up into a ball. His hands formed fists, and his body started to shake. I was afraid he might die, maybe right on the sidewalk," Damon told me.

"Oh my gosh!" I cringed, my eyes staring at the long grass under our feet. I couldn't look at Damon. This was the one thing not even the ER doctor mentioned; yet his loving behavior, holding my hands as we walked into a room to talk, conveyed what Damon was telling me now. Tony had been in grave danger. I had sensed there was something the ER doctor wasn't telling me at the time, and now I was getting the whole story.

"I thought I was going to have to dart him," Damon continued.

To "dart" means to relieve air pressure built up in the lung using a needle. Tony's chest was expanding because of the rib punctures to his lung; multiple holes made it impossible for the air to escape. That explained why El Doctor inserted the chest tube. I'm glad I didn't know then how close Tony was to this risky treatment.

Looking back, it's hard to read any of the posts from the Caring-Bridge blog, because even when I was upbeat, I was still honest about his state. I am not the same person I was right after the accident. My stomach turns to stone with even a sliver of the memory entering in my head. The injuries and uncertainty seemed manageable back then, because I felt as if I was swooped up and wrapped in a protective blanket. I had to be strong, or I could not have been the rock for my family. I had to roll up my sleeves and think, "OK, what do we have to do to get him better?"

Sitting beside the lone female of the station-crew, I wondered what went through the mind of a firefighter during an emergency call.

"How can you handle traumatic event after traumatic event in your job?" I asked the lone female of the station crew.

"Well, not every call is grim. Sometimes we rescue baby ducks from the sewer," she mused. "But seriously, I'm just like you. I go into a mental zone, and I want to do everything in my power to save or help a person. If I looked back at pictures, I would have a hard time stomaching the situation," she told me. She sounded much like me looking at pictures of Tony from the first night in the NICU. Even years later, I do not need to look at those photographs. I just don't.

When Tony was first injured, I was surprisingly unemotional. I didn't react, because I didn't know what I was reacting to; I convinced myself to keep calm. I kept telling myself to not spin into a tizzy of what-ifs. When I met face-to-face with the ER doc, he didn't share much information right away, as if the truth would be too much for me to handle. I wanted to know *everything*.

The firefighter smiled at my confusion. She had seen this before. She told me about a boy who fell from a tree and was badly injured. His mom insisted she be told *exactly* what was wrong with her son, no matter how horrible. The firefighter could not believe this calm, determined person was the *mother*.

With my new friend, I felt like I could relax about how I really felt at the time of Tony's accident and not be judged. In her experience, my reaction was not unusual. She gave me peace and validation. I always wondered why I was strong and positive instead of teary-eyed or forlorn. There is something inside a person that transforms them into a rock of steadiness in seconds, as if someone threw an override switch to counter hysteria. I don't think it matters what level of gore or brokenness is staring you in the face. A superpower takes over, a power you don't know you have until you are smacked with awfulness.

From the outside looking in, a terrible accident is extremely hard to digest. But the part no one sees, the upside, is that the person most protected, thankfully, is the victim. Some force helps the injured to forget the horror; Tony can't remember much from the first few weeks. But there is also something at work for the caregiver. I marvel at how comforted and safe I felt at a time that honestly could have been my worst. So many obstacles popped up making our journey more difficult, such as Scary Office or inept nurses. Despite the frustrating setbacks, we maintained a positive attitude. We fixed each issue and moved on, focusing on what we believed to be the end: A healthy, cycling Tony.

The last thing we learned from our visit with the firefighters: they often wondered if the person they rescued survived and went on to live a normal life. Seeing Tony walk in with trays of grilled meat was the kind of miracle they hoped to see. Meeting Tony's family, especially the boys, was icing on the cake, or cookies in this case.

CHAPTER 26

Cyclists and Saints

Five Months After the Accident,
December

AFTER THE CYCLING TEAM'S HOLIDAY PARTY, I could feel the tight bond Tony had with his teammates, exponentially more than in the hospital. The club was one huge family, chiding each other one moment and hugging each other the next. Every single one had a giant heart and sense of selflessness.

Before the accident, I looked at his time on the bike as a way of exorcising the stress demons from his mind and infusing oxygen into his body. I liked working out for the same reasons. Mental and physical fitness were almost as valuable to us as food and water. But Tony's workouts were so much more to him because he factored his teammates into the equation. As if in his world, 1 + 1 added up to 3.

"Riding is a head-to-toe, inside-and-out, experience. The sense of flying and freedom I feel by being in nature is a euphoric release," Tony described to me one time.

"Hmm. Swimming isn't quite the same," I said.

"What do you mean?" Tony asked with a quizzical smile.

"I can't say I feel free and appreciate nature while I'm staring at the black line at the bottom of the outdoor pool—even if I can feel raindrops on my face during backstroke. I *do* feel feather light from head to toe *after* the workout."

"Well, you might feel closer to nature if you swam in a lake," he laughed. He knew how I felt about swimming in open waters. I didn't want to be anywhere near fish or kelp. The black line in the pool brought me comfort, because I could see to the bottom and anything that might come after me. Which was nothing.

Of course, Tony was grateful for a ride but also for the incredible beauty that seemed only to exist for him. Tony rode early to avoid the tangle of cars and impacting the family schedule. He snapped photos of a rising sun or a blanket of fog below the mountaintop he climbed and posted them to Facebook. Sometimes the views spanned so far and wide it was like seeing the earth, just after its birth. A thin mist lifted from the green, rolling hills, the skies tinged in pale pink with hints of baby blue at dawn's break.

Riding in the Bay Area was a blessing, the varied terrain and beauty attracted professional cyclists from all over the world to train. Tony could cruise through a redwood forest ten minutes from our house in one direction. Or he could go twenty minutes in another direction to ride up and down grassy, rolling hills sprinkled with old farms and windmills. Other excursions might display sweeping views of Oakland to the Golden Gate Bridge and down the peninsula. Rides could be long or short. A lengthy trip was seventy to a hundred miles for race training or short, twenty to thirty miles, for a quick postrace recovery. Hill climbs were often three to five thousand-foot ascents—a triumph. The reward for reaching the top, a forty-five- to fifty-mile-an-hour descent down a mountain like Mount Diablo, where Tony could carve corners on switchbacks faster than cars.

"Very few sports offer the rush, fitness, exhilaration, and the *wheeee* factor," to quote Tony.

I'm glad he could see it that way. I'd be exhausted before I ever started a climb up a steep mountain and scared out of my wits on the downslope. I was very happy to send him out for epic rides with his friends. "Better them than me," was my thinking.

Cycling is a great sport for middle-aged guys with bad knees when running isn't an option any more. There are two types of riders: cyclists and racers. Cyclists ride for pleasure and racers ride to compete. Both types invest in a badass bike as if buying a sports car during a midlife crisis. In a cycling club, there's a built-in group to ride with for motivation to get out on the road and to train in hopes of earning a place on the medal platform. Competition pushed a rider to be more fit and faster. Tony uses an acronym for guys like him that were sucked into cycling: MAMIL—Middle Aged Men in Lycra. To me, the sport was cheaper than a Ferrari, so I didn't mind a guy in stretchy black shorts and a fancy two-wheeled "ride."

After a cyclist has been riding awhile, he often discovers he "needs" more than one bike. Tony owned three road bikes and one mountain bike. So how many bikes does a guy really need? I asked Tony once, in his goofy engineering and cyclist way he answered: the proper number of bikes a cyclist should own is $n + 1$, n being the number of bikes you already own.

Cyclist or racer, cycling was a brotherhood, a deep connection with a common passion. The community was so vast, Tony would always see someone he knew whether he went out for ten miles or forty.

"I'm never alone out there," Tony would say after a ride. "It's like one giant playground." He repeated these words often, as if it was the first time every time. The same thing could happen to me. Sometimes I ran into a girlfriend on a walk through the neighborhood or shopping at the grocery store. There was a thrill in impromptu chats with buddy after buddy.

The brotherhood of cycling elicited genuine concern for one another's health, whether it was an injury keeping them off the bike or getting enough time to meet their training goals. They cared about one another's equipment, spending hours discussing a new cogset or latest time-trial wheels. That waterfall of biking information happened in front of me anytime one of Tony's buddies came for a visit.

"Sorry. Don't mean to talk so much bike technology," his friend Ron apologized.

"Not to worry," I said with a smile. "I'm the same way with clothes when I'm with a fellow clotheshorse."

Tony shared a sweet and deeply personal take on his passion.

"Cyclists are so tightly linked that their greeting for each other is, in a way, similar to a common greeting in the Chinese culture. Having suffered great famine in years' past, Chinese will greet each other with the question, "Have you eaten today?" For a cyclist, the greeting is "Have you ridden recently?" My insides melted when he made that comparison to me.

For Tony, cycling was more than just pedaling a bike, but I could only see the physical part before the accident. Afterward, I saw what Tony tried to describe, the sport was steeped in a community of caring, acceptance, support, and friendship.

The brotherhood went to another level in the racing world. Teammates shared a common desire to win, so they rode as much as possible to make it happen. After a group ride, they strategized over coffee for the next race, reviewing prior competitions in their heads like it was game tape of a football game. Cycling might look like an individual sport, but it isn't. Every team has only a few riders trying for podium, a medal-winning position. The front rider uses 30 percent more energy than someone in the peloton, or group of cyclists, so members take turns at the lead to conserve the top rider's energy. The individual racer can't win without fellow teammates.

During a race, the most common role for Tony was the team leader. Someone needed to guide the team, directing a rider to take a front position. It wasn't easy. "It's like herding cats. Some riders forget the team goals and just get caught up in pedaling. That's where a leader coaches the team into position." Tony could ride and strategize at the same time. Which didn't surprise me, because he managed me on our rides too, never letting me fall too far from his sight. He waited for me to catch up or he followed behind me, sacrificing a harder or faster ride for my sake.

After the accident, many people thought Tony would hang up the jersey and quit cycling. They also thought if Tony didn't stop voluntarily, surely his wife would forbid Tony from riding ever again. Neither of us thought quitting was an option. *How could I ask or demand him to quit?* Especially after seeing the stream of cyclists visiting him in the hospital, the compassion flowing from the comments on the CaringBridge blog posts and the crowd at the team holiday party. To take cycling away from him would be like ripping him away from his family or cutting off an arm or a leg. Cycling saturated his being. It was his everything. He used every spare moment to ride, leaving little time for anyone or anything else. To take that away from him would be completely selfish.

The only thing I could do was to find some way to keep him protected and keep me from worrying. I was always nervous when Tony went out for a spin. I'd say a prayer every time he went out. *What could I do now to make us both feel safe?* I wondered.

My Catholic friend from Masters swimming gave me an idea. The church she attended in Berkeley offered special blessings on the feast day honoring a patron saint.

They were about to host a blessing of bikes for the feast day of the Patroness Saint of Cyclists, Madonna del Ghisallo. I learned through a Google search, a vision of the Virgin Mary made an appearance in a tiny town in Italy called Magreglio during medieval times where she saved a Count Ghisallo from robbers. Ever since, travelers and eventually cyclists stopped at the shrine for good luck. Eventually a small church was built that displays cycling memorabilia left behind by visitors. The site is the finish line for the annual Giro di Lombardia race and sometimes a stage in the famous Giro d'Italia bike race, the Italian equivalent to the Tour de France.

The special blessing triggered memories from my Catholic upbringing. I remembered seeing small medals dangling from a chain with carvings of Saint Christopher, Jesus, or the pope. In my research, I learned some cyclists strung a Madonna del Ghisallo medal on a chain and wrapped it around the stem of their bike for protection.

I decided to look for a medal Tony could wear underneath his jersey. I found a beautiful pewter Madonna del Ghisallo medal at Catholicstore.com. Somebody suggested a lucky rabbit's foot, but I always thought they were gross and it didn't matter if it was dyed hot pink, another favorite color. A pewter necklace adorned with an embossed saint was a prettier "good luck" charm and probably more powerful.

I engraved the back with the inscription: "Keeping you safe ALWAYS. Love Frances."

Of all the Christmas presents I had given Tony, this one was the first to make him misty-eyed. I blinked back tears too, not wanting to put a damper on the fun in front of the boys. We both swear the necklace works.

The medal offered a sense of heavenly comfort. Just like the words of the inscription, he ALWAYS wears his medal and when he does, he ALWAYS feels safe.

Tony said it best: "When I wear the medal for cyclists, I know I'll be all right."

Me too.

CHAPTER 27

Love Is All Around

Five Months After the Accident,
Late December

AFTER GETTING THE DEVASTATING RESULTS from the Frankenstein Lab, we were desperate for cheery distractions. It didn't take much. Friends and family filled our hearts with a lot of sweet moments while we waited for Tony's nerves to grow.

PT Man gave Tony the best news.

"Tony, you are doing so well you can move to the next step. I think you should hit the trainer to strengthen the upper body," said PT Man. He was watching Tony pull the red band toward and away from his stomach, an exercise focused on strengthening Tony's shoulder.

"You don't have to tell me twice," Tony beamed. He suddenly grew two inches taller. At least it looked like it because his posture was a perfect as you can get with a sagging shoulder resembling a ragdoll with all the stuffing torn out of it.

The trainer is a metal stand that holds the back wheel of a bike, similar to a stationary bike at the gym where the rider pedals to nowhere. In the days before the accident, Tony set up his personal cycling session on our front porch when it rained or if the roads were icy. The roof and wooden railing protected him from the elements and gave him a sense of privacy. He'd follow a training video on a portable DVD player that was strapped to the fold-out shelf of a stepladder.

Because of the accident, we had to make some adjustments. His neck wasn't strong enough to hold his head up to look at a screen; he could only look down. At first, we thought we could move the DVD player to the ground or paste pictures of cycling rock stars to the patio pavement to keep him motivated. Then we realized Tony could only last for thirty minutes, so he didn't need anything elaborate. He was so ecstatic to be riding again that the abundance of happiness was more than enough to pump him up. The neighbors were excited for him too. His brightly colored cycling clothes easily caught their attention whenever they walked past our house. Their faces lit up while they gave a wave or thumbs-up. The thrill of Tony getting on a bike again turned the bad news of the nonfiring axillary nerve into a back-burner worry.

He pedaled like nobody's business for four days straight. Sweating for the sake of exercise was so satisfying compared to the drug-fueled pools he experienced in the hospital bed. Tony felt like a wobbly novice, his shoulder and neck so weak and tender it was difficult to keep his balance on the bike. It didn't seem to matter that he'd lost all of his cycling muscles in his legs either. I took pictures of him grinning from ear to ear, working himself back into shape. I refrained from profile shots as he'd gained a spare tire around his waist after three months of eating yummy carbs, sweets, and big dinners. I focused on the joyful parts; the rest would come in time.

His new exercise program was easily portable and also a great way to take in a Giants' game. We moved the trainer to the back patio where we opened up the French doors to the family room. With the big screen TV with surround sound, it was almost like being at the game. He couldn't look at the screen much because he would have to lift his head up to see, but he could listen. Sometimes one of us would watch with him. We'd grab a furry blanket to keep out the early evening chill and cheer on the San Francisco Giants, now in the World Series. Watching a game while Tony took a spin was an exciting and comfy date.

Little by little, Tony was moving back into his old life, spending quality time with his family and his bike thanks to the trainer. He missed his cycling friends, since he couldn't go on group rides or compete in any races. I felt for him. I couldn't relate to the cycling world like his buddies, but I gained an appreciation for their passion for the sport and each other from their visits right after the accident. When Tony was in the hospital, we had talked for a few minutes about whether he would ride again. We both knew the answer.

"It's like a brotherhood," Tony told me from his hospital bed while he was still connected to all the machines. "Every team rider is a kindhearted person. All I can think about is my next ride and talking about it with my friends."

The Taleo team holiday party could not have come at a better time. Tony could see a good number of his friends all at once; some he hadn't seen since the hospital—me too. Normally I would not have gone to the cycling club party, but I'd bonded so fast with many of his teammates either at the hospital or through the blog. I wanted to go. I needed to go.

The party was held at Sports Basement, a locally-owned sporting goods store catering to cyclists, runners, hikers, and swimmers. And as the name would indicate, the décor was no frills, like hanging out in an unfinished basement with concrete floors, metal shelves of stuff, and worn out couches. Coolers of beer and foldout tables of appetizers and wine were enough party ambiance for the casually dressed crowd of skinny cyclists. You could easily tell who was the member and who was the date. The skeleton-like bodies were members, unless you were Tony who was currently enjoying the carbo ride. The dates wore either a silky blouse or sparkly top because after all, it *was* a party. At least that's what "holiday" meant to me.

The party paused for recognition for team members and sponsors. The love among the members was palpable. Speakers mirrored exactly what Tony said to me in the hospital: cycling is a *team* sport, and the Taleo team in particular was packed with respectful members that felt like family. The team prided itself on attracting quality racing citizens who were also highly competitive. They lived it, and it showed. The team won awards year after year in the race world for being such an upstanding and talented team.

The team sponsors were equally humble. Not one of them used the opportunity to tout their product when they spoke. Instead they talked about the love of the Taleo team and how each one was like a friend.

"Taleo mirrors my company philosophy."

"The Taleo team allows us to be a part of a community of friendship and fitness. We are honored to contribute."

No big egos were in this room, just a BIG team that was growing because it had something everyone wanted to buy into, even if cycling wasn't their hobby. I was sold. I liked the team, but I wasn't ready to ride, yet. Tony could ride for both of us. I was happy being the not-so-skinny date in a sparkly top.

Tony and I felt like celebrities at the party, swarmed by teammate after teammate.

"I feel like I know your whole family from the blog," an older lady with long gray hair said to me. We had never met; I hugged her anyway.

"Tony! You're back!" exclaimed most of the crowd with a slap on the back or fist bump.

My favorite guest of all, was the famed "brutha from anutha mutha," Carlos. I had not talked to him since he called me to see how I was doing just a few days after the accident. Carlos wasn't much for technology, so he wasn't following the blog. Seeing Tony was as much of a thrill for him as seeing Carlos was for us.

"Hey Tony! You look good!" said Carlos. His girlfriend stood patiently next to him, almost the same height. She was pretty in her silky black dress and long dark hair. Her eyes sparkled. Carlos was so friendly, you couldn't help but smile around him.

"Thanks, Carlos! Hey, did you enjoy the GranFondo?" Tony asked. Tony had given Carlos his ticket to ride in Levi Leipheimer's GranFondo ("Great endurance" in Italian—a long, hilly race.) Levi Leipheimer is an accomplished professional cyclist who hosts the great race north of San Francisco in Santa Rosa. The event attracts professionals, amateurs, and novice cyclists. Entry tickets were hard to come by and pricey, so Tony's ticket was a special gift.

"Yeah, it was great! Did you get the pictures I sent? I'm not too good at e-mail," Carlos said. At the race, Carlos did something really special. He finagled three famous people into wishing Tony well: Levi, the race host; Taylor Phinney, possibly the next Lance Armstrong; and Patrick Dempsey, a TV star from *Grey's Anatomy* and an amateur cyclist. Each one held a letter-sized paper with the words: "Get Well T. Low."

I was learning Carlos befriends everyone easily, so I could see how getting the photos were no trouble at all. He was thinking of Tony the whole time. But *McDreamy*? Carlos really didn't know Patrick Dempsey from his next-door neighbor, but his girlfriend did.

"Oh yes, we got the photos. THANK YOU!" I piped up.

Carlos's girlfriend jumped into the conversation. "Carlos wondered if he needed to title the Patrick Dempsey file," she said with a giggle. "I told him, oh no. She'll know exactly who this guy is."

The McDreamy photo caught me off guard. Normally, in the cycling crowd my claim to fame was being "T. Low's" wife. I was touched and amused that Carlos would think of me while he was sweet talking celebrities into taking a picture. I loved Carlos, and he loved us.

Cycling was a happy place for Tony, but the boys and his great love for them always made him forget about his troubles. Their visits to the hospital erased Tony's pain even if it was only an hour. The boys had a goofy if not surprisingly wise way of looking at life. At home, Tony carried out the silly conversations over breakfast, his favorite meal to stuff into his kids.

"Hey, do you guys think the big breakfasts I make, make a difference?" he asked.

TJ stopped chewing for a minute. "Yes. They make a difference."

"Why?" Tony expected replies of "I have more energy," or "I'm doing way better in school."

Instead, TJ replied, "Because they're made with love." I didn't even know he could pronounce the word *love* or pack it into his vocabulary. If you tried to kiss him on the cheek he'd run away or hold up his tiny stuffed pig, Sniffy, for the smooch.

Maybe his weekly cotillion class was rubbing off. In seventh grade, the middle-schoolers can sign up for a weekly class to learn dating etiquette and ballroom dancing, like the fox-trot or box-step. He learned about offering a soda to the young lady before getting one for himself. Alex was tracking TJ's every interaction. He was in fifth grade, and he had already begun contemplating his romantic future.

"I think I will marry someone either a year younger or maybe a year older. I mean, come on! Can you really see me with a third-grader?" I burst out laughing. Social awareness was his strength, even in grade school.

We were enjoying the simpler parts of life where a sweet moment was thrill enough for the day. Tony was absorbed with his porch pedaling, and I loved peeking in on him from the living room window as I read or worked on the computer. He could see me too from the other side of the window. One of those times, I was particularly focused on my computer when I heard a "ping" on my phone. I checked the message.

"Luv ya!" I looked up at Tony. He winked.

CHAPTER 28

The Nerve of Nerves

Six Months After the Accident,
January

TINGLING FEELINGS SHOT UP TONY'S ARM on a daily basis now. We took this as a sign the nerve was coming to life, inching its way to becoming whole. Tony cheered the nerve on whenever the pinpricks or knife stabs jarred him to attention. Three o'clock in the afternoon seemed to be the magic hour for nerve disturbances.

"I think the nerves are asking for chocolate. I always want chocolate at three o'clock," I said teasingly to Tony.

Tony's medical team was hopeful, but nobody was as impressed as the new primary doctor, the New Doc, when we met for a follow up appointment. He was not letting Tony out of his care. He was going to see him through his injuries and beyond.

"Oh, the axillary nerve will be back in six to twelve months," stated the New Doc after we gave him the prognosis from the Frankenstein Lab.

"Um. Excuse me. You know you are the first doctor to say his nerves will grow back." I couldn't believe what I was hearing.

"Well, it's not a problem in the spinal cord, so the nerve should come back," said the almost-a-neurologist primary doctor. He studied neurology more than most medical students but didn't actually specialize in the field.

Tony and I didn't need a science background to believe the nerve would come back. We had good old faith. Really, it was our only choice to believe the nerve would come back. If there is no hope, there is no fight. We were in for the fight, hanging on to a feeling before we even knew what a nerve felt like when it was making a comeback. It was as if we were gardening newbies who saw tiny green shoots sprouting from the seeds we'd planted months ago. We were delighted to say the least. And to have it professionally validated—well, that was elation.

PT Man commented on Tony's unwavering positive attitude—that's how strong we were both holding on to hope. Tony saw PT Man the most, three times a week, so they were becoming quite tight. PT Man would know if Tony had a down day, and so far, he hadn't had one in four months' time. Tony still held his arm close to his body like Napoleon, so he had every reason to be down. But he didn't go there; he wasn't going to let it get in the way of his banter with PT Man or his everyday life. The sling-like pose would not last forever.

I think Tony enjoyed being with someone who spoke cycling, and really just guy topics in general like cars, cameras, and computers. We updated our home laptop and digital camera at PT Man's recommendation. We stopped short of buying a Ford Flex SUV; I would be the primary driver, and I wanted something smaller. I didn't care if it had cool rainbow mood lighting in the interior.

Time and physical therapy would take care of most of Tony's healing, but the torn rotator cuff needed to be repaired. The window of opportunity to fix it was drawing to a close; his shoulder could atrophy to the point of freezing in place forever. We opted for surgery just after New Year's Day, a Friday to be exact, so he wouldn't miss work while he was recuperating over the weekend.

We met with Ortho Guy a few weeks ahead of time to go over the details of the surgery, pre- and post-op. I wanted to know exactly what to expect, something I couldn't do during Tony's emergency situation, where I just had to roll with whatever came our way. I had nothing to compare the bike accident to, so I wasn't as discerning. Everything was new to me and to Tony. This time around would be different.

"So, exactly where on Tony's shoulder will the surgery take place?" I asked Ortho Guy.

He gave me a 3-D explanation, demonstrating on Tony's shoulder from the back to the front. He pointed to where he would make two small incisions. Since he couldn't show me in real life what would happen under the skin, Ortho Guy pulled out the equivalent of a medical Etch A Sketch. He drew on the digital tablet with his stylus, leaving spaces where spaces were meant to be, unlike the real Etch A Sketch that connected letters with irritating lines where spaces belonged. He drew a picture of a shoulder and the arm bone where the screw attached the tendon to one side of the shoulder and another screw attached the tendon on the other side. The screws were not small. Ortho Guy begged to differ; he felt they were smaller than a railroad spike and therefore petite. We, on the other hand, pictured tiny screws similar to the ones that held eyeglasses together. The shoulder screws were much, much bigger, almost an inch long. And to us, they looked gigantic and painful. And what about postsurgery care? Surely the incision would be huge to accommodate a screw that big—at least that's what we imagined.

"Will I need to buy a lot of waterproof Band-Aids so Tony can shower?" I asked Ortho Guy.

"He only needs extra coverage if he showers within the first two days of surgery," answered Ortho Guy. Since Tony survived twelve days without a shower in the hospital, two days seemed doable. I could skip the trip down the first-aid aisle at the drugstore.

I kept going, asking a bundle of questions of Ortho Man. How long will the surgery last and exactly what will happen? When do I need to be present? With every answer to my question, Ortho Guy added how it wasn't going to be that big of a deal. He'd been through this a thousand times. We knew it was not going to be anything like our summer hospital adventure, but we were gun-shy and wanted to be prepared. Especially pain management—that one got my ire up.

We had the prescription in our hot little hands. And just to make sure we were not screwing up by electing to have surgery on a Friday, only to run into a pain problem over the weekend, I asked him about his accessibility.

"I have a twenty-four hour answering service. You can call with any concerns." He assured us we were in good hands.

During our ten-minute exchange, Ortho Guy and I took turns looking each other square in the eyes to nonverbally assert our position on Tony's care. It was as if we were in a chess match of stares: Pawn to pawn or knight to knight.

"You ask very good questions. This is not going to be anything near what Tony experienced before. You are not going to remember this information in two weeks, when it's time for the surgery." Eye contact.

"Oh, yes I will." Very strong eye contact.

And back to Ortho Guy: "Well, you will be the top of your class." Strong eye contact.

And back to me: "It's all too fresh for me to forget." More eye contact.

We were cordial because we liked each other. We had the same goal, Tony's well-being. I just knew after four hours of outpatient surgery (including paperwork, surgery, post-op observation) the primary care person would be *me*. Ortho Guy was not thinking about home medical supplies, school pick-ups, piano lessons, and sports practices. MY OTHER JOB. Moms are excellent planners, but we have to know what to schedule. So, I *had* to ask a lot of questions.

In anticipation of the surgery, Tony was relishing every minute of his righty status. He was grateful every time he lifted his fork with grace and ease, a skill he wouldn't have in a few weeks when he was back in a sling. He was porch-pedaling incessantly, even if it was thirty degrees outside, typical morning temperatures in late December. He considered riding the trainer with a sling, but Ortho Man told him it wasn't worth the risk of Tony falling off the bike. Tony had to wait six weeks.

With much angst and anticipation, the surgery day arrived, January 7th, 2011. Fortunately, Tony got the first surgery spot at six thirty a.m. The earlier slots were usually awarded to the more complicated cases, and Tony won the prize. Pre-op started at five thirty a.m. where we confirmed with Ortho Guy what was about to happen to Tony. We saw a new side of Ortho Guy. He was so energized and full of smiles; he was clearly in his element.

The surgery lasted a little over two hours. I saw Ortho Guy again, about forty-five minutes post-op. He couldn't have been more reassuring and caring, no glares or stares. It was nice having a bit of history with someone before a traumatic event like an operation; the warm handshake was so much more heartfelt.

Ortho Guy explained the gist of the surgery. "It went OK. He's pretty messed up in there, a lot of stuff. I fixed up what I could and if the nerves grow back, he'll be quite capable. He can do a lot."

The word "stuff" was his word choice for loosening up scar tissue and lifting muscle from the bone to improve Tony's movement. PT Man won't have as much to do but I don't think he would mind and neither would Tony.

We had the cheeriest post-op nurse, with a blonde bushy ponytail. She was so happy I swore birds and butterflies followed her around like Cinderella. She was trying to help Tony into the stretchy V-neck tee, he was back to wearing. But even in Tony's groggy state he just took over because he's been through the drill so many times. If a bubble were over his head, it would say, "Rookie."

Tony was wheel-chaired to the car since he was a little woozy. Once home, I walked him into the house. He was more unstable compared to the last time I escorted him home from the hospital. I set Tony up in the family room in the big one-and-half chair with a side table for meds and TV remotes on his *left* side, his new hospital bed. I dressed in yoga pants and a jacket with pockets for my cell phone, my caregiver uniform. The timer was set on my cell phone for meds so we wouldn't get behind like he did in the hospital. We were pros and we were ready for anything, so we thought.

Tony slept a lot! We stayed ahead of the pain with a constant infusion of painkillers. By morning, he had so much energy he wanted to cook breakfast with the boys, lefty style. Cooking for the boys was his go-to mental release. The boys would avoid starvation since I was relieved of my breakfast duties. Although I think Tony fed them enough over the last few months they probably had reserves.

In the kitchen, Tony was like a bull in a China shop. The meds were making him loopy, a bad combination with someone so revved up. Two forces were trying to control him, like two magnets repelling each other. His jitteriness was putting me on edge. I tried to stay out of the way but if I had, TJ's cheesy hash browns would have made a splat-landing to the floor. I was so worried I called the Ortho Guy and got right through.

"Drop the prescription meds and load up on ibuprofen," he told us. Wow, this was so nice getting a hotline to the doc.

Tony was so easy. I kept expecting the numbing medicine from surgery to wear off and the real pain to begin along with Darth Vader's voice. It was not happening. We only had one body part to contend with not a handful. He wasn't wearing a neck brace so he could see what was on his dinner plate and bend his head over to eat it. He could get out of a chair without screaming in pain because his ribs were healed. My friend Sharon was going to keep me company while we watched over the patient. Instead, both Sharon and Steve came to dinner and all four of us sat around the table to enjoy the big pot of white bean soup I made earlier in the day. They marveled at his happy state.

Two days passed and Tony could shower. I thought, here it is, it's going to be back to me getting a shower while helping Tony wash up. I unwrapped the puffy bandage from his shoulder. The word "YES" was written in sharpie on his skin. I chuckled. Now I knew the surgeon's "low tech" reminder to ensure he was working on the correct limb. I removed the sticky tapes from the tiny incisions that were right where Ortho Guy said they would be, thinking Tony will wince when I pull them off. He didn't. He couldn't feel me rubbing his skin in those areas. Hmm. Maybe the nerves hadn't grown as much as we thought so that is why nothing hurt like we expected. We were prepared for the mother of all storms, tons of pain and medical screw-ups. The storm never came.

PT Man was in for a surprise too. He was pleased with the increased movement in Tony's shoulder. PT Man moved the arm gently *for* Tony, or *passively* in PT terms. Tony's arm would barely budge before the rotator cuff surgery. But the real surprise came at the end of the appointment. Tony was hooked up to an electrical stimulation machine to increase the blood flow and speed healing. An electrical current sends prickly shocks around the recovering muscles. The strength of the shockwave can be set by manually pushing buttons up or down.

"Can you feel that Tony? I'm starting at level 29." Asked PT Man.

"No. Not feeling anything yet." Tony replied.

PT Man kept bumping up the numbers and Tony kept smiling until the display read level 46. "No Way!" PT Man exclaimed.

We confirmed our suspicions at a three-week follow-up appointment with Ortho Guy. The nerves had not grown as much as we thought. We were learning nerves had a lot of nerve, throwing everyone off with their unpredictable behavior, including Ortho Guy.

"I've never had a patient without nerves. It's normally excruciating pain, especially for men." Ortho Guy told us. I had to hold my tongue on this one. I found two-thirds of this information interesting and the last fascinating fact about men and pain, hilarious and hardly a scientific break-through. Man-cold anyone? We looked at the lack of nerves as a blessing.

"Pennies from heaven," Ortho Guy stated in non-medical terms.

The best news of the day, Tony could move his arm a little bit, a tiny chicken dance move with the help of Ortho Guy. I wanted to do a chicken dance right there but I didn't. Ortho Guy wasn't as excited as I was but he had a higher bar than I did. I kept the celebration in my heart and tried to keep the professional mood of our appointment.

"What did you mean by the "stuff" you found in surgery?" I asked.

He showed us magnified, colored pictures of Tony's shoulder from the inside. We didn't get squeamish because honestly it looked like a raw, fatty steak, creamy-white and pinkish-red. Some of Tony's bicep muscle was adhering to the bone so Ortho Guy loosened it up. He only used one screw instead of two, and it wasn't placed anywhere near a nerve if we had thought Ortho Guy accidently severed the nerve in surgery.

When PT Man found out why Tony didn't have any pain, he told us, "Tony is the dream rotator cuff repair patient. No nerves means no pain. No nerves mean Tony can't accidently move his arm and tear up the repair." He felt Tony must surely be on his way to healing more completely. He was thinking ahead about what a healed shoulder could mean for Tony.

"I want to take your first ride with you Tony! We could do Mount Diablo!" PT Man offered.

"Sorry man. Only the flats to start," replied the hopeful but realistic Tony.

CHAPTER 29

Take a Walk in My Shoes: PT for Everyone

Seven Months After the Accident

SURPRISINGLY, THE LONGEST ROAD seemed to be waiting the six weeks post rotator cuff surgery. Tony was locked up in his sling again. Having his short stint of freedom taken away after just a few months, seemed almost cruel. Since it was winter, he wore a jacket draped over his shoulders like a superman cape, another inconvenience we didn't anticipate. It was just too bulky to wear a jacket inside a sling with a built-in armrest. A thick piece of foam serves as a shelf, a little away from the body, as if he was carrying a stack of books all day long. Even PT Man is sick of seeing Tony wearing the sling, like a favorite shirt that he never takes off.

Tony wanted to fling that sling to Singapore. That's how I imagine the drink *Singapore Sling* got its name. Somebody in Singapore was weary of wearing a sling, flung it across the bar and asked for a drink to celebrate. Kidding aside, we were all ready to get rid of it. I say we, because I sensed Tony's frustration when I heard him in the other room trying to lube his bike chain or something and I heard, "Man oh Man" or "Dang It" or worse, "$%^#." I think he would like to hold a ceremonial burning and toss in the V-neck stretchy tees too.

At the end of the long, long six weeks, Ortho Guy unwrapped the shoulder to check on his handiwork. He had Tony push on his hand in different directions and then, he had him do a tiny chicken dance, raising his arm ever so slightly. He did it! Ortho Guy is a little too serious to jump up and down or do a football dance, but he was mighty proud of seeing his work in action. His smile was so big and bright, the grin could have lit up a Christmas tree.

"Hey! It's firing! We're in business! Heh. Heh. You will be able to do so much now!" exclaimed Ortho Guy.

Tony lost ten pounds in a flash. I literally saw it float away and his t-shirt filled out as his chest puffed out and his shoulders straightened.

"Now you can do physical therapy with purpose," said Ortho Guy. I kind of wondered what we were doing before. Ortho Guy prefers to call it physical terrorist. It's kind of true because sometimes it really hurts when they are trying to break up scar tissue.

The next round of physical therapy became a new kind of doctor date for us. My shoulder was bothering me so I had PT Man take a look at it. Serving tennis balls and swimming caused my shoulder to ache every time I raised it above my head. Ironic. I kind of wondered if it wasn't God's funny way of helping me more fully understand what Tony was experiencing—empathy instead of sympathy. I told Tony we could go to PT together. He didn't seem too excited at first. I had thought it was a sweet and creative way to spend time together. I ignored his lack of enthusiasm and tried for a PT date anyway.

When I called, the caller ID must have shown Tony's name. Instead of "Hello, physical therapist's office," I heard, "Hi Tony!"

"Well, this is his wife," I said with a chuckle. "I have a shoulder problem too." I paused, thinking this would surely knock her off her swivel chair.

"Oh, this happens. It sounds weird, but it really isn't."

"Oh," was all I could muster. I was slightly disappointed, and I think she was too, for different reasons. She wanted to talk to Tony;

he's great at making friends everywhere. Tony was very proud of the fact he knew everyone in the office.

"What time did you call? I'm sure I know her," Tony asked me after I relayed the less-than-friendly call to the PT office. Tony was the longest ongoing patient. He knew the staff as well as PT Man and his partner.

We did get my first appointment together. Since Tony was out of his sling, he could drive. He was all giddy like it was our first date. He warmed up to the idea of us going as a twosome pretty quickly. All he had to do was drive us; the hard part was coordinating the appointment.

"OK. Time to leave. Make sure you have your insurance card." Tony was relishing his caregiver role. Tony had a shot at taking a walk in my shoes. (I think God was messing with Tony too. I wasn't the only one getting a lesson here.)

As we drove into the parking lot looking for a space, Tony piped up, "Hey, ya see that Green Bay Packers car? That means Emily is working today. She's from L.A., but she loves the Packers."

Tony escorted me through the door, and we stood at the check-in desk together. The office is one giant room, so PT Man, his partner, and all of the associates could see us.

"TONY!" we heard in stereo. I felt like we'd walked onto the set of the TV show *Cheers*, where the loveable character Norm was always welcomed. Tony left me at the desk so he could talk to PT Man and let him know he'd brought in his "gal." I didn't know what to do except wait in the waiting room like I'd done for the last six months and read *People* magazine.

PT Man finished up with his previous patient. He was ready for me. As he walked up, he called out to his work partner, "Hey, I'm about to get insider information on Tony Low. Heh, heh, heh."

I was led to a long bench where PT Man started his assessment. Mostly he asked me questions and had me show him where it hurt. Because it was all one big room, Tony had his eye on us while he did his exercises. He was looking out for me.

Tony called out questions to PT Man. I didn't know if it was to show me how cool it was to be there with all his new friends or to let PT Man know he was watching him. The questions were so frequent PT Man had to put a stop to it. "Hey, you are taking time away from your wife. It's her turn."

And so, the love triangle began. We were all laughing. I could see how Tony loved hanging out in the place. The banter made the months of PT seem less of a burden. Heck, I'd go just to hang out and catch up with everyone.

PT Man delivered his prognosis. I could not swim or play tennis for six weeks. So, those two things were *my everything*, and I was not happy. PT Man was sensitive to my body language and tried to compromise. He didn't really look at me.

"Maybe you just hit some backhands and forehands; no serving."

"Uh, ya can't really play and not serve," I stated matter-of-factly. We let the information sink in for a moment. He still couldn't really look me in the eye.

"Six weeks is nothing. Look at him," he said pointing to Tony. "It's been six months for him." I knew there was no way around this if I wanted my shoulder to heal. I was used to Tony being limited in his activity. I felt for him then, and I *really* did after PT Man's comparison of my situation to Tony's. It sure is a lot different when you are the one being denied your normal activities.

I considered my options. I swam because I couldn't run anymore. The only exercise left was the bike. The irony of my situation couldn't get any more ironic. I was going to get to know Tony's PT *and* cycling world. Tony couldn't wait to be my cycling guide.

"We could set up dual trainers!" Tony was trying to help. I could not ride a bike at ten thirty at night like he did. I opted for a six a.m. spin class at the gym.

"You might need more than one pair of bike shorts, if you really get into cycling," he said with the enthusiasm of a kid teaching his parents how to do something new. Tony and I used to mountain bike on the weekends before kids. I owned one pair of biking shorts that were probably twelve years old. I could get by until I decided if I was "really" into cycling.

My first spin class, I thought I was going to die; I was shocked. Swimming kept me in pretty good shape. A whole new set of muscles came to life: legs that propelled the bike and arms and core to hold me up. I had a whole new respect for the cycling enthusiasts. I learned from my first instructor, spin class is the third-best bang for the exercise buck, followed by jump roping and kick boxing. No wonder cyclists are thin, resembling live skeletons in cycling shorts.

Tony continued his excitement for me. "Now you will really drop the weight!" Most wives would think Tony was working towards serious sleep-on-the-couch time. I started what I call the "cyclist diet" of my own free will. I always want to lose ten pounds, but now I would finally do it. Tony was so skinny he could be mistaken for having a serious illness when he was cycling and watching what he ate. And if the irony knife couldn't twist any more, Tony was now stuffing his kids full of food to make up for the time he was in the hospital and starving his wife as if he was still in the hospital.

The cyclist diet is not official, as in a book or a website. I should probably call it the "Tony Diet," as it was something Tony adopted after tons of research on nutrition. The idea is to kick-start the metabolism so it is always working. Eating every couple of hours is ideal. So, after eating a sensible breakfast of oatmeal with dried cranberries and walnuts, I ate a handful of almonds two hours later. I ate a salad for lunch with lots of veggies and chicken. An afternoon snack was another handful of almonds or an apple with peanut butter. Dinner consisted of a small portion of protein, salad, and brown rice. That's it. Except when I realized how often I was eating the bad stuff. Stopping cold turkey turned me into nasty crank.

I gave up sweets, dairy, and chips and drank less wine; I couldn't give up wine completely. I dropped ten pounds in about a month. Several watchmen checked on me. Tony sent a text when it was time to eat almonds. If I looked a little too longingly at the last strip of bacon on the counter, Alex was on me.

"MOM! Don't eat that! You are going to ruin EVERYTHING!" exclaimed Alex. And if I happened to falter, Alex could sniff me out.

"I smell mint! MOM! Are you eating a Girl Scout cookie?!?" Who could cheat with this guy around? I couldn't even look at a photo of strawberry shortcake. I told Alex how much I just wanted to eat that dessert. He quickly flipped the photo over so I couldn't drool over it any more.

The boys helped Tony too. TJ massaged out the knots. Tony sat on the couch or the floor and TJ sat behind him rubbing him down. TJ loved this time with his dad. His new PT role allowed him to be close without losing his twelve-year-old tough guy image. A tween would never crawl into his dad's lap to chat, his arms dangling around his dad's neck. TJ and Tony had a good gig.

Alex helped Tony hold poses. Before the surgery, Tony never could move his arm away from his torso, like a jumping-jack move. His arm wouldn't move that way even if someone tried to move it for him. Three weeks after the accident, I couldn't get a washcloth under his arm or a towel. I used a blow dryer to dry him instead. Tony could move his arm postsurgery, but not voluntarily; he needed help.

Tony lay on his back on the floor, while Alex helped get the arm stretched out and up toward Tony's head. With each attempt, the arm could go a tiny bit higher and a tiny bit higher, and he would hold the arm up for thirty seconds or more. Tony could hold the pose all by himself. He couldn't have made Alex more proud. Alex scrambled over Tony's chest like a playful puppy. He looked at the arm from every angle; he wanted to make sure Tony was really doing this himself, no cheating. I don't know how Tony would have cheated, but nothing was going to get by Alex. He even took a little credit for the success.

"Mom! Look! Dad is holding his arm up all by himself!" He had to show someone the "joint" accomplishment.

For the next six weeks, we took care of each other and worked on physical therapy. We had a rainbow of stretchy bands for exercises. A yellow band was the easiest, and they got progressively harder with each new color: red, green, and blue. I was relieved to have Tony help me at home. I was given printed instructions with diagrams ,but I couldn't follow them. Tony stepped in to help.

"No jerky movements. One fluid movement like this," he'd say as he demonstrated the proper form and motion. Once I used the wrong color band, a harder one, and my shoulder was really sore afterward. PT was trickier than it looked.

Tony was more accepting of our dates with PT Man. I usually arrived first. I'd lay face down so PT Man could rub out the knots in my shoulder and neck. I knew when Tony arrived because I heard the greeting in surround sound, "Tony!"

PT Man teased Tony about coming late. He gave him a guilt trip about how his wife could be on time, but he couldn't. Tony was usually stuck on a call for work, and his appointments were longer than mine because they were more complicated. Tony always tried to squeeze more out of a minute than most people. He's late to everything. Hence, our date was literally just the little bit of the crossover time we spent together.

Mostly we watched the other from across the room. I witnessed how hard PT Man challenged Tony. He'd ask Tony to push on his hand and then move the target so Tony would have to move too. Tony was so focused, it was as if he was trying to lift five hundred pounds. PT Man didn't cut him any slack. We were both there to exercise. We didn't talk much, just made eye contact every once in a while.

PT Man caught us once. "Ahh geez! Are you two making goo-goo eyes at each other?" We both got a little pink. He didn't stop us though.

At the end of six weeks of joint PT, I learned how hard it was to fit in fifteen minutes of exercises every day. I hated it. I had so many other things I wanted/needed to do, but I did the exercises because it was good for me, like eating vegetables. The routine was boring and monotonous. Yellow band, red band, green band, blah, blah, blah. Repeat. We made snow angels together on the floor, part of the exercise regime. Tony had to put a towel underneath his arm so he could slide his arm on the hardwood floor. He couldn't get his arm to work on carpet—too much resistance. I liked to think we were sending an SOS to heaven: "Send us an angel! We're sick of this!"

I really appreciated Tony's stamina and discipline over the previous seven months. Even PT Man was in awe. "Most guys would be so depressed by now." After seventeen years of marriage, I thought I could not possibly be "wowed" by my husband. What was there to know at this point? I knew he was tough, smart, thoughtful, and all the reasons you marry a person. I just didn't know the depth of those attributes. He made me feel like I picked the most durable model on the market—one that would last forever.

CHAPTER 30

PT in Paradise

Seven Months After the Accident,
Spring Break

IF WE HAD KNOWN—OR WORSE YET, PT Man had known—the precarious circumstances we would find ourselves in, I'm not sure we would have done what we did. We spent spring break in Belize. Honestly, we thought we would hike through the jungle gazing at playful monkeys and exotic birds. Belize is known for exceptional bird-watching, so it made sense to us we were in for a semi-active vacation. We both thought Tony would get behind on his exercises but experienced completely the opposite. PT Man came up with creative exercises, but he could not top our version of PT and not nearly the thrill or alluring setting.

Tony had planned a dreamy destination, because he knew life could end in a minute; his accident was proof enough. Why not reach for the stars? I'd like to say he was always considering the boys and their engagement, but I think he factors himself into the action-adventure vacation. He wasn't going to let his limitations limit his fun with family. Luckily, the tomboy half of me went along with the program. The last eight months of being stuck at home or in doctor offices was getting to everyone.

We stayed deep in the jungle in a tree-house resort. High above the ground, we were eye-to-eye with the branches and leaves, the canopy we usually sat underneath for a picnic. Half the walls were screens to keep the cool in and bugs out. The corrugated metal roof was a perfect medium for falling debris or lively monkeys skipping from tree house to tree house, clattering awake the slumbering guests. We ate buffet breakfasts and dinners in a communal lodge, meeting guests from all over the world. At dinner, a host came around with a clipboard to ask us what we wanted to do the next day. By morning, we knew what to wear, hiking boots or a swimsuit, and jumped on a bus with other guests with similar adventure tastes.

Our first excursion, cave tubing, was a must, a friend told us. We rode in an army-green bus down a bumpy, dusty road for about an hour. After disembarking, the four of us dug through a pile of inner tubes, looking for the most perfectly round one. Most had some kind of bulge, like a knot on a tree. Anyone with open-toed shoes was asked to choose a pair of bright white basketball shoes from a box. Sizes were limited. Both TJ and Tony picked a pair.

"I feel like Shaq!" said TJ as he stared down at his feet that were now six inches longer.

We were looking forward to the cool water to wash the heat and grime from our skin. Floating down a slow stream, in and out of caves, sounded easy and relaxing. Unfortunately, the bulk of the river was dried up; there was very little floating. We carried our tubes down a narrow dusty path to what was left of the river's edge. Julio, our husky guide, instructed us to paddle backward into a blackened cave. When it was too shallow to float, we carried our tubes again, splashing through the puddles in Shaq shoes or Keen closed-toe sandals. Then we would paddle some more and drop the tubes at the shore to explore on foot—all with headlamps clamped to our white plastic helmets.

For a fully functioning person, cave-tubing didn't sound particularly challenging. If you consider how someone with still very limited arm extension and mobility would accomplish this trip, Tony came up short, literally. It was like one fin was shorter than the other, barely flicking the water away. Instead of advancing with great surges with each row, the tube spun a bit, gliding side to side and advancing only inches. Alex's kid-length arms couldn't extend far enough past the tube either, so he was basically all hand and wrist motion, like a hummingbird instead of an eagle. Tony and Alex made good paddle buddies: two baby ducks chasing the flock. The short strokes forced Tony to move as if he was holding a stretchy PT band, the water the resistance. PT Man would never think of sending us up the river in a tube.

The adventure became even more challenging. We explored the crevices of the cave on foot, down narrow paths that required all fours for balance. If you were Tony, and one arm was basically useless, you had to be mighty creative to figure out how to get at least three body parts touching the ground or cave wall to make your way over jagged rocks, slippery clay, and around sharp corners. But poor Tony was stuck in a pair of borrowed slick-soled sneaks made for basketball courts, making the exercise nearly impossible. I swear, this was the only safety rule of the entire trip: closed-toe shoes. Slipping to your death seemed a bigger threat than losing a toe.

Hugging walls and boulders sure beat PT Man making you push against his hand while he moved it all around like the sign of the cross. The expert guide told you exactly where to step or place your hand. For Tony, he made himself into a spare platform, like a frog that needed an extra lily pad to get across the pond. Julio bent over, staring down into the abyss while Tony pushed off his back. At one point, we were practically pressed into a wall to get around a corner. Julio the guide held your foot still so you could brace yourself and step ever-so-carefully next to a hole-to-nowhere and over to safety. The hole was so deep and dark, it was best not to know any more or you could lose your balance thinking about the bottomless possibilities.

Alex went first for everything. His preference. I grew accustomed to Julio getting us around and watching him help Alex so I'd know what to do. It was pitch dark. You could only see right in front of you. I made the mistake of shining my headlamp beyond Julio to take a look. Nothing. No wall. No railing like in America. Down was the only thing close, *way* down. *CRAP!* I couldn't chicken out, because to me, it was more frightening to sit in the dark with the bats and scorpion spiders (all harmless) *all alone.*

Forget my babies making it across—how was Tony going to do it? Julio made like a human lily pad again with amazing strength, balance, and agility. No net. PT Man would never think of doing a push-up off someone's back while scooting around a narrow path. Hindsight being 20/20 was an understatement. We didn't know what to expect, and finding ourselves in the middle of potential trouble was an exercise in faith and positive thinking. Mind control, ten thousand prayers, and Julio got us through.

Our next PT exercise led us to the Mayan city of Tikal: ancient ruins hosting three great temples in Guatemala. We rode in a van for several hours, crossing the border from Belize to Guatemala. At the border we made a bathroom stop while officials checked our passports. An attendant stood at the door of the restroom, selling toilet paper by the square.

Inside the national park, we walked for twenty minutes from the parking lot to a collection of limestone ruins, still intact after centuries. The pyramids reach as high as 230 feet and date back to 732 A.D. The heat and humidity drenched our skin and clothing, making us look as if we came out of a waterfall instead of from a short walk. Our guide, Edgar, took us to Temple I and told us if we wanted to go to the top, go for it. It was too hot for him, so he waited for us at the bottom. He wasn't sweating like the rest of us so, I seriously doubted his reasoning. Locals are used to the tropical climate. He added it might be tough for those with a fear of heights, the real reason he didn't go to the top, in my opinion.

I had about thirty seconds to debate my decision. I thought to myself, *We've come this far. Hmmm.* Tony was kind of afraid of heights. I knew this from the days we lived on the top floor of a San Francisco apartment. When we locked ourselves out, he climbed three flights on the fire escape to our bedroom window we always left open. He didn't have a choice, so he did it.

My thoughts came to an abrupt stop. "CRAP!" I said to no one in particular. The boys were off and half way up the very, very steep wooden ladder. Somebody had to go after them quick! It had to be me, given Tony's fear of heights and his physical limitation.

The ladder was equipped with handrails, providing me a tiny bit of relief, a little more protection. *Just look up,* I told myself. About every twenty steps was a three-foot platform, giving my racing heart a tiny break from my terrified self.

The boys were out of sight. I reached the top and practically kissed the wall to shimmy the three-foot wide path to the middle where the boys were sitting on receding steps, no railing. One couple stood in fright, flat against the wall, so I had to shuffle past, splitting the difference of the path and holding my breath.

We sat for a few minutes. All I could think about was getting down. The boys and I ended up being part of a family picture to a family we weren't related to—I wasn't going to move. We met the tall, blonde family from Minnesota at the jungle lodge later, and they graciously told us we were part of their family now. It worked for me; I smiled really big.

I thought Tony would stay below, but he'd popped up to take pictures.

"ARE YOU CRAZY?" I cried out.

"Ah, I'm not going to miss out!" he answered back with a chuckle. He had suddenly lost his fear of heights and all of his common sense. He was just like his boys, thinking without a frontal cortex. PT Man wanted Tony to get as much up and down arm movement as he could, but he would never say, "Go climb a 154-foot ladder with a camera strapped to your back." And we were worried his PT would regress on vacation.

The handrails going down were exceptionally smooth, as if sanded to velvety perfection. The soft surface, however, was from hundreds of death grips squeaking down the ladder each day. My entire body shook for at least thirty minutes after reaching the ground. At a beverage cart, I tried to ask for four waters in Sesame Street–level Spanish. I could barely spit out "quatro aguas." Why couldn't I say two simple words? I couldn't believe I could become so rattled. Nothing had ever scared me so much as my family and me being inches from free falling to the dirt-packed ground. We climbed the other two temples in the park, but they weren't nearly as scary. They were taller but wider; zigzag staircases to the top made them much more approachable. At the top, a cascade of deep steps made it possible for us to sit without fear of getting knocked off the ledge, possibly plunging to our deaths.

The rest of the trip seemed uneventful by comparison. We rappelled down a three-hundred-foot rocky cliff, a sinkhole leading to a haunted cave. Our guide told us a couple spent their honeymoon night at the cave. They didn't sleep well, as "something" shook their air mattress in the night. My fear and the boys' excitement doubled with this bit of folklore. The boys peeked around the cave, hoping to see a heavy rock levitate or a wispy human image emerge from the darkness. I kept my eye on the boys. I'm not sure how I would have saved them from the paranormal, but I was ready to leap to the rescue with my mom superpower.

Surprisingly, rappelling had tons of safety measures in place, like we were used to in the States. Straps wrapped around our bodies, helmets secured to our heads, and guides at the top and the bottom took the edge off, a little. I was still scared but not nearly as scared as I was at the top of Temple I. Alex dropped down first, so he could show his petrified mother how it was done. The family looked up as we watched Tony glide down, using the rope and gravity to stretch out his arm, like the rope over the door at home only much longer. Every day delivered a new exercise for Tony's shoulder.

After our jungle excursion, we spent a few days on an island just off the coast. We slept in our own private cottage, with two tiny bedrooms and a tiny bathroom. Meals were served in a lodge with six other guests. It felt a little creepy being one of ten people on an island with one man managing the place. He even controlled the seating arrangement. Our family gathered at a round table for four while the others sat at a long table with him, the "king." The other guests had arrived a few days earlier, so the hierarchy was set. I didn't mind; it just felt a little like a page out of a horror novel: A sinister man entertaining unsuspecting guests on his private island. A place where guests couldn't leave their bungalows at night or they risked a run-in with a saltwater crocodile. We saw evidence of the crocodiles in the mornings, a long line in between sets of footprints in the sand.

Our days were spent snorkeling and eating. After breakfast, a boat would take us out into the postcard-perfect waters of turquoise blue. The water was warm and inviting. We saw schools of brilliantly colored fish: blue, purple, yellow, orange, and red. Once in a while our Jamaican guide, Too Sweet, would grab your arm and point out an eagle ray hovering on the white sandy bottom or a sea scorpion hiding in the rocks. Snorkeling was the best PT exercise in all of Belize. Tony could swim at his own pace, moving his arms up and down and around in small strokes. It was OK to go nowhere fast since we were anchored in one spot. He could kick to make up for what his arm could not do. The ocean leveled the playing field.

After snorkeling, we headed back for lunch and a rest. By two p.m., the boat took us to a new location for another two-hour snorkel tour. In shallower waters, the boys picked up orange-red starfish the size of frying pans, eclipsing their faces as they looked closely at the bumpy texture. And then we returned for a shower, cocktail hour, and dinner. By nine o'clock we'd locked ourselves in our bungalow, lest any crocs attack us in the night. Snorkeling PT and sun were tiring. This was the cycle of island life for us for two days, and it was pure bliss. Our troubles were far away.

On this trip, there was no time to weigh risks or discuss parental judgment. If a guide said, "go," the boys did, immediately. And they never looked back at Tony or me to see if it was OK. As a mom, I was looking after my babies, but from really far behind. They were growing up and could swim and climb faster than me. I could only catch them if they fell, maybe, or fight off a ghost in a cave trying to snatch my kids, maybe.

Tony was just being his usual tough self, never complaining or letting his shoulder keep him from following his family into an adventure. Because he kept up with us, we were freer to explore, even if it scared me half to death. Nobody thought about the icky journey we had experienced for the better part of a year. All of us would agree this was the best trip *ever*. Tony had never looked so happy to do PT in paradise.

"I have to pinch myself to know it was real," exclaimed Tony.

CHAPTER 31

Dr. Downer

Nine Months After the Accident

THE SHOCK DID NOT COME from the nerve but the doctor. The formerly happy-go-lucky neurologist who had told us, "I'm not going to say it will come back. I'm not going to say the nerve will never come back," had changed his tune. He took one quick visual scan at Tony and said in a clipped tone, "It's not working. Your other muscles are compensating."

After nine months, we checked on the status of the nerve. Did it grow the predicted inch per month from the neck to the deltoid? Was it firing? Hence, our visit to the neurologist with the Frankenstein Lab. Dr. Happy was now named Dr. Downer in our eyes.

Before we could even process the negative blast of news, Dr. Downer added insult to injury: "Did you fall?" He couldn't remember what happened. When we explained the bike accident, his next question was even more ridiculous, given his quick assessment of Tony's condition.

"Oh, so you are back on the bike again?"

"Uh, no," Tony said. We both looked at this guy as if he had just crawled out from under a rock. He really didn't remember a stitch about us and seemed surprised to see us back once he made the connection. We went on to tell him how Tony had had rotator cuff surgery, when he interrupted us.

"Whoa! Your doctor operated on a shoulder that doesn't work?" he asked with an incredulous smirk. We learned right then and there the competitiveness of the medical field and the seeming importance of proving to patients who is the smartest doctor. He trashed Ortho Guy and told us how we needed to see a far superior orthopedic surgeon. To us, it was more like a competition of who was the most pessimistic, and we were looking right at the winner.

Tony only had a short window of time to get rotator cuff surgery whether the nerve was firing or not. Dr. Downer didn't say conclusively the nerve would never come back, so why should we have believed otherwise? Ortho Guy would never, never recommend surgery unnecessarily. He was keeping Tony's options open. Dr. Downer's lack of professionalism, diplomacy, and team spirit was shocking. *Whose side is he on, anyway?*

Whenever someone told Tony he couldn't do something, he'd prove them wrong. Tony always found another way when faced with an obstacle, even in a traffic jam. Before Google Maps, he whipped through pages of the *Thomas Guide* to find another route. A lot of people would just wait out the traffic jam singing along with the radio to kill the time, like me. The same reaction happens at medical appointments; it's easier, if not expected, to trust an expert because that's what we know. We were not most people any more. Once again, we were learning to take matters into our own hands.

In the nerve situation, Tony knew Dr. Downer did not have X-ray vision. He couldn't see or *feel* the tingles deep inside Tony's shoulder. Some doctors can only see black or white, like this one. Ortho Guy told us he'd never seen anything like Tony's situation before, but he was willing to stay positive and open-minded. If the answers weren't in the textbooks, you could always be human and plain old hope.

The only way to know for sure was to enter the Frankenstein Lab again. Two weeks later we were back in the Lab and the nice side of Dr. Downer was back. His memory was not however.

"Hi! I'm Dr. Downer. I don't think we've met?" he said while re-introducing himself.

In just two weeks, how could he forget us? I grumbled inside my head. I could almost understand drawing a blank after a nine-month gap, but two weeks? We were unique in so many ways. I kept thinking of all the clues he had about us. First of all, how many couples go to all the appointments together, especially a distinctive looking couple like us, Asian and Caucasian. Secondly, how many patients were run over by a truck and suffered nerve damage? Put those factors together, and we are about as one of kind as a snowflake, only more obvious. Restaurant owners remember us, even if we haven't been in for nine months, and all they have to go on are appearances.

The only difference, is that I wore street clothes instead of yoga pants, and I wore lip gloss. I've run into friends in the grocery store who ask me if I'm working because I'm wearing lip gloss in the middle of the day. Maybe, this threw Dr. Downer?

After the "introductions," Dr. Downer went about running his tests. He inserted the needles, slapped on the painter's tape, and marked Tony up with a Sharpie. The neck was firing but the axillary nerve: zero. The axillary nerve allows the arm to throw a ball like a baseball player, hold a car over your head like Superman, or push somebody out of your way like Tony wanted to do to get the heck out of the office. We both hated that Dr. Downer's prediction was correct.

As a patient, Tony had to take control of the situation. Had we taken Dr. Downer's advice from the start, Tony would have been forever locked up and in pain. He would never get back on a bike. He would be doomed to a black cloud of existence because an "expert" told him he was all washed up.

"Hey! Look at the bright side. You are alive and everything else seems to be working OK," Dr. Downer offered. We were looking at the bright side, but we were not going to settle. Our old mantra, "alive and fixable," morphed into "never give up."

After an Internet search on axillary nerves, we learned if it is not working, something is blocking the neurological path. Surgery can help and a full recovery was possible. We had been contemplating alternatives. The nerve results and Dr. Downer's negativity were our catalysts.

CHAPTER 32

A New Hope: Acupuncture

Nine and a Half Months After the Accident

IT WAS TIME TO CREATE our own happiness again. Dr. Downer had fired us up to carve a different path to fix Tony and find hope. So far, Western medicine worked for Tony, saving his life and bringing back some shoulder function. However, we'd reached an abrupt dead end, forcing us to take matters into our own hands. Thoughts of alternative methods, like acupuncture, had crossed our minds before, but we had held back. How would we find the right person for the job in a practice so unfamiliar in America? Given the circumstances, we knew we had to explore the possibilities.

The mom-network was not much help. My girlfriends had plenty of acupuncture recommendations if Tony wanted to get pregnant. Tony's only experience with Chinese medicine was a ghastly-tasting black tea for a sour stomach. We stored the medicinal tea alongside the Celestial Seasonings Sleepy Time, Vanilla Honey, and Yogi Green Jasmine teas in our kitchen cupboard. Sometimes we had small vials of tiny mauve-colored pills in cardboard sleeves inside a bigger box. Those pungent beads worked wonders on a digestive system running amok. The tummy and intestinal remedies came with my husband when we were married, and they were his only exposure to Eastern treatments for illness.

Fortunately, Tony relished research. He sensed our relationship with Western medicine might be coming to an end, and Dr. Downer confirmed Tony's beliefs. He googled "nerve growth" and found his way to acupuncture. His early searches turned up practices for weight loss or quitting smoking, sort of an acupuncture light. Most of the acupuncturists he found studied in the United States and were not of Chinese descent. He knew he wanted someone trained in China to help him, someone old-school and authentic. After a few more Google searches, e-mail exchanges, and phone calls, he found a good fit: an instructor from the Academy of Chinese Culture and Health Sciences, trained in Shanghai in traditional acupuncture, who had practiced Chinese medicine for twenty-five years. We nicknamed him Doc Hope because no matter the circumstances, Tony looked to him as a sign of hope.

Tony interviewed Doc Hope over the phone. We couldn't read up on him like other physicians because he didn't have a web presence. He said he'd helped lots of patients like Tony. Slivers of doubt entered our minds, since previous doctors had said they rarely saw someone in Tony's shoes. As long as he could help, we didn't really care about experience with exactly the same injury. Apparently, Doc Hope worked on a horseback rider who'd injured her leg in her twenties. Forty years later, she came to Doc Hope, and he fixed her up, unblocking the nerve so she could walk without a limp. The story sounded promising to us. Plus, he was covered under our insurance plan. It was worth a try.

We fully expected a dusty apothecary storefront with aromas of herbs and dried roots, and dark examination rooms. In our experience, shopping for Chinese cookies, medicinal teas, and whole fish in California Chinatowns, the markets were replicas of those in Hong Kong going back years. So, it wasn't out of the question that our idea of an old-school office would be accurate, especially since it was located on the fringe of Oakland's Chinatown. We were completely wrong. Doc Hope practiced in a three-story building with bright and cheery modern décor. Accents of lime-green walls, bamboo screens, and a large front window flooding the building with natural light extinguished any scary thoughts of walking into a house of hocus pocus.

The waiting area was long and narrow, with a reception desk at the end, belonging to the owner's wife. The remaining space was filled with cloth-walled cubicles—the examining rooms. We could hear and smell the treatments. The odor wafting through the air was reminiscent of a rock concert. To us novices, we really thought it was medical marijuana, but it was an herb called moxibustion with the same aroma. Moans and groans made us feel like some other illegal activity was taking place too. What the heck was going on in here? We tried not to laugh out loud.

We were handed paperwork by an older Chinese lady, dressed in black with coifed hair like my mom wore in her Final Net hairspray days. Files were kept on patients like a western medical office, only the questions were slightly different. Tony focused on filling in the personal profile. Every once in a while, he read a question out loud, because it was so different and comical to us.

"Are you married, single, divorced, or separated?" Tony read to me. How many ways can you slice up love status? We held back more snickers. If we could hear the patients, they could hear us. We tried to be polite. I looked around for something to read, to take my mind off our humorous surroundings. I could not find one *People* magazine, not even one hopelessly out of date. The only reading material available was a Chinese newspaper. I can't read Chinese, and there weren't very many pictures for me to guess what was going on in the story, so I just looked around the room, trying to tune out the R-rated noise.

At last, a short and trim Chinese man, who was old enough to be Tony's dad, greeted us in the waiting room. His gold wire glasses reminded me of all the physicians we met at the hospital, a uniform worn in all kinds of medicine.

"Hello. You can come back now," Doc Hope said as he shook our hands. He walked us back to one of the examination "stalls," leaving us there for a few minutes to check on a patient.

"I gotta go," Tony whispered. He walked the twenty feet to the reception area where he was instructed to take off his shoes before climbing the stairs to the bathroom. When Tony returned, he was grinning like a Cheshire cat.

"Hey! It's really clean up there. I took a picture." He pulled out his smartphone to show me a sign written in English and Chinese.

"Do Not Use the Bathroom for More than Three Minutes."

In fits of giggles Tony spat out the question, "What happens after four minutes?" We were holding our hands over our stomachs and mouths, trying to be quiet. The more we looked at each other, the more we laughed, as if we were two kids in church listening to a boring sermon.

Doc Hope returned and asked for our story. Tony barely got out the word accident when Doc Hope stopped the conversation.

"Do not tell the insurance it is related to car accident," Doc Hope commanded. "They won't pay."

"The accident is covered under our insurance plan. It's OK," Tony replied in defense.

"No. You tell them you here for pain in neck," Doc Hope stated firmly.

We still couldn't find common ground, so he walked us to the lobby to talk to his wife, Mrs. Doc Hope. She echoed her husband. After about fifteen minutes of back and forth, I looked pleadingly at both of them.

"OK, we do not care about the money. We really want you to help us. We need you," I implored.

Mrs. Doc Hope let out a sigh and offered a compromise. "OK. You send to insurance. They listen to you. You pay cash."

"I will do my best for you," Doc Hope said to us.

We returned to the examination room, and Tony finally got his accident story out. Doc Hope explained the acupuncture process for about a minute.

"I will treat you four times. If no results, we stop and . . . ," Doc Hope explained before Tony grew impatient and interrupted him.

In a loud and fast voice, Tony exclaimed, "What?!? You give up after four appointments?" Quitting was not part of Tony's vocabulary. I stepped in to sum it up for everyone.

"Just try it a few times, and we'll know by then if it's working." I looked at Tony and went on to tell him to try not to think beyond four visits, just see what happens and trust this guy. Next thing I know, Doc Hope was looking at me to explain and deliver information. I became the official interpreter of Acupuncturist English to Husband English.

Finally, Doc Hope could begin his work. Tony lay on his left side on the examining table. Doc Hope manipulated Tony's arm, moving it up and down and around. He probed Tony's shoulder with his elbow, pushing down and moving in circles. "Ah. You muss-o-man (muscle man). You go to gym?" Tony looked pretty good despite the lack of exercise in nine months. After a bit, Doc Hope tapped nine needles into Tony. One needle went into the neck and another in the forearm. The remaining needles were scattered around the shoulder. Doc Hope placed a heat lamp over Tony and walked away.

"Hey! When is he coming back? I feel like french fries. Is there a timer for this?" Tony joked. Snickers filled the cubicle.

I stared at Tony's backside. "Uhh, are you hedging your bets? You've got on lucky four-leaf clover boxers *and* Lucky Brand jeans?" More giggles rose from the cubicle.

Doc Hope returned twenty minutes later. The needles he removed worked as an irritant to bring the blood to the surface and stimulate the nerves. Acupuncture activates the nerve when the body is inefficient or nonfunctioning. Doc Hope climbed up on the table with

Tony, digging his elbows into Tony's shoulder even further, rocking and rolling him. He was desperately trying to break up the scar tissue that was cemented into one big glob. Doc Hope would have preferred we came sooner so he wouldn't have had to work so hard to loosen Tony up.

"First I break up scar tissue. Remove pain. This blocking movement and nerve." We about fainted with this news. Isn't that what we've been working on for the last nine months? PT Man would never be as aggressive, because Western medicine is more cautious; potential lawsuits hold physicians back. Ortho Guy would not prescribe PT on the neck for that very reason. "Something might get messed up."

"Phase two: we get angle," said Doc Hope. He meant wider movement, even passive. The last phase focused on the nerve. He pushed down on the shoulder from the top.

"You feel tingling in fingertips?" Doc Hope asked Tony.

"Yes!" Tony practically shouted. I clapped my hands. Bravo! Doc Hope was pleased. He continued to push on Tony's shoulder, more rock and roll. Again, Doc Hope commented on "musso man." He half meant Tony's tolerance for pain and not just physicality. Tony said it hurt a lot, about a nine out of ten on the pain scale but he didn't let on one bit, no yelps or tears.

"You must be a muscle man too, after working on so many patients," I kiddingly said to Doc Hope. He patted me on my shoulder and smiled shyly.

At the end of the session, Tony felt looser. We were so very grateful. The other patients had thanked Doc Hope profusely; we heard their words across the cubicles. Now we knew why they were so effusive. With such encouragement, we couldn't help but feel Tony was on his way. Doc Hope told us Tony had Big Chi, the energy of life. No wonder Tony was not going down without a fight, even from the very beginning. Big Chi was his superpower, and it had been driving him the entire time since the accident.

CHAPTER 33

Big Chi

Nine and a Half Months After the Accident, Post–Acupuncture Appointment

"YOUR HUSBAND HAS BIG CHI."

Well, I can't say anyone had ever said that at any of the medical appointments, not to me or to Tony, at least not in those words. I knew it was a compliment. I knew it had to do with internal energy. Doc Hope's assessment was dead accurate as I recounted in my head the miserable moments during Tony's progression from the ER to PT to surgery and now acupuncture.

Doc Hope did what no other doctor, nurse, friend, or even PT Man could do, explain Tony's positive attitude and superman threshold for pain. He gave the superpower a name, chi, the breath of life. Western culture would call it his spirit, but for some reason, spirit is never used in the context of assessing a person's well-being at a medical appointment like an appendage or heartbeat. It's more like an afterthought. "Wow. You sure are one tough son of a gun! You'll be just fine." Or, "Such a happy guy! That-a-boy."

Chi *is* part of an acupuncture appointment. It's not like Doc Hope had a device to size up Tony's spirit, like a water diviner or metal detector; he could sense a specialness in Tony through his touch as he worked on him. He pressed very, very hard on his shoulder, and Tony could take the pain in a way some of his other patients could not. We knew Tony was resilient, but we had no fancy way to explain it.

It's not like Big Chi just showed up for the accident either. Tony was probably born that way, but he was never tested in a way that we saw his gift as remarkable. I think cycling over the years honed Tony's chi—showed him what he's got. It's not a sport for the fainthearted. In fact, Tony told me cyclists are some of the toughest athletes out there. Those packs or pelotons of riders on the road might look more social than physical, but they are maintaining an incredible pace to stay together. No matter how much the legs turn to jelly or the lungs feel ready to pop, a cyclist has to push past the pain or be left behind.

Spin class gave me a glimpse into Tony's world. Cycling is a constant tease; a push to see how much stamina and mental strength is inside a person, even on a stationary bike. Rodney, my favorite spin instructor, constantly reminds the class we are stronger than we think. He'll prove it too. After a hard set of twenty ten-second sprints, every rider is panting and dripping with sweat. Rodney will not let us quit.

"Let me show you something," he shouts. And he cheers us on to do another five ten-second sprints. "You can do it! It's all mental."

I can't do what Tony can on the road, pedal hard without a cheerleader telling me I'm awesome; I can barely hang on in class. Heck, I can't even endure pain like Tony does either. I've had my share of minor shoulder injuries over the last few years. I'll complain absentmindedly, "Man, my shoulder still hurts, and it's been three weeks!"

And Tony will say, "That's me for the last seven years." *Ugh.* I want to snatch back my thoughtless words. Tony is so good at masking constant pain and compensating for his inabilities that I think he's 100 percent healed. I'm still in awe of his inner strength and motivation to just accept and move forward.

Tony's Big Chi was and is a gift. It's remarkable.

CHAPTER 34

Super Doctors, Super Friends

Ten Months After the Accident

TONY AND I WERE NOT THE ONLY ONES searching for alternative solutions to get him back on a bike. PT Man called his connections to see about a special brace to hold Tony's shoulder in place. The expert shopper, PT Man, found a brace so thick and with so much coverage Tony's torso looked like a black mummy. It was similar to the Octopus sling but with a lot more straps, like solving a Rubik's Cube by comparison. Now Tony could ride and even run with this special Velcro T-shirt, and his shoulder barely moved from its forced perfect posture. I rather liked the added protection in case of a crash, like a helmet for the chest.

The mummified Tony went out for a road test on his bike, the same flat road in front of our house where our boys had learned to ride bikes. I wasn't so sure about this experiment.

"Does PT Man know you are out on the road?!?" I asked, wanting some authority to be aware of Tony's actions.

"He told me I could! Only flat roads," Tony justified like a child to his mother.

And just like the boys, he teetered up and down the block, past three houses and back. His shoulder was very weak when he tried to steer clear of our white Sequoia SUV or the Great White Bus, as I liked to call it. But the smile and the sparkle in his eye made up for his lack of strength. Hope. Hope you could see and feel. For the last eleven months, not the three months as predicted in ER, we only dreamed of Tony riding on the road before this day. Now everything we had been working and praying toward played out over Tony's face. Mostly, it showed in his beaming eyes. Joy, from deep within, illumined the patch of road where he stopped to look at me watching from the porch. I smiled back at him, excited for his triumph but more than anything, to see the happiest man on earth. Tony's Big Chi got a power boost—not that he needed it. He tasted his future and would do anything to make sure he rode again.

Not to be outdone by PT Man, Ortho Guy had one more avenue to try; he wasn't ready to throw in the towel any more than Tony. He went that extra research mile to find a super doc to fix Tony's nerves.

Ortho Guy made some calls to help Tony get accepted into medical school, as a patient. The University of California at San Francisco is a teaching hospital with world-renowned doctors, ranked in the top ten in the United States according to *U.S. News & World Report.* In Tony's case, he had to apply for admission, or at least be approved for an interview. Ortho Guy left a phone message on a Saturday morning to deliver the good news. He suggested talking more about it over a Little League baseball game and hot dogs. He was also our friend, going above and beyond his medical expertise; he was not leaving us to the wolves to figure out how to survive the next phase.

The late May sun was beating down on the baseball fields, bleachers, players, and parents. Buckeye Fields is a social hub for families and friends. Two fields are side by side, so the chances of seeing a friend or two or more is highly probable and makes the slow game of youth baseball pass by quickly. Our sons were on different teams but we parents comprised a different kind of team. We sat next to each other, glancing at the players for a play or two and then zeroing in on Ortho Guy's words.

"I called a few people and found a neurosurgeon at UCSF, a well-respected expert in his field. I told him your story and he agreed to review your case," Ortho Guy told us. "Not everyone is eligible. You'll go through a series of tests and questionnaires, and if the results prove you're a good candidate for a nerve transfer, you're in."

"Thank you! Thank you!" we both exclaimed. We didn't really understand what a nerve transfer was exactly but we didn't care. We were game for anything to get Tony back to normal. We were not giving up on Doc Hope; we were adding to our solutions. A nerve transfer could make the goal of acupuncture move along more quickly, freeing up the neuro-passageways.

Unlike a regular interview, Tony couldn't brush up on company facts or practice his answers to potential questions. He could only be himself. The interview process would take about four hours. Between paperwork, waiting and testing and waiting and more tests and waiting, we would meet the wizard of neurosurgeons, the Great Oz.

We named him the Great Oz mainly because nobody had ever seen him in our medical circle. His grand reputation preceded him. Little did we know, the UCSF campus was like going to Oz in this case, a huge hospital campus with fog-enshrouded buildings carved into the hills of the Inner Sunset district of San Francisco. Blustery winds howled through the streets most of the year, especially in summer. Every service imaginable was available within a two-block radius: restaurants, banks, barber, copy services, or coffee.

"Geez! This place is its own city within a city, like the Vatican is to Rome. I bet they have their own zip code!" I quipped to Tony. We were a little lost, as building numbers were not really obvious. I, the wife, finally asked a group in white lab coats for directions. Once we reached our destination, a chipper desk clerk with gravity-defying, red-tipped hair greeted us like the gatekeeper at the original Oz, only more welcoming.

"Hi! Which department are you here to see?" she asked us. When she confirmed we were in the right place, Neurological Studies, we were invited to take a seat with fifteen other people waiting to be seen by some type of wizard doctor.

We had never seen so many diverse kinds of people in one room. As we looked around, we realized it wasn't just illness or injuries that differed. The only trace of American suburbia seated in the waiting room seemed to be us. Once again, we found ourselves a short distance away from a real prisoner. The first time was in the NICU where two policemen had watched over a sleeping inmate. Now, a wide-awake version was just eight feet away from us. My heart jumped as he shuffled past in his bright orange jumpsuit, ankle shackles, and handcuffs. His police escorts, with tattoos wrapped around swelled biceps, made us feel a little safer, but it was still a little unnerving. I tried not to stare, so I looked in another direction only to find yet another suburbanite shocker. I glanced just long enough to see a young man with fully tattoo-sleeved arms wearing a Marilyn Monroe T-shirt suggesting an X-rated act. My face flashed red, and I swung my head in the opposite direction. A Hispanic family was pushing their head-bandaged toddler in a stroller toward the elevator. My heart ached. Where was a *People* magazine when you needed one? I didn't know where to look without either being rude or bursting into tears.

We felt like this hospital was home to the brainiest people on the planet. Otherwise, why would so many people from all walks of life and from all over the world be in the same waiting room? All of us were desperate for expert help we couldn't find in our hometowns. We wondered what was so wrong with the other patients that they had to come to Oz in search of hope, just like us.

After a long thirty minutes, we were called back to start Tony's nerve testing and EMG-- the all-too-familiar examinations from the Frankenstein Lab. A petite resident with auburn shoulder-length hair and glasses greeted us and quickly became an instant friend since she grew up next to our hometown of Lafayette. Her lab was brighter than the one where we'd had our more creepy experience with Dr. Downer. A floor-to-ceiling window let in just enough daylight to take off the spooky edge, despite the fog-filled skies. Since UCSF is a teaching hospital, the resident called in her professor, also a practicing doctor at UCSF, to explain her findings. We learned the results alongside the goateed doctor.

In short order, the tests determined there was not even a flicker of conductivity. Zero. A panel of doctors and residents would discuss a plan, delivered by the Great Oz to us. We went back to people-watching in a different waiting room, trying not to look at a guy with a half-shaved head and multiple surgical scars across his barren skull. We settled on a family dressed in shorts, gawking at the Golden Gate Bridge out the window.

"Clearly, they are not from around here," I said to Tony. San Francisco must be the number one seller of sweatshirts in the world, as visitors always think they are coming to sunny California. The blustery cold fog catches visitors off guard, and reluctantly they shell out twenty bucks for a hoodie with "San Francisco" emblazoned across the chest.

"I heard the family say they were from Ohio. We are so lucky we only drove over a bridge into the hospital parking lot. They flew or drove for miles and miles to get treated here," Tony said with a touch of guilt.

An hour later, we were called back into a tiny examining room with hospital off-white and taupe walls. One chair and one examining table took up most of the space, and somehow six of us, four doctors plus Tony and me, stuffed ourselves into the room, standing the entire time. Standing seemed to keep things very clinical and brief, or maybe it was out of respect to the Great Oz. I expected a pudgy white-haired old man to make a grand entrance. Instead, we got a movie-star handsome doctor with dark hair and slightly graying temples.

We finally heard him speak.

"A nerve transfer is the best solution. A nerve will be snipped from the triceps and grafted to the axillary nerve for the deltoid," the

Great Oz announced in his silky voice. I imagined it being a similar process to grafting a rose bush to produce a more beautiful bloom.

He continued to explain how there are several vines to the triceps; snipping one would leave Tony a little weaker, but not noticeably. The triceps rippling along the back of his upper arm would turn to jelly. My imagination took me back to elementary school when the lunch-lady's arm muscles hung loose, swinging with every scoop of mashed potatoes plopped on to my lunch tray. If Tony's arm ever extended again, he wouldn't mind a little jiggle.

"The success rate for a nerve transfer is 50 percent. We had another patient in a similar situation; he did not have success. Of course, there is the risk of infection with surgery," the Great Oz stated as if he were a sterilized medical instrument. He spelled out our risks as if the downside would preclude us from moving forward. Not us; there was no doubt in our minds that surgery was worth a shot and our only chance. Besides, we just might be on the good side of the 50 percent.

The part we didn't like: the bleepin' sling. Tony would become a lefty again for the third time in ten months. It would only be a two-week stint this time instead of six weeks. We dreaded it like being forced to eat broccoli when all we wanted to eat was ice cream. At least it was an outpatient surgery, so Tony would not stay overnight with chancy nurses we didn't know. The boys were still in school, so I'd only have to ask a friend to pick up TJ from school. Alex could ride his bike home.

Our superfriends, Ortho Guy and PT Man, were excited for us. The experience was so unusual that they both wanted to watch the surgery. Being a teaching hospital, it was possible to get a ticket to the surgery show. Doc Hope told us his phone was "open" all day; he wanted to hear the outcome. He was behind Tony too, even after just a short time. He did not let his Eastern belief system stop him from reaching across the medical-discipline aisle for the good of the patient.

With only a few weeks to enjoy his two-handed functionality, Tony made plans with the boys. Most of the activity took place forty-eight hours before the surgery, over the weekend, as the surgery date was set for a Monday. What better time to buy a new monster-sized grill, monster assembly required. TJ and Tony spent an entire afternoon poring over directions and screwing in parts.

The next item on the to-do list: painting TJ's ugly old orange bike. Tony had bought TJ a new bike, and Alex would inherit the old one. Because Alex hated orange, Tony and Alex shopped for neon green and purple spray paint. For best results, they would take the bike apart. I would not have the patience for any of those activities. But Tony's patience explained how Tony could live through his injury with unbelievable positivity. Step-by-step progress, like following assembly instructions for a grill would bring good things in time. The nerve transfer was a stride toward perfection for Tony's shoulder.

Ortho Guy called Tony to see how the appointment went and got me on the phone instead. Tony was out. "OK. Now I can get the real story." He wanted to know, "How does he do it? How does he stay so positive?"

"There is nothing to tell. Just like I said to our lawyer, Tony is not hiding in his office in tears or crying into his pillow at night," I answered.

"Hmm. There's nothing?" he said with surprise and slight disappointment. I think he was hoping for the insider's scoop and came up empty. He really had expected Tony to be down in the dumps at home, away from public view. Other friends asked the same questions.

"Look at you two. You talk about the accident like it was a simple broken bone. You don't seem sad or angry at all," our friend Monica said in amazement.

"Well, he lived. That's kind of a biggie. And he's not completely broken," I said, defending our cheery outlook. Anyone perplexed by our upbeat attitude should take a visit to Oz; their perspective would change.

Besides, we had already been through the worst of the healing process and were medically savvy now. Another surgery wasn't going to send us over the edge. We could handle anything after facing the accident and its aftermath. If surgery would get him back on the bike, Tony would endure, despite the return of the blasted sling.

CHAPTER 35

Déjà Vu

Eleven Months After the Accident,
Surgery at Oz

EVERYTHING WAS TAKING LONGER. The surgery scheduled at ten thirty a.m. didn't begin until one p.m. Imagine waiting all morning with nothing in your stomach since eleven p.m. the night before. As if the delay wasn't bad enough, a few nonpatients thought eating sandwiches with a side of fries in the waiting room wasn't a big deal. When I saw the anguish on Tony's face, I couldn't stand the wafting aroma of greasy potatoes any longer.

"Excuse me," I said politely as I stood in front of the group of three with sandwiches resting on their laps.

"Yes?" one responded as he wiped his mouth with a paper napkin. His friend slurped icy soda through a straw in a supersized cup.

"Maybe you didn't notice, but there are signs that say to refrain from eating in the waiting room." I carefully pointed out the signage in different directions like a flight attendant pointing out plane exits. "My husband is waiting for surgery and so is that lady over there. And he hasn't eaten since last night," I said with a forced smile.

"Oh. Sorry," apologized another in the guilty party. They hastily wrapped up their food and slunk out of the room. When a party of four entered the presurgery waiting room, I jumped up before the lunch ever made it out of the bag.

"Hi. Do you mind?" I asked with a courteous smile, resuming my flight attendant pointing at the "no eating" signs. Much to our relief, Tony's name was *finally* called.

We followed a nurse dressed in bright-blue scrubs into pre-op. Tony slipped into the familiar hospital gown that looked like faded wallpaper—the same patient ensemble he had worn before. We were shown to a stall-like waiting room with barely enough space for a gurney, surrounded by thin white curtains. I waited by his side trying to avoid pushing into the "room" next to us. While we waited, we couldn't help but overhear a patient and her doctor talking over her surgery.

"The tumor will be extracted through the nose," explained the surgeon in a slow and caring voice.

"So, my nose won't look the same. That's OK; I just want the headaches to go away," she confirmed with herself as much as the doctor. We were in awe of her acceptance, no trace of fear or loss in her voice; the pain must have been unbearable.

Tony and I just looked at each other, our eyes speaking our thoughts. Once again, we were thanking our lucky stars Tony wasn't suffering as much as he could have, given his circumstances. The nurse and anesthesiologist felt the same way after we described to them what happened to Tony.

"Wow. You are lucky to be alive," said the nurse.

"No kidding. And you are here for a shoulder and not more," responded the anesthesiologist.

Tony and I could only nod in agreement. Almost a year after the accident, we forgot about the effect Tony's injuries, neck brace, and sling had on others. The memories were tucked away like childbirth. We didn't want to remember the hard parts. Instead, we stuck to our mantra, "alive and fixable," even if the fixing was still happening. We were different people now, more trusting that things would work out. Even the delicate surgery to reroute nerve threads didn't bother us.

Tony was given a presurgery cocktail to erase any memory of the operating room or going under. I called the drink truth serum. A few minutes later, as the pre-op team wheeled the gurney to the doors entering surgery, Tony let everyone know what he thought of the place.

"It's a mess around here!" Tony said in disgust. Everyone laughed because it was true. Narrow walkways were stacked haphazardly with boxes of supplies on either side. When we reached the entrance to the operating room, our two new pals told me they would take care of my sweetie and disappeared behind the swinging doors. Like in a dramatic scene out of a movie, I stared at the doors for a minute, tears welling.

Crap! I better get out of here before I am mistaken for a hospital rookie, I thought as I dabbed my eyes.

My emotional reaction surprised me. I never cried during the worst times, ER or ICU, when Tony was bandaged and broken. With so much uncertainty about Tony's condition and energy spent keeping the boys worry-free, there hadn't been room for tears. This time, I knew Tony would be OK after the nerve transfer, but the nurturing side of me, the bodyguard, the loving wife, did not like being even the four floors down from him, but that was my closest option. I never ventured far from the hospital during all the hours of waiting. Cute shops and fantastic restaurants, normally a magnet for me, were only two blocks away on Irving Street. But I didn't want to go. I couldn't. I needed to be as near as possible. I was never bored. All the waiting never angered me. I just couldn't leave.

The surgery took longer, over three hours instead of two hours. It made sense that surgery delays were a regular occurrence, since patients here were special cases and often with unpredictable outcomes. But I was relieved a nurse called me hourly on my cell phone, or I would have shot up the elevator to find Tony.

The last call was from the Great Oz.

"Mrs. Low?" The silky voice asked when I picked up the call.

"Yes, this is she," I said with a slight wariness in my voice. *Was it bad if the surgeon called instead of a nurse?*

"Everything technically went fine. Tony is still under anesthesia." He answered the most important questions on my mind first. Then he went on to explain the surgery. As long as an axillary nerve didn't mind being fired up by a triceps nerve, he told me, Tony's prognosis looked good.

"Can I see him now?" I asked.

"Yes, he's in post-op. You can go on up," the Great Oz answered caringly.

The recovery room was dimly lit. The crisp white sheets of the hospital bed popped against the wheat-colored walls. Equipment was attached to Tony that I didn't bother to ask about. In my mind, I was right back in the ER where Tony was so loopy, he repeated himself: "What happened? What happened?" It was a déjà vu of déjà vus.

"My incision is eight inches, not four," Tony croaked in his sleepy voice. He said it twice. *His Big Chi must be powering him up again. How does he know this*? I wondered.

"The surgery took longer. That means it's going to hurt a lot," he told me twice.

"Can you IM PT Man?" he asked me twice.

IM? I was glad he said it twice. I translated IM to mean text, a technology I skipped over back in 2007.

Then I thought, *PT Man?!?* He said it twice!! *Does he ask about me twice, to anyone?!?* I shrugged it off to the anesthesia fog.

The post-op recovery would take longer too, six hours instead of one hour. Tony would have to stay the night. I was beat after ten hours of sitting on pins and needles in the waiting rooms of Oz. But before I left, I clarified Tony's overnight pain management. A Darth Vader–Tony was a déjà vu I did not want to repeat. Then, just like the nurse in ICU, the recovery nurse told me to go home because he wouldn't remember I was even there. He didn't, both times.

The next day, after the release from Oz, Tony wanted real food, not hospital cuisine. I wasn't surprised. The last time I drove him home from a hospital, he wanted a giant frozen yogurt. He was like a little kid getting a lollipop after a vaccination shot. He deserved a reward, again.

"You can eat anywhere you want. What'll it be?" I asked.

"I want noodles from Japantown!" exclaimed Tony. He was starving.

"You got it!" I said. I was happy to feed him anything at this point. All he had eaten in the last twenty-four hours was the most delicious popsicle at two a.m.

Tony was still groggy from the anesthesia, but his appetite won out over his partially drowsy brain. We ate at his favorite spot: Mifune for Japanese soba noodles in beef broth. He was back to using his left hand with a fork. No tricky chopsticks for him.

Once we were home, a sinking feeling reminded me I had not received any calls about the pain prescription. Before we left Oz, I made sure we were squared away.

"We will get your prescription filled. Don't worry sweetie," promised the in-house pharmacist. She must have been fifteen years younger than me, but I let the condescending reference slide.

"Thanks," I bristled. The pain meds were more important. I never doubted her word, because everyone had been so attentive throughout the surgery. But hours and hours later, I had to place some calls to an assistant and another resident and back to the assistant to get the prescription. *Why is pain medication always the snafu?* Déjà vu.

The third round of recovery was quick compared to the accident and rotator cuff surgery. He slept for a day, then his Big Chi spurred him into action. We had timed the surgery around a job change so Tony had two weeks to relax and recuperate before starting at a new company. Just like his nerves, the old job wasn't working for Tony either, so he made a switch and sought out a new opportunity.

As a sales rep, commissions were a large part of Tony's compensation. Sales deals took time, so he wasn't going to be earning anything extra for a while. However, the job transition was a little less risky, knowing after months of negotiations with the insurance company that a settlement had been reached in our favor. The White Knight gave us the good news.

"Hey, Francie! How is everything? Tony all fixed up now?" asked the White Night on a check-in call to me.

"Well, he's not *completely* fixed up. He's just had surgery on his shoulder, and hopefully he'll be fine after that," I replied. "What's going on?" I was a little nervous something might have changed with the traffic ticket.

"We got a settlement from the insurance company. The young guy didn't have much coverage, but at least it's something," he answered. I wasn't expecting any compensation, so this was good news.

"Wow, thanks!" I said. "That will buy a lot of frozen yogurt sundaes, Tony's favorite reward after surgery." We both laughed. Things were slowly getting resolved. Tony and I both hoped for a happy ending for the other driver too.

While Tony dreaded going back to one-arm status, the new sling wasn't as intrusive as the others, with far fewer straps and no foam shelf to carry around like a football. It was just a simple blue cloth, over-the-shoulder model, similar to wearing a shirt-sleeve with a wide cotton strap. Even *I* could get all the parts in the right place; I didn't need TJ to help me. Again, with only the shoulder to worry about and not a concussion, broken ribs, and cracked vertebrae, we hardly felt the imposition.

The unveiling of the incision was more gruesome than all the others. Alex got the honor of peeling off the bandage. Underneath was one badass, Frankenstein-like scar. After the leftover, whiskery stiches dissolved, a jagged stripe the length of a number 2 pencil streaked down Tony's arm. He could pass it off as the result of a knife fight or whatever tale he wanted to spin to sound more frightening than a nerve reroute and less complicated than the accident story. With the accumulation of scary scars, I had a new nickname for him: the Intimidator.

A vacation from work for Tony meant a vacation for the boys. He took Alex and a bunch of friends to Water World. He laid in the shade reading cycling magazines, shelling out bucks for lunch and snacks while the kids swooshed down the curvy slides or splashed in the giant wave-making pool that simulated the ocean. TJ was treated to an entire day of eating through Japantown with Tony, returning to Mifune for noodle bowls and buying fancy, pastel-colored tofu candies in pretty boxes.

Our staycation allowed us to sleep late in our own beds and make fancy breakfasts. We played the card game Killer Bunnies, the one we bought a year earlier as therapy for Tony's brain recovery. The games went faster and were more animated; nobody felt guilty for beating dad anymore. We watched movies in the family room, stretched on the couch or bean bags.

Tony was just so thankful to spend quality time with his family. He was grateful for the latest round of support while he was at Oz, mostly from his bodyguard wife. He kept thanking me over and over for staying with him at the hospital. I even heard him telling his mom on the phone, "Mom! She stayed at the hospital ALL day!"

I didn't feel like I deserved so much attention, even if it meant earning gold stars in my mother-in-law's eyes. Where else would I be?

So, it was only fitting I would escort Tony to the last two appointments with the Great Oz. We learned more about nerves than we'd ever imagined.

"No PT for at least two more weeks. The nerve is extremely delicate and slow to grow, about one inch per month," the Great Oz continued our Nerves 101 class with us.

"PT Man is going to be bummed," lamented Tony. "I know, I'll bring him and his team lunch!" Tony could not stand to be away from his buddy.

"You can ride a stationary bike; that's cool," the Great Oz countered. Tony smiled at the permission to ride a bike, even if was only on our front porch.

The last appointment at Oz took place a few months later, going the way of many of our medical experiences. The conversation was brief. Tony's arm wasn't moving, *yet*. The Great Oz had done his job, and there was nothing left for him to do. He didn't request a follow-up e-mail or any further updates. I was kind of bothered given the cutting edge operation and the fact it was a teaching hospital. Wasn't he the least bit curious?

We were on our own, *again*. Déjà vu. This time, we knew exactly what to do. PT Man, Doc Hope, and the bike were patiently waiting in the wings.

CHAPTER 36

On the Road Again: Riding for Real

One Year After the Accident

"SHUT UP!" MY FRIEND CAROL AND I stood on her front porch in the late August sun, watching Tony pedal up the street. She pushed her long blonde hair behind her ears. She wasn't going to miss this miracle moment one month after nerve surgery and a little over a year after the accident. Carol ran inside to get her husband, Mike, so he could witness the miracle too. The three of us stood on the sidewalk as if we were waiting for the Queen of England to ride past in her open carriage.

Tony had ridden all the way from our house to Alex's swim meet and back, about six miles total. Alex worried for his dad as much as I did. Busy intersections, known for drivers running red lights, freeway entrances, and heavy traffic made us fear for his safety. We wondered if his arm was strong enough to hold up his torso in a hunched position and his neck upright so he could see the road. Tony told us he would know within four blocks if he could make it. Of course, his determination and excitement to ride again gave him all the strength he needed.

Tony made it to the swim meet just in time to cheer on Alex in the fifty-yard backstroke. The break to watch Alex swim was just what his weakened muscles needed to tackle the three-mile journey back home. Alex and I arrived home first, ample time to meet at Carol's for the one-man parade coming our way.

When Tony could look far enough ahead to see his cheering squad, he coasted up in his bright green-and-white Taleo bike kit with his patron saint dangling from his neck. We were all glowing, Tony more from exertion. The mummy shirt PT Man ordered for him made him look ten pounds heavier; his bright green Taleo team jersey stretched to one size bigger than intended to accommodate the extra inches of padding and straps. I noticed, even with the brace, his right shoulder was shaky, forcing him into extrawide turns like a six-year-old learning to ride.

"You made it! How was it?" I asked eagerly. Slap after slap of high fives filled my heart, and my eyes were peeled, ready to catch every expression of Tony's happiness.

"It was the most freeing moment. I feel like I came out of a fog," Tony said between breaths and sips from his water bottle.

"Anything hurt? Your shoulder?" asked towering Mike, his toothy smile almost as big as Tony's. Carol and I were beaming.

"Yeah. I didn't know the ribs and neck supported me too, until they 'spoke' to me," he answered with a sigh. "But it's a happy pain. If I can ride, I don't mind a little achiness."

Tony was officially on the road again. In just one week, he pushed his mileage up from six miles to twenty-five—flats only, no hills. I kept my phone close whenever he rode. My eyes barely left the clock, checking to see if he was out too late. I hunted him down one evening at dusk, the riskiest time of day, when shadows, bushes, and cyclists without lights blended together. I know he had not anticipated the sun going down so early, and I could just imagine some tired driver headed home from work, drifting into my sweetie.

I spotted him on a dark and windy stretch close to home. I stayed behind him, headlights on to guide him out of a tunnel of eucalyptus trees. It wasn't pitch-dark, but the little bit of light left in the sky was not enough to see potholes or worse, to allow a car to see him. He didn't know who was following him until we turned at the next intersection.

"It was you!?!" Tony said half grateful and half annoyed as he pedaled alongside the SUV.

"Of course," I said quickly looking at him and back to the road. "I'll see you at home." We were just a mile away with wide roads and streetlamps to show us the way.

Tony made it back safely from his twenty-five mile ride, minutes after me. He burst through the front door, exploding with glee.

"I passed a recreational rider!" Tony exclaimed triumphantly. Sure, he was just a guy out for fun on his bike, but Tony's competitive spirit could taste the future. He would race with his team in no time. Tony was fired up, ready to pick up where he left off. He was so inspired, he signed up for Levi Leipheimer's GranFondo, the sixty-five-mile ride he missed the previous year, when his brother-from-another-mother, Carlos, rode in his place.

Getting back on a bike after a year would have been incentive enough, but the GranFondo was like a set of booster rockets. With six weeks to prepare for the race, he was fiercely determined to compete, no doubt about it. His alternate rider, should the distance and steep hills prove impossible, was me. I would ride in his place. I decided right then, *I* was fiercely determined for him to get in shape for the race too; I didn't really see myself covering sixty-plus miles of road in anything but a car.

I had built up mileage in spin class over the last six months, so I wasn't completely hopeless. My respect for cyclists grew as I tried to keep up with the faster beat of music and high resistance that simulated hills. My usual exercise was in the pool, so I thought I was amply prepared, swimming a mile and a half, three times a week. But I had never sweat so much in my entire life, water dripping off my nose, chin, and ponytail. I grew to love spin and all the weight that fell off with each class. Now I was going to take my spin skill onto the road with Tony.

Our first trip together was on a weeknight ride from our house to the top of Pinehurst and back. It's thirty miles through a canyon thick with tall, shadow-casting pine trees and up a steep, squiggly hill. For the serious cyclist the ride was short, but for me, the distance was intimidating. How far did I ride at the gym? I didn't really know, as the odometers on the stationary bikes were always broken.

I rolled out my Wilier, a present Tony got for me when he bought his first road bike. After wiping off the dust, Tony oiled the chain and pumped up the tires, as my bike rarely made it out of the garage. Once Tony caught the cycling fever, I couldn't keep up with him anymore; we rarely rode together. Riding to Pinehurst was a treat for both of us, despite the challenges we faced: Tony's lack of fitness and my amateur cycling skills.

I dressed in my safety-pink jersey, a sweet date-night color. It was my favorite and one to accentuate my femininity in the presence of cars if I rode solo. When a pink rider came into view, I imagined drivers would glide cautiously around me. It was a sexist perception, but I wasn't ashamed to work every angle. I also thought the likelihood of getting help would increase in my princess hue if I got a flat. Tony had tried showing me how to fix a flat tire in his home-office bike shop. The complicated plastic levers to remove the tire from the wheel and capsules of goo to shoot into the tube to stop up the air leak made my eyes glaze. I told him to expect a call from me; he was my bicycle AAA.

Dressed and ready to go, I confidently climbed on to my bike, sure I could keep up, given Tony's physical condition. If I was going to ride with him, now was a good time, before he was too fit to be with me. However, I hadn't ridden on a bike that moved in forever. I had to relearn how to shift gears, using more than the big red knob on a spin bike. And my confidence in unclipping my shoes from the pedals to stop was about as shaky as Tony's right shoulder. At five o'clock, I usually had a glass of wine, so my energy level was set for relaxation at that hour, not exercise. I tried to put images of a chilled glass of sauvignon blanc out of my mind. If Tony could ride, so could I.

Tony was an excellent and patient guide. He rode in front most of the time, pointing out road hazards like potholes, manhole covers, or dead creatures; his index finger drew an imaginary circle around the lumps and bumps. Needless to say, I was very grateful for this cycling courtesy I didn't know existed and never had to consider in my spin class.

As the flat canyon road started to ascend, I shifted down through my gears. The hill grew steeper and steeper. I geared down and down and down. I panted a lot. My goal was not to stop, no matter how many switchbacks and blind curves tricked my mind into thinking the end was near, only to see another stretch of incline. Tony probably felt stopped, his bike teetering at my slow pace. We were not even close to the top, and I was breathing hard.

"How many gears you got left?" Tony asked cheerily.

No answer was my answer. It was wine-o'clock for me, but I wasn't going to complain.

"You can draft off of me. It's thirty percent less work!" Tony kindly offered.

The only problem for me: to get any benefit, a cyclist has to ride about two feet from the rider in front. That was way too close for me. I needed room to wobble. I came up with a solution: ride three feet back instead of two.

"It's a good thing you have a big butt right now! That's all the blocking I need," I teased. Tony thought he was overweight and out of shape, but in my eyes, even from the back, he looked great.

At last, we reached the crest. I stopped immediately, no coasting around to find the best patch of shade to rest. I couldn't talk. My head was light. Tony pumped me up with, "You did great!" "You're so strong!"

I wasn't feeling great or strong, disappointed in myself was more like it. I made it to the top, but slowly. I am much better at five a.m.

than five p.m. Thankfully, the hardest part was over. Most cyclists call the downhill the reward, but I'm very cautious. I don't want to waste the payoff by careening off the road and down the side of the mountain. We plummeted down, Tony behind me so he knew where I was at all times.

"Get on the drops!" he called out.

"What's that?" I yelled back. I thought it was some sweet spot in the road, a cool cycling term to keep the rider safe.

"It's the curved part of the handle bars," Tony answered back.

What?!? The curve of the handlebars serves a purpose? I quickly learned it made a rider more aerodynamic. For me, who was scared out of her wits riding down any steep hill, I didn't want to go any faster nor did I want to be inverted to that degree. Staring down at the pavement, just a few feet away from my front teeth, frightened me to death. I practiced on the bunny hills, but on the giant hills, I kept my hands on top, close to the brakes.

Tony got us home safely.

"I hope it wasn't too bad," I apologized.

"Oh no, it was easy!" He misunderstood.

"No, what I meant was, I hope it wasn't too easy for you, as in *slow*."

"Oh no! Perfect!" he quickly responded. "I'll ride with you anytime."

I knew he meant what he said. The steep incline of Pinehurst was a warm-up for an even bigger ride. His next challenge was with his cycling team up Mount Diablo, 3850 feet tall and forty-eight miles from our house, round trip. Ten miles of uphill climbing at 6 percent grade was grueling for anyone, but the last hundred yards was three times harder at a very sharp 18 percent grade. The translation: Tony was skeptical, but his team was going on this ride and he was not about to let anyone down. I kept my cell phone ready, as always.

Twenty of his Taleo cycling teammates met at the base of Mount Diablo, clad in their matching jerseys. Tony told me he never felt so humbled and honored to be surrounded by so much green and white. After a round of "welcome back" and "great to see you" the ascent to the top began. His friend Carlos stayed behind the pack to coax Tony through the zigging and zagging to reach the top, much like Tony did for me on the less steep and much shorter ride to Pinehurst. He never called me for help. The excitement of being with his team and climbing a familiar and special mountain he used to ride up three times in one trip was fuel enough to make the full forty-eight miles.

Tony got so strong so fast I was beginning to understand why Doc Hope was enamored by Tony's Big Chi. I thought for sure I would never be invited back out to ride with him. He gave me the honor of a warm-down—a recovery ride from Mount Diablo the day before. Thankfully, we went in the morning, when my body was used to working out. We rode for thirty-six miles, my energy boundless past the golden grassy fields and new home developments of Danville. I attacked the hills with gusto, none as big as Pinehurst. Feeling stronger gave me the confidence and freedom to ride for enjoyment.

"You better save your energy. Bigger hills are coming," Tony suggested.

"Really?!? Darn it!" I said, only half believing him. Nothing could be as hard as our last ride.

"You're excited. I can tell." He was complimenting me. I *was* excited. I wanted to show Tony I could do it, and I was much stronger than my previous performance. The wide roads allowed us to ride side by side and chat a little about the beauty or the thrill of being outdoors. We spotted a female cyclist ahead of us.

"Go git 'er!" Tony tempted me. I looked up at him to see if he was serious. He nodded. I rode as fast as I could, but to no avail. It was fun trying, to test my prowess. As we pedaled along, we ran into several guys from his team and our neighbors, another cycling couple out for a ride just like us. Their eyes lit up when they spotted Tony, a sight no one was sure could happen.

"It's like a playground out here. You never know who you'll see, so you are never really riding by yourself," Tony said with delight.

He was sharing his cycling world with me, a rarity. Our adventure included a stop for coffee, like a regular date, me dressed in my safety-pink jersey. Coffee and cycling go together, I discovered. A dozen cyclists lounged in the sunshine around us, bikes resting against building walls or tables. Cycling was a very social sport; no wonder Tony loved it with all of his heart.

We ended our date ride with a smooch, in a not-so-romantic spot next to our brick mailbox, straddling our bikes.

"I don't do that with any of my teammates," Tony sweetly informed me.

"Good," I said, grinning from ear to ear.

CHAPTER 37

GranFondo: Coming Full Circle

Fifteen Months After the Accident

TONY WAS READY ENOUGH. He would ride the middle distance course of Levi's GranFondo, sixty-five miles of winding, hilly climbs along the Sonoma County coast. *Gran fondo* is Italian for *great challenge*. I liked to think the race name translated to "Great Tony." In the past fifteen months, he'd had his own kind of "great challenge" ride; now he would do one on two wheels with a much easier time of it by comparison.

The original Gran Fondo took place in Cesenatico, Italy, in 1970, I learned on Wikipedia. Ours would be in Santa Rosa. The course is broken into three levels: Piccolo (30 miles), Medio (65 miles), and Gran (103 miles.) Professionals, amateurs, and recreational riders can pick a distance that suits them—undoubtedly a monumental test for each. Tony would test everything he had: lungs, legs, arms, shoulders, neck, heart, and mind as a Medio competitor.

I was relieved. If Tony had not been strong enough to ride, I was signed up to take his place. Now I could observe how the race was done rather than jump immediately from spin class to racecourse. The family had never seen Tony compete, as he convinced the boys and me we'd spend most our time waiting around for a blur-of-a-dad to ride by.

"You would be bored to death," Tony told us. He was sensitive to our happiness and to his own needs. I'm sure it would take the thrill out of racing if an impatient image of the family lingered in the back of his mind as he rode in a cluster of cyclists through the scenic terrain of a racecourse.

But we were not going to miss this coveted event and Tony's grand debut. We set out the Friday night before, leaving after seven in the evening to avoid commuter traffic. Our SUV was stuffed with four helmets, four duffle bags, backpacks, tire pump, extra bike wheels, pillows, favorite blankets, DVDs, and snacks and snacks and snacks. Even at eleven and thirteen, the boys cherished an abundance of chips, beef jerky, and DVDs for road trips. They sat on their nest of bed pillows, covered up with a blanket, plugged into their headphones. We had the drill down.

Tony and I talked in the front while driving along and listening to eighties music, the Cure, Eurythmics, New Order—the bands we danced to in college and in Tony's opinion, the best decade of all time. About an hour into the trip, TJ reached behind him looking for Cool Ranch Doritos when his head jerked to attention, his eyes wide with shock.

"DAD! DAD! There are sparks coming off the road behind our truck!"

I spun around to look. A bike was bouncing in the road, emitting white, sparkly puffs like fairy dust.

"Mom! That's your bike!" TJ exclaimed. The bike was bobbing behind us as if it were a water skier attached to a boat. Tony locked all our bikes together with one long cable, but my beautiful purple Electra retro bike with gold, swirly trim on the fenders and stem had slipped off the trailer.

Tony pulled over to the emergency lane of the highway, my bike scraping to a stop. The cute, natural wicker basket was gone, blowing in the wind like something out of a *Wizard of Oz* tornado. The deeply scratched handlebar held only the clamp to the gear shifter that probably followed the way of the basket, tumbling into the brush. The black plastic-coated wire connecting the shifter to the gears was sheared open, exposing wires much like a damaged nerve. My three-speed had become a one-speed, locked in second gear. The brakes worked the old-fashioned way, back pedal. I hopped on and found I could still ride.

Ironically, the name of my cool Electra bike as written in curly, cursive letters on the frame was *Karma*. Better my bike than Tony's? At least my bike still worked after such a brutal tumble. I had to believe that without Karma, something worse could have happened.

We made the rest of the trip intact, checking into the hotel by nine p.m. We wheeled the bikes into the room and dragged every bag inside too, to prevent theft. Exhausted, we ate a late dinner at the hotel restaurant, not wanting to go anywhere near a car or anything with wheels for that matter.

In what seemed only minutes, our sleep was interrupted by the alarm clock set for six thirty a.m. The race started at eight a.m. We reloaded the truck with 700 bags and triple checked the clamps holding down the wheels of the bikes on the trailer. With 7,500 riders, the closest lot we could find was a mile away. The plan was to ride to the starting line with Tony.

We strapped on our helmets and climbed on to our bikes. Nobody was on the road so early in the morning. We glided through the downtown city streets of Santa Rosa as if we owned the place, the businesses dark and shades pulled. Sometimes we rode in the middle of the street and sometimes four across instead of single file. This was a "crazy cool" highlight of the day for the boys.

"We are breaking the rules and our parents are too!" cried TJ.

We stopped when we reached the towering, black, air-filled arch labeled "Start." Clusters of riders were lined up and ready to race, while other cyclists walked around with their bikes, chatting.

"I think we should take a picture here," I suggested.

"Looks good to me," Tony said.

Tony straddled his bike while the boys and I parked our bikes a few feet away. My cute, retro kickstand, still whole, held my bike upright while the boys tossed their mountain bikes to the ground, too hip for such an accessory. I found a lone cyclist to take our picture, a nice man with gray hair shooting out of the sides of his helmet.

"We have surprise T-shirts underneath our real clothing," I whispered into his ear. "Can you try to capture my husband's expression during the unveiling?"

He nodded and took my cell phone, ready to shoot.

As the boys and I stood around Tony, we unsnapped our helmets and pulled off our shirts, Superman style. Tony looked at us quizzically.

"What are you guys doing?" he giggled. And then his face lit up. We had donned matching black T-shirts with a pancake-sized headshot of cyclist Dad wearing his green-and-white team jersey, bright white helmet, and sunglasses. The caption in emerald-green letters, all caps: "GO DAD!"

Tony's eyes were darting from T-shirt to T-shirt, absorbing the silly sight.

"Who made those for you?" Tony asked, cracking up.

"Me," I said.

Another round of giggles erupted from Tony because he couldn't fathom my newly found skill. I am not a techie, and he knew full well I was handicapped by anything past Microsoft Word. He *loved* the shirts all the more.

"How did you do that? I don't even know how to make a T-shirt."

"Well, we couldn't carry around posters on our bikes, so I thought, why not wear the posters? I got iron-on printer paper and T-shirts at the craft store," I answered triumphantly. While Tony packed, I ironed on the design in Alex's room. I was scared to death Tony would walk in at any moment. But he never even raised an eyebrow at an ironing board in an eleven-year-old's bedroom.

"Have you got your good luck charm?" I asked Tony.

"Yep." He pulled out the pewter necklace of Madonna del Ghisallo, the patroness of cyclists, from underneath his green-and-white jersey.

"Good job!" My skin tingled. With evidence of heavenly protection and a quick smooch, I knew he was safe to ride.

Thirty minutes before race-start, Tony waited in the sea of cyclists with two of his buddies. He wasn't riding alone, thank goodness. His teammates were too fast for him, so he rode with his casual riding friends—my kind of riders. The boys and I stood along the sidelines, snapping pictures with our cell phones. Asian drums rumbled in the background, playing an ominous beat to motivate the cyclists for the toughest race of their lives. Those drums were inspiring; a deep tribal energy inside me was awakened. I kind of wanted to be riding now.

The race host and former cycling champion, Levi Leipheimer, stood on top of an event van. He competed with the best in the world, the likes of Lance Armstrong, and now Levi turned and waved ever so slowly so everyone could get a photo of the skinny biking god. He seemed familiar with the drill, as if he had lessons from Miss America. His celebrity friend, Patrick Dempsey from "Grey's Anatomy," joined him. They had no idea a suburban-paparazzi-mom was targeting the two for later.

I planned to follow in Carlos' footsteps, getting snapshots of Tony with Levi and McDreamy holding a sign that said, "Welcome Back T. Low," to mirror the original, "Get Well T. Low." I was determined to come full circle. It would be the perfect ending to a horrific year where he was not only riding again, but he was riding in a coveted race surrounded by family, friends, and celebrities. I desperately wanted him to have the experience documented.

Finally, an announcer called out, "Go!" and the cyclists were off as if in one giant peloton creeping to a start then slowly splitting up as each cyclist gained momentum. I snapped photo after photo, so I thought. Somehow, I unknowingly slipped into video mode. I was only starting and stopping video with each click.

"Mom! Give me that phone!" said Alex horrified. He showed me how easily the camera function could change. Alex checked my phone the rest of the day; we could not afford any more photo faux pas.

With four hours to burn until we saw our favorite racer at the finish line, the boys and I asked around for a good breakfast place. The cereal bars from our stash of snacks were wearing off. As we rode, TJ couldn't help but notice how fast my feet were spinning around and around like a hamster on a wheel, my legs rapidly pumping up and down as if I were being chased. With only one gear left from the tumble off the trailer, I had to pedal fast if I wanted to keep up.

"Mom! You look like the Wicked Witch of the West!" I was certain he was referring only to the action and not the physical features.

The cozy country diner was in a strip mall, surrounded by small shops dating back to the sixties. We chose a window seat so we could peek out the blue-and-white checkered curtains to check on our jumble of bikes. I don't know who else would have wanted a scraped-up cruiser with one gear and used up Karma, but I needed my Electra cruiser that day, even in its poor state.

Tony was too far away for us to watch him during the race, so we killed time biking around town, ending at a gourmet grocery store for fizzy fruit drinks. We tootled our way back to the event venue, stopping at the ten-foot blowup slide in the kiddie area to kill some more time. I got plenty of practice taking good photos of the boys diving head first down the cushy, steep incline into a pile of smiles and laughs at the bottom. We wound the clock down to thirty minutes before Tony crossed the finish line. I did not want to take any chances missing Tony after coming so far.

We ended up waiting closer to two hours, as Tony miscalculated. I wasn't worried exactly, but this was taking a long time. He or one of his buddies could have gotten a flat. Or maybe Tony, ever the follower of good cyclist etiquette, stopped to fix a stranger's flat. I wasn't going to lose faith.

I cringed more for the boys who were bored to death, as Tony predicted. After an hour, they gave up looking for Dad and curled up underneath a nearby tree to nap. I kept watch. The first cyclists coming through were mostly from the piccolo course, thirty miles long. I was inspired by the variety of race participants who came in all shapes and sizes. It didn't matter if you were five or seventy-five, fifty pounds or five hundred pounds. Anyone could ride.

Fans were hanging over the white plastic barriers, cheering or ringing cowbells. Rattling cowbells at cycling races was a European tradition, and I wanted one of those bells. The boys showed me an app on my phone, a digital version that rang when I shook my phone. It wasn't as loud as a real cowbell, but I loved it anyway.

After so many false sightings, and back and forth of "Is that Dad?" and "No, it's not him," it was pure joy when Tony finally did appear.

"It's HIM!" Click. Click. Click, click. Alex was too slow to check my camera so I hoped for the best. Cowbells were ringing all around as if we were at the Tour de France.

Never had we seen Tony so ecstatic. His smile filled half of his face and lasted so long I wondered if he would ever get his lips over his dried out teeth. He glided over to his family, full of hugs and kisses.

"The scenery was so beautiful. The Pacific Ocean, the hills, fog, everything," said euphoric Tony. "This ride and every ride is a gift."

"Tony was a MACHINE!" his buddies cheered and high-fived all around. I didn't doubt it after all we had been through. I knew Tony was super tough, able to crank out sixty-five miles after fifteen months off the bike. He was fueled by his Big Chi—the stuff most cyclists were made of or they wouldn't stay in the sport.

At such a fancy venue, we could park our bikes in a guarded area, like a coat check. We were free to roam the festival filled with food tents, beer, and music strewn across green, green grass. In between,

Tony talked with fellow riders he knew from years of cycling, recounting tales from the course. This was my chance to head over to the VIP tent to see how I could get a photo with Tony and Levi.

I had my own idea how to make The GranFondo a great celebration. I was as determined to fill his heart with happiness as I was to save him from bodily pain during the icky days. All the practice protecting my husband from medical mishaps had empowered me. I was not afraid to march right up to the VIP tent and plead my case to Levi's personal assistant. I stumbled through my words, "husband," "accident," "picture."

"Come back in fifteen minutes. He's in a press conference." I couldn't tell if he was giving me the brush off or not. I had no choice but to take his word and return fifteen minutes later, Tony straggling behind me, still talking to his teammates. Fifteen minutes turned into thirty. I watched the personal assistant's friends walk in with bike jerseys to be signed. Pretty girls with long waves of silky hair dashed inside the tent too. I overheard a lady going off in a condescending tone with one of the marshals, "Some people will say anything to get into the tent."

Was she talking about me? My eyes narrowed, and my mouth tightened.

Here I was, looking as if I didn't have a shred of credibility, in my homemade T-shirt with the jaggedy-edged, iron-on mug of my cyclist hubby, claiming a sob story to get a picture. I probably did look like a modern-day pauper spinning tales to get a shilling. I didn't care. I could hardly contain my boiling blood, blinking back my tears of anger and humiliation, doing everything in my power to hold back months and months and months of stress and trauma.

Tony was by my side, still talking to yet another fellow racer. The boys were painfully shifting from foot to foot, wiping sweat from their brows with a sigh. I felt bad for them, but I wasn't ready to give up. As we waited, who should stroll up but *McDreamy*! Patrick Dempsey was still in his bike helmet, toting a black backpack over a Specialized bike T-shirt and rolling his bike with him—just like a regular person. I marched right up to him before he got inside that blasted tent.

"Hi! Would you mind taking a picture with my husband?" I asked kindly and politely, trying not to think about my haggard look as I stood next to one of the most handsome actors in Hollywood. He nodded. I was in such a hurry to corral Tony next to *McDreamy* I forgot the "Welcome Back T. Low" sign. I tried to explain the "whys" of taking the picture, but he wasn't getting it. I think he was anxious to grab a cold beer like all the other cyclists. The quicker he posed, the quicker he could get his liquid reward. Click! I got the shot.

The boys were growing even more impatient.

"Mom, when can we go?" they whined.

"As soon as Dad is done talking to his friend we can split. I don't think the Levi thing is going to happen." My voice was filled with disappointment and resignation.

A nice man wearing a dark polo stamped with the word "Marshal" in white stitched letters overheard us. "He'll come. He's really nice. It's just bad timing."

"Thank you," was all I could muster.

Two minutes later, the nice marshal called to me, "He's coming!"

THERE HE WAS! LEVI! The personal assistant came out of the tent towards me, the cycling celebrity in tow. Levi was smaller in person than he looked on top of that van, the same height as Tony and thinner. He wore fresh clothes: black zip-up jacket, blue jeans, and a black baseball cap. He looked nice and he *was* nice, just as the marshal described. I took back every nasty thought in my head. I got to shake Levi's hand and introduce myself like a respectable person. I hurriedly explained our story and how the picture would bring us full circle. I dragged Tony over to Levi, remembering the "Welcome Back T.Low" sign. Snap. Snap. Done! We got the picture in less than thirty seconds.

"Oh, thank you! Thank you! Both of you!" I said to Levi and his trusted personal assistant.

So much stress, angst, and emotion fell away. I was exhausted and elated at the same time. The plan had been lodged in my head for months. I wanted to make this special for Tony, beyond the ride and being there to support him. The homemade T-shirts and following Carlos' paparazzi footsteps was like a GranFondo for me. Chasing down celebrities was draining enough, my brain and ego fried; I don't know how Carlos got his pictures in addition to riding a long race. But it was worth the effort, a way to come full circle and a trophy for Tony, proof he was healed.

Now we were all ecstatic. The GranFondo was a grand accomplishment for anyone, but for Tony it was monumental. He didn't need me any more for doctor appointments, surgeries, showers, bandages, neck braces, slings, pain pills, stretchy V-neck tees, or protection from bad nurses. Tony was back on the bike and well on his way.

The race was over for me too.

Epilogue

Eight Years After the Accident

"HEY, CAN YOU COME SIT ON MY ARM?" Tony asked at halftime during the Warriors game. He laid on his back on top of a beach towel in the family room. Tony was doing his nightly stretching routine; surrounded by dumbbells, foam roller, stick roller, and a lacrosse ball.

"Yes, but I'm pretty heavy," I replied with raised eyebrows. Eight years later, Tony's accident arm could not perform a 360-degree rotation so he swims like Nemo. Nor could he flash his biceps in a strong man pose. I gingerly sat on his forearm, palm up, fearing I would push his shoulder out of socket or crush a bone like a boulder with my big bottom.

Tony groaned as his arm mashed into the ground under my weight.

"Holy crap. Your arm is so tight!" I said, surprised.

"I know! It's worse if I don't stretch every day." Tony mentioned this fact to me over the years, but until I sat on him, I couldn't relate. He was not a complainer. After five minutes, I got up. His arm snapped forward like a screen door slapping shut.

"Yikes! Are you trying to grab my ass?" I teased.

This was the first time Tony asked me to sit on him versus pushing down on his arm with my hands. The thick scar tissue in his shoulder prohibits him from holding his arm flush to the ground unless he places a thirty-five pound dumbbell on his forearm, like a paperweight. Or, on some nights, he'll decide a greater than thirty-five pound paperweight, a wife, is better.

Tony has come a long way in eight years. He can lift up his bad arm about 75 percent towards the sky, enough to shoo a fly from his face or put the glasses away in the cupboard. Any higher, he's trained his left arm to paint the crown molding or change a light bulb in the ceiling. And most importantly, he rides his bike as often as he can, carving corners like a pro and using his own strength, no mummy shirt. We forget, or rather his family forgets, Tony is still not 100 percent normal.

"My shoulder aches. Is it supposed to rain?" he'll ask. Or, "My shoulder hates travel! It's so stiff," he'll say as he hammers his shoulder with his right fist. He's constantly trying to free his shoulder from the smothering scar tissue. His broadcasts or deep pounding are the only way his family knows he's not having a good day.

In addition to acupuncture, Tony found a deep tissue chiropractor to adjust him back into place, a protocol he stuck with for many years. Just when he thinks he can't get any further, he'll discover another technique. The latest is a big guns chiropractor that uses deep penetrating ultrasound to break up the scar tissue, a common practice in Europe but not in America, and not covered by insurance.

"I have never felt looser! I can move my neck!" Tony exclaimed after his first appointment. His new physician resembles Mr. Clean: brawny and bald. He discovered Tony is locked up in scar tissue all over his torso, not just his shoulder. Mr. Clean ordered an X-ray. The films showed Tony's spine is crooked like multiple soft curves on a windy hill. Unless a physician looks at the entire body, it's impossible to pick up additional ailments.

"You have a higher purpose," Mr. Clean told Tony after hearing how he became so mangled.

"Funny, that's not the first time I've heard that," Tony said. "I feel the same way."

Tony has evolved into a healer. His experience with different medical disciplines and lots of Google searches has taught him a lot about the human body. If something hurts, a sore knee or a tweaked back, the common response is, "Ask Dad." He'll rub out a neck kink or suggest a roll on a lacrosse ball if he can't dig deep enough to release the irritating bulge. In addition, he will prescribe a veggie and fruit smoothie to bring down the swelling.

Instead of stuffing his family with a panini or breakfast burrito, he's drowning us in anti-inflammatory and anti-cancer smoothies. Eighteen ingredients make up this magic elixir to help fight cholesterol, feed the brain, and calm the muscles. Everything is organic. We feel more energetic and our eyes see more clearly, as if someone turned up the lights in a dim room.

"Cancer is not going to get my family!" proclaims Tony. His favorite T-shirt in Yale University blue, says it all: "Kale." We eat "bottomless salads," as the boys call them. Each night, Tony packs a soup bowl for each of us with romaine, kale, arugula, purple carrots, purple cabbage, radish, fennel, and dried cranberries with homemade vinaigrette. The salad goes on forever. We are addicted.

When any of us travel, boys included, the first thing we crave is a salad. Alex is almost mad at Tony for training him to eat tons of fruits and vegetables and very few glutens.

"If I eat pizza with my friends, I feel like crap afterward!" Alex scowled at Tony.

A prideful smile crosses Tony's face. He was equally pleased to see TJ pack up the old NutriBullet for college; the family had graduated to the supersized, superpowerful blender that cranks out smoothies by the half dozen. The top shelf of the refrigerator is lined with glasses of plum colored concoction with color-coordinated tops. My customized smoothies come with a shot of iron and are marked by pink or purple lids.

Tony's health mission for his family was born out of "fixing" the broken parts deemed unfixable from the accident, and still fixing. And my mission, inspired by the encouraging comments on the CaringBridge posts: writing. Composing newsletters had always been fun for me, but I never had the courage to do anything more. Until that fateful day when I had to turn a tragic story into something informative and palatable in a technology I didn't know existed—a blog. The response was life changing.

"You're a great writer!" "How did you learn to write like that?" Little nuggets of praise made me believe in myself and work toward perfecting the craft through classes and writers' groups. Learning is never-ending, but eventually, *Alive and Fixable* was born.

"In a few more days, I'll be back to a full-time housewife," I said to Tony. I was looking forward to finishing my nearly three-year book project and resuming home improvements and purging closets.

"No, you are more than a housewife. You are an *author*," cheered Tony, the proud husband.

"Ha! Funny guy," I said, my eyes misting up and face flushed.

The things Tony absorbs always surprise me, kind of like a parent not knowing what will stick in a child's head until one day, the knowledge blurts out. Smack. That's how I felt when he was quick to remind me about the importance of helping others during a trying time.

"Do you think I should bring Kelly soup? I don't want to intrude," I'll ask after a friend's hand surgery.

"You always say, 'Community is important. Food brings community together. Do something, even a little something.' Right?"

"Yes. That's what I say."

TWO YEARS LATER

First Reflections

Last blog post—March 2012

It's hard to love. It's hard to know love; to know you are loved. You can't intellectualize it, which many of us do. I do. It's a feeling not really a word. It's a life lesson, a learning process to figure this out. Sometimes it comes at you in a most unlikely, ugly event, and crazily, in a loving way.

My neighbors and friends love me. God loves me. My husband and sons love me. I felt this when my husband was tragically run over on his bike. The scene was horrific, I'm told. That part I don't want to feel or know. I chose to love him and care for him, to make him feel safe.

My friends cooked for me. Mowed my lawn for me. Took my kids for me. They loved me and made me feel safe. I felt it. I didn't hear it or read it. I felt God in those acts, because how could my friends and in some cases, complete strangers, know what I was thinking or needed. I didn't ask. They just came. No words exchanged.

To me this is love. It's kindness, upon kindness upon kindness. Every day of those first few weeks after the accident brought vivid, palpable love to my family and me.

Excerpt from Personal Essay, 2012

"Love is selfless. It's something you do without thinking. Something you want to do and can't imagine otherwise. It is not work. It is not drudgery. It's not self-indulgent. You don't even know you are reaching out to someone in the name of love or that there is a choice. This is love. It is our instinct, our nature. We are so busy we don't even think to label our actions as such and that's OK. To know the truth might scare some off and for others it's a revelation of epic proportions. It's a beautiful lesson in the midst of tragedy. It is something so touching, so overwhelming it can almost make you cry more than a bundle of injuries. I'm not glad for the accident, but I'm glad for the amazing window into our hearts, to see and to feel. Amen." —Francie Low

TONY'S TEAM THANK-YOU

Tony Low

One Year Later—Post–Mount Diablo Ride,
September 2011

For all that showed up on the Sunday ride I wanted to thank you, it was so good to see each of you out there and be surrounded by all that Green! However, I also want to thank all those that weren't there but have been sending me your prayers and positive thoughts. I needed every one of them and am thankful for all you have done.

I keep pinching myself to see if my Sunday ride was just a dream and am glad that it was not. I am so humbled and honored for the warmth that was surrounding me on my first team ride after thirteen months off the bike. I cannot say enough of what that means to me. Each of you individuals that make up Taleo have been an unwavering inspiration for me. From day one, the outpouring of humanity that came from Taleo has been simply amazing, and I am very moved by it and the spirit of this team.

Recovery is easier, with the constant reminders that all you Green guys and gals are out there doing what you love. Over the past year, there must have been a million times I saw one of you on the road and I told myself, "I'll be there again." Whether or not you knew it, you have been the source of my daily motivations for recovery, and I am forever grateful.

I will remember this past Sunday for the rest of my life. It was a huge victory for me just to make it to the parking lot to join the ride. There were many times this past year I wasn't so sure I would ever be able to do that. Though I still don't have a functioning right shoulder, I can ride, and for now, that's enough. And for all of you out there on your own recovery, you can bet there's a bunch of us in Green pulling for you to get back on the road!

Thanks to all, it's good to be back.
TLow

Acknowledgements

TO MY EXCEEDINGLY COMPASSIONATE and supportive husband, Tony, thank you is not enough for the countless hours you spent listening to my drafts while cooking the family dinner and reliving that horrific fifteen months of rehabilitation. Your encouragement and belief in me as a writer make me cry. Writing *Alive and Fixable* helped me realize how much you were keeping your pain to yourself and staying incredibly positive. You kept us all guessing, "How does he do it?"

And to our sons, TJ and Alex, thank you for enduring the repeated question over and over, "Do you remember….?" so I could fill in the gaps where my memory lapsed. Your parents are eternally grateful for your patience and kindness during that awful time. You kept us laughing and focused on the future. You make us so very happy and proud.

Thank you to my dedicated writers group, The Januaries: Teresa Caldwell and Joanie Kibbey. Without your positive and constructive feedback, I could not have kept up my three year marathon of writing. You never tired of reading revision after revision.

Elizabeth Fishel, my forever mentor who welcomed me into the world of writing in the gentlest of ways. You kept my confidence up and the love flourishing. I'm grateful to the group of writers who sat in your living room for Wednesday Writers and the ongoing friendships I formed there, in particular, Jeanne Halpern, Ellen Newman and Alicia Young. Alicia, your over-the-top encouragement and advisement was a generous gift.

My community of readers, Elinor Cheung, Annie Hebert, Colleen Miller and Casey Sasner who read the rawest of drafts and cheered me on to revisions, you are saints. To my pool of proofreaders, your enthusiasm to help was overwhelming. And to the fastest friend I have ever made over the Internet, Laurie Chittenden, my editor. You enriched the book beyond what I could see and helped me believe I could touch someone I didn't yet know with my words.

Thank you to Colleen Weems for introducing me to the online world of publishing professionals and answering my endless questions. I will never forget the serendipitous morning I spotted you at my coffee house office. Your impact made all the difference.

Lisanne Mueller, I am so grateful for your immediate response to text after text of medical questions for over two years. And to my favorite barista and owner of Papillion Café, Brenda, I could not have written thousands and thousands of words without the caffeinated supply of soy lattes stamped with a swirly, foamy heart to pump me up.

A huge load of gratitude to the medical professionals, firemen and cycling buddies that kept Tony's eye on the prize of riding again. Special shout out to our lawyer who made our medical bills disappear; you made an empty mailbox a joyful sight. To our families, thank you for your understanding and belief that we could handle everything. Lastly, thank you to the Lamorinda community for supporting my family during a scary time and for supporting me, the writer for years after. You are very much a part of *Alive and Fixable.*

CPSIA information can be obtained
at www.ICGtesting.com
Printed in the USA
BVHW082012110319
542317BV00003B/416/P